Prelude to the Guardianship

Prelude to the Guardianship

How 'Abdu'l-Bahá prepared
the young Shoghi Effendi
for the office he was destined to assume
as Guardian of the Cause of God

by

Riaz Khadem

George Ronald
Oxford

George Ronald, Publisher
Oxford
www.grbooks.com

© Riaz Khadem 2014
Reprinted 2022

All Rights Reserved

*A catalogue record for this book is available
from the British Library*

ISBN 978–0–85398–582–2

Cover design: Steiner Graphics

Dedicated to my father,
Zikrullah Khadem,
whose life's yearning was to attain
the good pleasure of
Shoghi Effendi,
and to my mother,
Javidukht Khadem,
his lifetime companion, deputy and helper

Contents

Acknowledgements ix
Preface xi
Introduction xv

Part I: Early Years 1
  1 Childhood and Youth 3
  2 Syrian Protestant College (SPC) 8

Part II: Learning from the Master 21
  3 In the Service of the Master, Autumn and Winter 1918 23
  4 In the Service of the Master, Early 1919 34
  5 In the Service of the Master, Spring 1919 63
  6 In the Service of the Master, Summer 1919 70
  7 In the Service of the Master, Autumn 1919 90
  8 Last Months with the Master 107

Part III: France and England 129
  9 Recuperation in Paris 131
  10 Arrival in England 140
  11 Matriculation and Student Life at Oxford 150
  12 Michaelmas Term 1920 156
  13 Hilary Term in Balliol 162
  14 Spring Vacation 1921 170
  15 Trinity Term 1921 173
  16 Long Vacation 1921 178
  17 Michaelmas Term 1921 191
  18 The Last Days in England 198

Part IV: At the World Centre 203
  19 The Beloved Guardian 205

Appendix: Shoghi Effendi's Address to the Oxford University Asiatic Society 227

Bibliography 241
Notes and References 245

Acknowledgements

I owe a debt of gratitude to Marion Hofman, the tireless and devoted worker in the Cause of God who encouraged me every time we met during the period I was a student at Balliol College. Her indomitable husband David Hofman, member of the Universal House of Justice from 1963 to 1988, continued the same loving encouragement by instilling a vision of the importance and necessity of this work and constantly urging me to finish it as soon as possible. Coincidentally, I am now working with their daughter, May Hofman, who has been assigned by the publisher to help me with the current version of this book. I am grateful to her for her meticulous verification of all the sources and for the organization of the additional material into the book. This book owes much to the Hofman family!

My gratitude is extended to the National Spiritual Assembly of the Bahá'ís of the United Kingdom and especially to Hugh Adamson for giving me access to the Archives of the National Spiritual Assembly. I thank the Balliol Society for providing the names and addresses of Shoghi Effendi's contemporaries, and E. V. Quinn, Balliol librarian, for his assistance in the initial research. I thank David Lewis and Mary Perkins Gray for taking the photographs of buildings in Balliol and Oxford, and Christine Nicholas and Anne Thorne Munro for their assistance in typing letters to two hundred Balliol men. I thank Balliol and St Catherine's Colleges for allowing documents to be photocopied and I am indebted to those men and women who have written their recollections of Shoghi Effendi.

I am grateful to the National Spiritual Assembly of the Bahá'ís of the United States and to its Bahá'í Publishing Trust for permission to quote selections from *Blessings Beyond Measure* by Ali M. Yazdi, published by them in 1988. I am also grateful to the Bahá'í Publishing

Trust of the United Kingdom for permission to quote selections from *The Priceless Pearl* by Rúḥíyyih Rabbaní.

Once the original version of this book was published, several Baháʾí friends sent me supplementary materials. I thank Cyrus Alai for sending me the Persian text of the supplication of Shoghi Effendi to the Master written from Manchester. I am grateful to Brent Poirier for sending me documents from Shoghi Effendi's student days at the University of Beirut. And I wish to convey special thanks to the Research Department of the Universal House for the source of Shoghi Effendi's article to the Asiatic Society at Oxford. Finally, I wish to express my gratitude to the Secretary of the National Spiritual Assembly of the Baháʾís of the United States for permission to visit its Archives and use its materials.

I am grateful to Blackwell Publishers for permission to reprint the map of Oxford drawn by Brian Cairns in 1966.

I also thank the members of my family who have encouraged and assisted me with this work, especially my daughter-in-law, Názanin, for helping me with the organization of the material, and my wife, Linda, for her careful editing.

Preface

This book is the expanded version of an existing title, *Shoghi Effendi in Oxford and Earlier*, published by George Ronald in 1999. On the eve of the publication of that title, I discovered that an important source – an inch-thick diary by Shoghi Effendi – had been overlooked inadvertently. This was in the form of a transcription made by Lucy Hall in the early 1970s and now in the Archives of the National Spiritual Assembly of the Baháʼís of the United Kingdom.

This discovery caused me a dilemma: should I delay the publication until this important material was incorporated into the book, or should I proceed with publication as scheduled? My dear mother Javidukht advised me to proceed with the publication and to update the book later. I thank her for that advice, as otherwise the access of the friends to these precious materials would have been delayed.

The present volume includes excerpts from the missing material I had access to earlier[1] as well as other documents that have emerged, including the supplication of Shoghi Effendi in Persian sent to the Master from Manchester, several documents from the days when Shoghi Effendi was a student at the University of Beirut, the article he presented to the Asiatic Society when he was at Oxford, and other documents and letters written by Shoghi Effendi.

The idea for the original version of this book was born one evening in 1965 during a Baháʼí meeting in London when a friend, Mr F. Taghizadih, approached me and asked if I had considered conducting research about the life of Shoghi Effendi at Oxford. I had not, and his question started me on a course that has led to the publication of this book.

The search began one autumn afternoon as I was looking at some old college albums stacked in the Balliol College Junior Common Room.

PRELUDE TO THE GUARDIANSHIP

I was curious to see whether Shoghi Effendi's picture might be in one of them. Suddenly my eyes fell upon the face of Shoghi Effendi in the middle of a group of students. I cannot describe the feelings of joy and reverence that overcame me at that moment. With this precious album in hand I hastened to the college office to obtain permission to make a copy of the picture. Permission was granted, and I took the album to Gilman & Soames photo studio. When the photograph was copied, I submitted it to the Universal House of Justice. It now appears in Amatu'l-Bahá's wonderful book *The Priceless Pearl* and is included here.

The discovery of this precious photograph encouraged me to continue. I approached the Balliol College office to see if they had any records of the student days of Shoghi Effendi. The immediate response was negative. Little was available in the college records after the passage of some 43 years, except a brief description of Shoghi Effendi in the Balliol Registry, and hearsay about the room he had occupied in college. Neither did the Local Spiritual Assembly of the Bahá'ís of Oxford have very much detail about the year Shoghi Effendi spent in Oxford. The Balliol College office had been approached before by Bahá'ís. However, the search had not produced significant results and the college offered no encouragement for further search.

I approached Mr Russell Meiggs, Fellow of Balliol and tutor of ancient history, and asked him if he would assist by writing with me the account of Shoghi Effendi's year spent in Oxford. I hoped that Mr Meiggs would help find possible sources of information and would enhance the work with his scholarly approach as an historian. Mr Meiggs graciously accepted my invitation and commenced the joint project by approaching several eminent Balliol men of 1919–21. He was keen to unearth information that would be appropriate for a biography. However, the joint effort did not produce sufficient material and the project was abandoned.

The status of the project was then referred to the Bahá'í World Centre. The response was a letter from the Universal House of Justice stating that 'it was indeed a pity that he [Russell Meiggs] was not able to find sufficient information for you to undertake a biography'.[2]

This letter prompted me to resume the work on my own and to begin a systematic and sustained search. I approached the Balliol librarian, E.V. Quinn, and asked him if he would mind me going through old, dusty archival material in the college library. He consented. This

PREFACE

search led me to a few letters about Shoghi Effendi written by his tutor at the Non-Collegiate Delegacy. Upon tracing the history of this institution, it became clear that it had evolved through several stages into St Catherine's College. I then approached St Catherine's College office requesting information about Shoghi Effendi. Most of the important documents presented here were kept in their archives.

Initially, this project was intended to cover only the Oxford period of the life of Shoghi Effendi. I intended to finish the project during my three years of study at Balliol and the subsequent two years I spent at the University of Southampton. However, in the course of the research, I decided to write to the registrar of the American University of Beirut to see if there was any information that would be relevant. By return, the registrar sent some valuable materials including the university transcripts of Shoghi Effendi. As these materials became available about the Guardian's studies in Beirut, I decided to expand the research to include the Beirut years.

An important source, though perhaps less reliable than documents, is the recollection of individuals who had known Shoghi Effendi and could provide anecdotes related to the time they had spent with him. I began looking for professors or other individuals who would have been with Shoghi Effendi at the time but found no one in Oxford. The idea then occurred to me to track down Shoghi Effendi's contemporaries who lived outside Oxford. To do this I needed an address list.

I was pleasantly surprised to find in the college office the names and addresses of 205 men who came to Balliol in the years 1918 through 1921. Those who came in 1918 would have been in their third year when Shoghi Effendi arrived and those who took up residence in 1921 would have had the opportunity of knowing him for three months. I wrote to them all, enclosing a biographical sketch and copy of a college photograph in which Shoghi Effendi's face was circled.

I was surprised and delighted to receive 135 replies, 52 of which contained some information about or recollection of Shoghi Effendi. I compiled these responses and sent the originals to the World Centre.

Despite diligent search to find the exact room Shoghi Effendi occupied while in Oxford, I was unable to discover any conclusive evidence. There was a rumour attributed to Maurice Keen that Shoghi Effendi occupied the same room he himself had occupied in 1969. Maurice Keen said that he had heard it from his father, Hugh Keen, a Balliol contemporary of Shoghi Effendi. Yet the letter I received from Hugh Keen did not support this view. References Shoghi Effendi had made to pilgrims indicated the general location of the western staircases facing the Martyrs' Memorial.

After much discouragement, I came to feel that perhaps Shoghi Effendi, in his great humility, did not wish his room to be given special significance.

In 1971, having compiled all the available material, I sent the documents to the World Centre for preservation and thus felt that my work was completed, leaving the task of writing a biography to future historians.

Without the continued insistence of two people, my wife, Linda, and Mr David Hofman, I would not have produced this manuscript. I did in fact put it aside for years for two reasons. First, Rúḥíyyih Khánum's book *The Priceless Pearl*, which is and will always remain the definitive book on Shoghi Effendi, was published; and secondly, I felt that despite all my findings, my search had produced only fragments, tiny pieces of information not sufficient to make a book. I was finally persuaded that all the little bits were priceless too and would be of interest to Baháʼís. During his visit to our home in Peachtree City, Georgia, Mr Hofman reinforced this decision and advised me to commence immediately the task of writing a book based on the original research. In subsequent correspondence and visits with Mr Hofman his advice was amplified.

I started work in 1993 and produced the first draft of the manuscript in 1995. Upon the commencement of this task, I wrote letters to both Balliol and St Catherine's Colleges, where I had found valuable documents 27 years earlier, to see if by chance they had become aware of the importance of documents related to Shoghi Effendi and had collected the material. However, to my disappointment, both colleges informed me that they had practically nothing of real significance.[3] I was surprised that they did not even list the documents they had given to me some 30 years earlier. Therefore, I assume the items I had collected are misfiled in the college archives. Sometime in the future, no doubt, these two colleges will realize the significance of what they had in their possession and will cherish the legacy of Shoghi Effendi.

Introduction

This book is written in a simple style by an ordinary Bahá'í with the assumption that the readers are also mainly believers. Other readers will find the book of interest once they become familiar with the terminology used in Bahá'í literature.

It is a great privilege for me to write about this subject, a topic that has been dear to my heart all my life. As long as I can remember, the mention of Shoghi Effendi and the attainment of his good pleasure have been the central themes of my life.

During my childhood and youth I learned of Shoghi Effendi through my father's eyes. Later, in 1956 on my own pilgrimage to the presence of the beloved Guardian, a gift I received from my father and mother upon reaching the age of maturity, I had the bounty of confirming through my own experience what I had learned from my father. That pilgrimage allowed me the soul-stirring, priceless and unforgettable experience of standing before the Guardian, gazing at his countenance, walking behind him in the gardens of the shrines, hearing his melodious voice chant the Tablet of Visitation, and pondering his words of counsel and wisdom – words that are still fresh in my memory after the passage of more than half a century.

Ten years after that pilgrimage, the experience of walking on the same ground Shoghi Effendi's feet had walked, of eating in the same hall where he had taken his meals and studying in the library where he had studied filled my days with feelings that are impossible to describe. I was continually reminded of his presence and the memory of my pilgrimage was vivid throughout my own sojourn in that great academic centre.

To provide a historical context for the reader, I have included a brief history of Balliol College and described some features of that remarkable institution which were unique in 1920 and remain unique today. I have added a few points concerning the attitudes of the British upper class of the time to serve as appropriate social context for the study of Shoghi Effendi's sojourn.

The transliteration system used in Bahá'í literature is adopted throughout this book except for quotations dating to the period before 1921. These quotations, which are mainly translations of the Tablets of 'Abdu'l-Bahá by Shoghi Effendi or letters by early believers, are produced in their original form. There are a few quotations from Persian manuscripts which I have translated and these are indicated explicitly in the endnotes.

Significant events in the early life of Shoghi Effendi as a student both in Beirut and at Oxford are noted. The book is divided into four parts; of which the first three, containing 18 chapters, survey a period of 24 years in the life of Shoghi Effendi with particular emphasis on his educational experience not only academically but more importantly, from 'Abdu'l-Bahá.

Part I, *Early Years*, is about Shoghi Effendi's elementary and secondary school years and his experience as a student in the preparatory school of the Syrian Protestant College as well as his undergraduate education.

Part II, *Learning from the Master*, consists of six chapters covering the period of about one-and-a-half years during which Shoghi Effendi served the Master as secretary and translator. These chapters draw heavily on Shoghi Effendi's diary letters recorded by him in Haifa and which he shared with the friends at the time.

Part III, *France and England*, covers the period April 1920 to December 1921, from Shoghi Effendi's arrival for a period of four months of rest on the outskirts of Paris to his return to the Holy Land following the passing of 'Abdu'l-Bahá. Chapter 10 describes his arrival in England and his meeting the believers there. Chapters 11 to 18 are all related to Shoghi Effendi's work at Oxford and are based on records found at Oxford University, letters he wrote, and recollections of his contemporaries. During his stay, and particularly during his vacations, Shoghi Effendi took the opportunity of visiting Bahá'ís in the United Kingdom; he was particularly impressed by his visit to the Bahá'ís of Manchester, described in Chapter 16.

Part IV, *At the World Centre*, consists of one chapter only. It provides

INTRODUCTION

an overview of the period after Shoghi Effendi left Oxford until his passing on 4 November 1957. This chapter conveys my own limited understanding of the unfolding events during this early period of the Formative Age of the Bahá'í Dispensation.

I hope this book will help you draw closer to the beloved Guardian, will assist you in gaining a deeper understanding of the workings of Providence in his life, and will help you appreciate the significance of Shoghi Effendi's contributions to the establishment of the World Order of Bahá'u'lláh.

I

Early Years

1

Childhood and Youth

Shoghi Effendi was born on 1 March 1897[1] in the house of 'Abdu'lláh Páshá in 'Akká, situated in the vicinity of the barracks where Bahá'u'lláh was imprisoned in 1868. This date of birth is consistent with the information Shoghi Effendi provided on his registration form for the Syrian Protestant College in 1915.[2] Shoghi Effendi's father was Mírzá Hádí Shírází, who was a descendent of the family of the Báb. His mother, Ḍíya'u'lláh Khánúm, was the eldest daughter of 'Abdu'l-Bahá.[3]

In a Tablet from 'Abdu'l-Bahá we learn of His prayer that God may confer upon His grandson the name Shoghi:

. . . O God! This is a branch sprung from the tree of Thy mercy. Through Thy grace and bounty enable him to grow and through the showers of Thy generosity cause him to become a verdant, flourishing, and blossoming and fruitful branch.

Gladden the eyes of his parents, Thou Who givest to whomsoever Thou willest, and bestow upon him the name Shoghi so that he may yearn for Thy Kingdom and soar into the realms of the unseen![4]

The title 'Effendi' or Sir, added as a term of respect, is an integral part of Shoghi Effendi's name. The Master required everyone, including Shoghi Effendi's own father, to add the title Effendi to the name and always to address him as Shoghi Effendi.[5]

Shoghi Effendi was one of the 13 grandchildren of 'Abdu'l-Bahá nurtured in the household of the Master. Aware of Shoghi Effendi's great destiny, the Master protected His beloved grandchild by treating him on most occasions the same as the other children. The surname 'Rabbání', which means 'divine', was conferred upon him by the

Master to distinguish him from the other grandchildren, who used the surname Afnán and Shahíd.[6]

The earliest records of Shoghi Effendi's schooling are based on the accounts written by Amatu'l-Bahá Rúḥíyyih Khánúm. She writes in *The Priceless Pearl* that from childhood Shoghi Effendi had the great desire to write and to learn.

> . . . one day Shoghi Effendi entered the Master's room, took up His pen and tried to write. 'Abdu'l-Bahá drew him to His side, tapped him gently on the shoulder and said, 'Now is not the time to write, now is the time to play, you will write a lot in the future.'[7]

Because of Shoghi Effendi's desire to learn, classes were arranged in the household of the Master for the grandchildren. These classes were taught by an elderly Persian believer. At one time the children were taught by an Italian, who acted as governess.[8]

When Shoghi Effendi was a young boy the Master sent him with a nurse, Hájar Khátún, to live in Haifa. There he registered in the French Jesuit school, Collège des Frères.[9] Dr Habíb Mo'ayyid, a devoted Persian believer who was in the Holy Land during this period, was assigned by 'Abdu'l-Bahá to look after Shoghi Effendi. Dr Mo'ayyid first met Shoghi Effendi in 'Akká in 1907 and thereafter spent considerable time with him. He states that Shoghi Effendi was not happy in this French school.[10] Shoghi Effendi did complete his studies at this school and then went to another Jesuit boarding school in Beirut for advanced studies. A trusted woman was sent by Shoghi Effendi's family to rent a home in Beirut and look after him. But this did not improve the situation, as he was still unhappy in this French school.[11] Here Shoghi Effendi's unhappiness grew to such a point that 'Abdu'l-Bahá arranged for him to transfer to the preparatory school attached to the Syrian Protestant College of Beirut.

While attending school in Beirut, Shoghi Effendi spent his vacations in Haifa, often in a small room next to the room occupied by 'Abdu'l-Bahá. He would spend hours studying and reading. At times his lamp remained turned on late at night, and the Master would get up and go to his door, saying 'Enough! Enough! Go to sleep!'

Ali Yazdi was a school friend of Shoghi Effendi, whom he first met in Ramleh, Alexandria, in 1910 when Shoghi Effendi was 13 and Ali

Yazdi was 11. Shoghi Effendi had gone to Ramleh to be near 'Abdu'l-Bahá. Here are Ali Yazdi's recollections:

> We slowly started to get acquainted; you know how children are. Then we got to know each other better. I would see him at 'Abdu'l-Bahá's house, and gradually we became friends. Even as a child he was always dignified, but he was also friendly.[12]

Aborted Journey to the West with 'Abdu'l-Bahá

When 'Abdu'l-Bahá returned from His first visit to Europe in 1911, He decided to take Shoghi Effendi with Him to America. At this time Shoghi Effendi was a boy of about 14 years of age. The Master ordered long robes and two turbans for Shoghi Effendi and was pleased to see him try them on.[13] Ali Yazdi recollects Shoghi Effendi's eagerness about this journey to America.

> Shoghi Effendi was in seventh heaven. He had heard so much about America, and he longed to be with the Master as He travelled throughout North America and gave the Message. He looked forward with great anticipation to the experience.
> The day before 'Abdu'l-Baha left, Shoghi Effendi came to see me and asked, 'Sheikh-Ali . . . do you want to go to the ship with me and see my cabin?'
> I said, 'Surely!' So, with some other believers, we took the electric train to Alexandria and then to the harbour. Before us was the *Cedric*, a White Star liner.
> It was a beautiful ship . . . Shoghi Effendi and I went on the boat, and he took me upstairs and showed me his stateroom, the dining room, and everything on the ship. He was extremely happy, and so was I very happy for him. I made him promise to write to me when he got to America, and he said he would.[14]

On 25 March 1912 Shoghi Effendi sailed with 'Abdu'l-Bahá from Alexandria to Naples to commence the long journey to America. However, in Naples the Italian health officials asked him and two other companions of 'Abdu'l-Bahá to leave the ship and return to the Middle East. They said that Shoghi Effendi had trachoma. However, he had never had trouble with his eyes and there were no signs of trachoma. When Shoghi Effendi returned to Ramleh, he consulted doctors who said emphatically that he had no problem whatsoever with his eyes. Yet the damage was done. The young Shoghi Effendi was heartbroken. His separation from the Master was painful. He lost weight and became sick and it took him some time to regain his health.[15]

Dr Mo'ayyid relates that after Shoghi Effendi was denied passage with 'Abdu'l-Bahá to the United States, he went to Beirut:

> From Naples Shoghi Effendi proceeded to Beirut to attend school . . . I learned that Shoghi Effendi was not happy with school. He used to pay weekend visits to the Bahá'í students at the Syrian Protestant College (SPC) and stay overnight in my lodgings.[16]

A picture of Shoghi Effendi from this period appeared in *Star of the West* on 2 March 1912. In this picture Shoghi Effendi is standing in the second row among the Bahá'í students studying in Beirut.

In spirit, Shoghi Effendi was with the Master during His North American journey. He followed the account of 'Abdu'l-Bahá's travels by carefully studying a map of the United States, reading with keen interest every copy of *Star of the West* and tracing His itineraries.[17]

'Abdu'l-Bahá's thoughts were also with Shoghi Effendi. He was concerned about Shoghi Effendi's welfare and his happiness. In letters written to the Greatest Holy Leaf, He enquired about His beloved grandson, as these excerpts from different Tablets indicate:

> Write to me at once about Shoghi Effendi's condition, informing me fully and hiding nothing . . .

> Kiss the light of the eyes of the company of spiritual souls, Shoghi Effendi.

> Kiss the fresh flower of the garden of sweetness, Shoghi Effendi.[18]

Furthermore, the Master revealed a Tablet for Shoghi Effendi from America that reflects His love and concern for this precious grandchild:

> Shoghi Effendi, upon him be the glory of the All-Glorious! Oh

thou who art young in years and radiant of countenance, I understand you have been ill and obliged to rest; never mind, from time to time rest is essential, otherwise, like unto 'Abdu'l-Bahá from excessive toil you will become weak and powerless and unable to work. Therefore rest a few days, it does not matter. I hope that you will be under the care and protection of the Blessed Beauty.[19]

2

Syrian Protestant College (SPC)

When 'Abdu'l-Bahá learned of Shoghi Effendi's unhappiness with the Catholic boarding school in Beirut, He arranged for his transfer to the preparatory school operated by the Syrian Protestant College.¹ Dr Mo'ayyid describes Shoghi Effendi's joy at the prospect of transferring from the French school to the American school:

> I remember Shoghi Effendi took Arabic for his entrance examination into the SPC. He was very happy and always smiled.²

A record of Shoghi Effendi's registration at the preparatory school of this college shows his entrance in October 1912.³

Background to the Establishment of the Syrian Protestant College⁴

In the middle of the 19th century, friction between Syrian Muslims and Christians, which had intensified during the period of the separation of Syria from Ottoman rule and its subsequent return to Ottoman control, had reached a crisis point necessitating the intervention of the European powers.

The French Government interceded by sending French troops to Lebanon to oversee the situation and to influence the restructuring of the administration of the area. Syria was divided into two provinces, with governors appointed directly by the Sultan, and Lebanon became a separate district with a Christian governor appointed by the Sultan but acceptable to the European powers.⁵

The new political system opened fresh opportunities for the American missionaries in the region to expand their influence. They became aware of the need to increase their numbers and therefore visualized opening a training centre, an American-style college that would combine Christian ideals with modern practices of Western education.

This training centre would not only supply the needed missionaries but would educate knowledgeable leaders for the country. Designated as the Syrian Protestant College, positioned in the city of Beirut, it was established in 1866 and formally opened its doors to 16 students on 3 December of that same year.[6]

A preparatory school was added in 1872 to improve the level of high school graduates who entered the college. By 1902 the enrolment of the college had reached 600, of which half were students in the preparatory school. The college continued to grow into a full university and later became known as the American University of Beirut.[7]

Shoghi Effendi at SPC

Shoghi Effendi attended SPC high school during the period 1912–13. It was a turbulent period in the entire Middle East region. The Italo-Turkish war spread to the area and brought devastation to the shores of Syria. On 24 February 1912 two Italian warships bombarded Beirut and caused large civilian casualties. The Syrian Protestant College, flying the American flag from its buildings, became a place of refuge. Shoghi Effendi was protected in this environment.

During this period Shoghi Effendi completed his high school senior year at the preparatory school and graduated in the early summer of 1913. Upon graduation, he hastened to travel to Alexandria to meet his beloved Master, who had returned from His long journey to the West. The period of separation from his beloved was over, and with great longing Shoghi Effendi attained the presence of the Master in Ramleh on 1 August 1913. At this time he was a youth of about 16.[8]

During the next two-and-a-half summer months the young Shoghi Effendi lived again in the household of the Master. He enjoyed the sweet experience of serving Him by taking down letters He dictated, running errands, receiving visitors at the railway station and occasionally accompanying visitors to the famous park and zoo in Alexandria.[9]

In October 1913 the summer vacation was over and Shoghi Effendi returned to Beirut to commence his college education at the Syrian Protestant College. The course of study he chose to pursue was Bachelor of Arts. His aim was to prepare himself for his future services to the Cause. Most of all he wished to please 'Abdu'l-Bahá, who expected Bahá'í students to exemplify a praiseworthy character and to achieve high standards of academic excellence.

During the first semester of his freshman year at SPC, 1913–14, Shoghi Effendi studied English, Arabic, French, History, Geometry and the Bible. During the second semester he continued with the same subjects, except that History was replaced by Biology.[10]

During the second semester of this academic year Shoghi Effendi participated in a declamation contest. This was conducted in four languages: English, Arabic, French and Turkish. Shoghi Effendi was the winner in the French language contest held on 12 May 1914.[11]

Shoghi Effendi became actively engaged in the Students' Union activities of this college. He was nominated as a secretary of the Union and contributed several articles for publication in the *Union Gazette*. Below are excerpts from an article he wrote which was published in 1914–1915. The title is 'Function of Sport in Life'

> If we consider sports from a general point of view and consider their relation to the life of the ancient people we must inevitably come to the conclusion that sports, if well conducted, have always raised the standard of the nation to a very high degree.
> ... that athletics, a branch of sports, is of great advantage to life is evident to the experienced student of modern European colleges ... Athletics are necessary if not indispensable for the future success of the nation as well as of the individual. 'A sound mind in a sound body' was the motto of the Greeks and in the model of the strong, healthy and vigorous Spartans ... Athletics refresh the body, tranquillize and enlighten the mind, and develop moral character. As a concrete example let us take a student in his college activities. The student who does exercise is always fresh and vigorous, he seldom gets sick and tired. His jovial character, his good disposition and his interest in life are his chief characteristics.
> Moreover in exercising, the student gets animated, his blood is purified and consequently his mind becomes more apt to receive the ideas and thoughts found in his lessons. The health which he acquires will help him to work harder and he becomes more successful. A weak person seldom can endure the hardship

SYRIAN PROTESTANT COLLEGE (SPC)

of school life, the trouble of memorizing and persevering in his daily lessons. Lastly when a student is busy with athletics during recess time his ideas do not deviate any more to the path of impurity, to think of such trivial things and the health and strength which he acquires will help him in overcoming such temptations. Generally a healthy person is endowed with a will stronger than that of a weak person . . .[12]

Shoghi Effendi was also involved in theatre. On 13 June 1914 the Students' Union presented *The Tragedy of Julius Caesar* at the West Hall Auditorium. Shoghi Effendi's name is mentioned in the cast list under 'Senators, citizens, soldiers and attendants'. It is not clear exactly which roles he played.[13]

The Bahá'í students attending the Syrian Protestant College expended their utmost to excel in their studies and to devote time to their Bahá'í services. It is clear that Shoghi Effendi played an important role in guiding the services and inspiring the lives of the small group of students. In a letter from Beirut on 3 May 1914, he wrote:

> Going back to our college activities, our Bahá'í meetings, which I have spoken to you about, are reorganized and only today we are sending letters, enclosing glad tidings of the Holy Land, to the Bahá'í Assemblies in various countries.[14]

In addition to sending letters to Bahá'í Assemblies, Shoghi Effendi wrote to individual believers in the West sharing with them the glad tidings of the health of the Master and other news he had received from Haifa. One such letter was written to Miss Kaukab MacCutcheon on 14 August 1914: Shoghi Effendi thanks this spiritual sister from the West for sending him volumes of literature in accordance with the wish of the Master. He signs the letter as Shauki Rabbani, son of Mirza Hadi Shirazi. Here are a few paragraphs from this letter:

> My very dear Spiritual Sister:–
> Before anything else, I should like to announce to you the glad-tiding of the health of Abdul-Baha. He is improving physically and he is ever happy and joyous.
> The news of the rapid progress of the Cause in the East and in

the West fills his heart with joy, encouragement and assurance. The fragrant breezes wafting from America as well as from Europe bring with them the sweet, ever expected news of the unity and amity reigning among the believers and maid-servants of Baha'Ollah. This causes indescribable and infinite joy and bestows upon our lives a new vigor, power and efficiency . . .

I wish to thank you . . . for the books which you have kindly sent me, this being in accordance with the desire of our Lord.

I have received 10 Books or better 10 volumes of the masterpieces of Literature and 12 volumes of the World's best Literature with some other pamphlets.

Indeed these highly esteemed books have been very useful and profitable. I am getting a great deal out of them. They form a very well equipped, important and fascinating library. I hope that I will keep them in a good condition and increase, through them, my knowledge and widen the sphere of my information.

Again, I most heartily and sincerely thank you for the great trouble you are taking to send them and mail them to me . . . [15]

After completing his freshman year at SPC Shoghi Effendi returned to Haifa for the summer. He corresponded with friends from different lands who had written to share the news of the progress of the Faith in their areas. One of these believers, Siyyid Muṣṭafá Rúmí from Burma, wrote to Shoghi Effendi sharing the glad tidings of the Cause of God. Shoghi Effendi describes the joy that the news brought to the Master:

. . . a Holy tender smile ran over his radiant Face and his heart overflowed with joy. I then came to know that the Master is in good health for I recollected his sayings which I quote now. 'Whenever and wherever I hear the glad tidings of the Cause my physical health is bettered and ameliorated.' I therefore tell you that the Master is feeling very well and is happy.[16]

The war in Europe began in August 1914, while Shoghi Effendi was spending his summer vacation with the Master, and gradually spread to Turkey. In late October there were rumours that the war would spread in the region and that Syria was unsafe. These rumours caused many students of SPC to drop out and the numbers enrolled at the college fell from 970 to 817.[17] However, the rumours did not affect Shoghi Effendi's resolve to go back to Beirut to begin his sophomore year. By contrast with many other students, Shoghi Effendi was calm and happy. His peace of mind and spiritual orientation are reflected in this letter to George Latimer from the Syrian Protestant College on 31 October:

> My very very dear spiritual brothers: –
> I am so happy to get this occasion to write you this letter. I feel so grateful and comforted whenever I remember your visit to us on Mount Carmel. That really was a wonderful and an inestimable time: During our vacation, the Lord with us, the students including Habib and Aziz among us, all was perfect, a most peaceful immemorable time we had. That should never be forgotten ...
> We students are in the College busy with our lessons, receiving at intervals the refreshing, life-giving breeze wafting from the Holy Land ...[18]

The immediate result of the declaration of war was the closing of the French and British schools and the enrolment of some 60 former students of the French schools in the Syrian Protestant College. There was fear among the Christian population that the Turkish Government, backed by the Germans, was attempting to stimulate a holy war against the Christians in order to attract the Arab world to their side. In early November a *jihád* was proclaimed by the Shaykhu'l-Islám and was confirmed on 11 November by the Sultan. Many Christians at the Syrian Protestant College anticipated a general massacre. However, the *jihád* failed as Husain, King of Hijáz and the Grand Sherif of Mecca, refused to endorse it.[19]

In December 1914 orders came from Damascus that all members of British and French communities were to be deported. This affected many friends of the faculty of the Syrian Protestant College as well as three doctors who had taken refuge on the campus.

Jamál Páshá, Commander of the Fourth Army and supreme Turkish authority in Syria, inspected the college, was impressed by the relief work being done there and allowed the medical doctors to return to Beirut. Soon after, the Government was informed that any wounded soldiers sent to the college hospitals would be treated free of charge. The offer was made possible through the Red Cross and Jamál Páshá accepted it, making the Syrian Protestant College a place of relative safety during the war.[20] Thus, despite the war, Shoghi Effendi studied in a relatively safe environment.

The contrast of this bitter war that had produced devastation and instilled fears in the hearts of men with the inner peace of Shoghi Effendi is remarkable. We can see the tranquillity of this beloved grandson of 'Abdu'l-Baha in the following paragraphs from a letter to George Latimer he wrote from the Syrian Protestant College on 14 March 1915 – having been away from home almost six months.

> Blessed is the Name which has bound all our hearts in love and sympathy and has drawn us together in perfect harmony and fellowship!
>
> I was exceedingly glad to hear of the brilliant career which you have set before you namely the propagation of the News of The Kingdom in the Islands of Honolulu, the furthest corners of the globe. In return I pray for you in his Holy Presence, I ask for confirmation at his Holy Threshold and beg for perseverance and steadfastness at His Holy Tomb . . .
>
> As to the news of the Holy Land may I quote some passages among the diary of Ahmad Sohrab written lately in Haifa: 'We have no news of the bitter struggle in Europe, we know here nothing but Peace, we sleep in Peace and we eat the Prince of Peace; we breathe the atmosphere of Peace, and live in a region of Peace . . .' That indeed is the case . . .
>
> While the Old Continent is busy with these horrible wars and carnage, may the new continent be guided to the Kingdom of El-Abha. While the former is darkened by the mists of superstition, hatred and irreligion may the latter be enlightened by the Light of Truth, by the light of Faith![21]

During the first semester of his sophomore year, 1914–15, he studied English, Arabic, French, History, Trigonometry, Physics and the Bible. During the second semester he studied English, Arabic, History, Analytical Geometry, Elementary Mathematical Analysis, Biology and the Bible.[22]

During this latter semester Shoghi Effendi participated again in extra-curricular activities. On 22 May 1915 the college conducted its

Shoghi Effendi during his early years

Shoghi Effendi as a youth

Shoghi Effendi, seated third from the right, with the Bahá'ís of Ramleh, Alexandria

Shoghi Effendi about the time of 'Abdu'l-Bahá's travels in North America

Number	Name		Date Oct 14
541	Shawki Hâdi Rabbâni		1916

	Name of Student, in vernacular	Name of Father, in vernacular
	شوقي رباني	ميرزا هادي شيرازي

Residence of Student	Vernacular	English
	حيفا	Haifa

Address of Parent or Guardian (with titles)	Vernacular	ميرزا هادي شيرازي حيفا
	English	Mirza Hadi Shirazi Caifa, merchant

Beirut Guardian:

Age	Religion	Nationality	Previous School	Department	Class	Day or Boarder	Scholarship Aid
19	Bahá'í	Persian	S.P.C.	Cg	IV	Roomer	

Vac 1916 Aug. Leaving May 14, 1917

Number	Name in Vernacular	طلبه نك اسمى	عدد
455	شوقي رباني		۵۰۰

Date Oct 9 1917	Name in English Shawki Hâdi Rabbâni	مكتبه دخولى تاريخى اكتوبر ۹ ۱۹۱۷

Place and date of birth	Residence	محل اقامتى	محل وتاريخ ولادى
Acre 1899	Haifa	حيفا	۱۸۹۹ عكا

Nationality	Denomination	Date of last vaccination	صوك آشيلاندبغى تاريخ	ملهبى	ملتى
Persian	Bahai	July 1917	۱۹۱۷	بهائى	ايران

Name, Title Occupation and Residence of Father or Guardian	Hâdi Rabbâni Business Haifa	هادي رباني	پدر ويا وليسنك اسم وشهرت وصنعت ومحل اقامتى

Beirut Guardian: Previous School:

Dep't.	Class	Day or Boarder	Scholarship Aid	Remarks
College	Grad.			

Shoghi Effendi's registration form for the Syrian Protestant College

Shoghi Effendi at the Syrian Protestant College

College Hall at the Syrian Protestant College, pre-1900.
Blatchford Collection, American University of Beirut

Shoghi Effendi, third from the left, second row, among students at the Syrian Protestant College

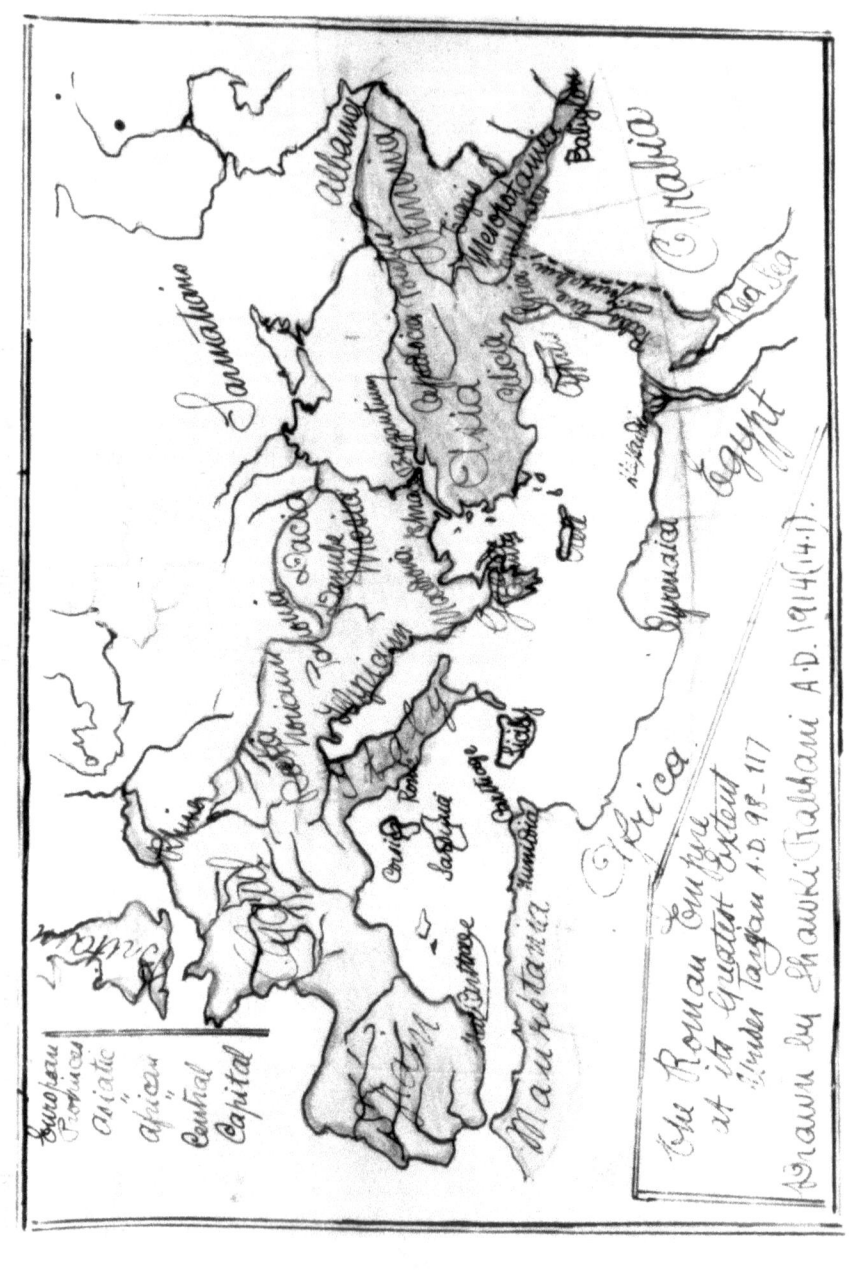

Map of the Roman Empire drawn by Shoghi Effendi

annual declamation contest in four languages: English, Arabic, French and Turkish. Shoghi Effendi was again the winner of the contest in the French language.[23]

As the war conditions and the blockade of the coast prevented the Bahá'í students at the Syrian Protestant College, most of whom were Persians, from going home, they spent their summer vacations in Haifa. The anteroom to the Shrine of the Báb was assigned to them. This reinforced their continued friendship with Shoghi Effendi, who would also go to Haifa during the summers. These students participated in the activities at the World Centre and frequently attained the presence of the Master.

The Master was pleased with the work of the students of the Syrian Protestant College and He revealed a Tablet in their honour:

> Praise be to God that the Bahai students in Beirut are well known for the beauty of their character, the purity of their deeds, and the loftiness of their morality. From whomsoever one enquires about the Bahai students, one will hear unstinted praise. This is through the favours and bounties of the Blessed Beauty, who has assisted you to attain such a high station. For you have lived in a manner conducive to the glorification of the Cause of God. Baha'o'llah is pleased with you; all the people are pleased with you; I am pleased with you, and the friends of God are pleased with you . . . If one asks any person concerning the Bahai students, he will answer: 'In reality they are intelligent, sober, industrious, diligent, displaying good manners and behaviour and concentrating all their attention on their acquirement of knowledge. They do not spend their time in frivolous amusements and distracting recreations.'[24]

This Tablet served to define the Master's expectations of Bahá'í students and to encourage the students at the Syrian Protestant College to excel in their studies and to strive to live a life that was pleasing to the Master.

Dr Habib Mo'ayyid, who himself attended the Syrian Protestant College, relates his recollections of the activities of the Bahá'í students there:

> The number of Baha'i students at SPC, many of whom were sent by the Master, increased to 35 during this period. As teaching the Faith

was forbidden in Beirut, Bahá'í activities consisted of meeting other Bahá'ís. The group of students often used to go on picnics with lunches packed by the school consisting of olives, dates, cheese and bread. The group went to the mountains and rivers in the vicinity of Beirut for the day and returned in the evening. Shoghi Effendi associated freely and on the same level with the other Bahá'ís. He was fond of walking, mountain climbing and swimming in the sea, and he played soccer.[25]

Ali Yazdi gives us a further description and paints a vivid picture of Shoghi Effendi's eagerness and joy while attending the Syrian Protestant College:

> At the college Shoghi Effendi was always jolly, optimistic, and hopeful. He had a wonderful personality. All of a sudden he would burst forth with loud laughter. Or sometimes a smile would break on his face. He had a very small mouth; beautiful, expressive eyes; and very regular, handsome features. He was bouncy. He just bounced.
> At college we were in the same dormitory. Shoghi Effendi's room was right across the hall from mine . . .
> We would converse on many subjects . . . We often talked to each other about the future. His vision was always of the Faith spreading all over the world and of everybody serving the Cause; these were his only ambitions.[26]

During the first semester of his junior year, 1915–16, Shoghi Effendi studied English, Arabic, Logic, Economics, Rhetoric, History, Ethics, Zoology and Chemistry. During the second semester he studied English, Rhetoric, Ethics, History, Logic, Economics, Physics and Chemistry.[27]

Shoghi Effendi participated again during this semester in the Student Union activities. The first issue of the 1915–1916 *Gazette*, dated November 1915, contains his article on 'Rules of Parliamentary Discipline'. The conflicts that apparently racked this student organization may have influenced his choice of this topic. Shoghi Effendi insisted on the importance for 'any deliberative assembly or organization' not only of adopting a constitution and bye-laws, but also of mastering them and practising them. In language that echoes down the years, he wrote:

SYRIAN PROTESTANT COLLEGE (SPC)

> In view of this indispensable fact . . . I find myself urged to state and explain some important points that shall assist an assembly to accomplish the work for which it is designed in the best possible manner.

And further on:

> My aim in this present article is to present to you, whom I hope have mastered the Bye-laws of the Union, a short clear satisfactory outline of Parliamentary terms and the order of its procedure . . .

Shoghi Effendi helped his fellow students understand the parliamentary rules for better functioning of the organization. He defined such terms as *meeting, session, call to the previous question, adjournment, amendment, laying a motion on the table, appeal, point of order*, etc. He concludes the article with a table classifying different kinds of motions.[28]

During the first semester of his senior year, 1916–17, Shoghi Effendi studied English Rhetoric, Arabic Rhetoric, French, History, Economics, Psychology, Engineering, Law and Astronomy. During the second semester he studied French, History, Sociology, Ethics and Law.[29]

The names of the professors and their assistants who taught these courses are listed in the college catalogue of 1915–16. According to this, the president of the Syrian Protestant College was Rev. Howard S. Bliss. Among the professors were: Jebr Mikha'il Dumit, professor of Arabic; Mansur Hanna Jurdak, professor of Mathematics; Julius Arthur Brown, professor of Physics; Rev. Stewart Crawford, professor of Bible and Ethics; Robert Reed, professor of Social Sciences; James Patch, professor of Chemistry; and Alfred Joy, professor of Astronomy.[30]

As stated earlier, Shoghi Effendi's diligent work at the Syrian Protestant College continued throughout a very difficult atmosphere of conflict. The war brought general misery to the whole region and caused a deterioration of economic conditions. Food supplies dwindled rapidly, even at the college. Actual starvation and disease surrounded the Syrian Protestant College and took the lives of more than 300,000 people in Syria.[31]

Shoghi Effendi was protected during the war because he lived in a college that continued to maintain its neutrality. However, this safe haven was always on the verge of disappearing throughout the whole period. Even during the last months before Shoghi Effendi's graduation, the College was in danger. It was informed that diplomatic relations with the United States had been cut off, and consequently, the College would be closed and taken over by the Government. A few days later, however, the statement was modified to indicate that the Government would not actually take over the College unless Turkey was at war with the United States. To protect the American institution from the fury of the mob, however, policemen were stationed at the gates. The College remained closed but student life continued as usual. On 5 May the College was informed that it could resume its activities on 7 May. Permission to reopen was partially due to the intercession of Jamál Páshá.

The reopening of the college enabled Shoghi Effendi to conclude his course of study and to graduate with the degree of Bachelor of Arts on 13 June 1917.

Shoghi Effendi was one of ten students listed among the graduating class of 1917. His fellow graduates were Fu'ád Amín 'Abdu'l-Málik of Beirut, Fá'iz As'ad of Beirut, 'Abdu'l-Husain Bakir of Haifa, Alexander Chorbajoglou of Constantinople, Murád Ibrahím Dishshi of Beirut, Taufik Yusuf Kashshu of Haifa, Aflátún Mírzá of London, Joseph Salám Rahwán of Cairo and 'Abdu'l-Rahmán Ramieff of Constantinople.[32]

Shoghi Effendi is registered on the college books again on 9 October 1917 as a 'Grad' student. He entered his name on the registers as 'Showqi Hâdi Rabbâni'. Even at this time he was aware of the necessity of accent marks in Persian and Arabic names when transliterated into English. Many years later he introduced the transliteration system now used in Bahá'í literature.

Three months later, on 15 January 1918, Shoghi Effendi wrote to the Master from Beirut. The English translation of this letter is quoted in *The Priceless Pearl*:

> I have resumed my studies, directing and concentrating all my efforts on them and doing my utmost to acquire that which will benefit and prepare me to serve the Cause in the days to come . . . my love and longing for you . . . I have sent you by post a piece of cheese, hoping it will be acceptable to Thee.
>
> Thy lowly and humble servant Shoghi[33]

SYRIAN PROTESTANT COLLEGE (SPC)

The summer of 1918 was a critical period in the history of the Faith. The Master's life was threatened. Jamál Pá<u>sh</u>á was determined to crucify 'Abdu'l-Bahá and His family. However, before this appalling act could be carried out, his design was frustrated by the rapidity of the British advance and the entry of General Allenby's forces into Haifa in September of 1918. 'Abdu'l-Bahá was safe.

Though the world war had not yet ended in the summer of 1918, Shoghi Effendi was ready to go back to 'Akká and render whatever service his beloved Master required. He left the American University of Beirut in the summer of 1918 after completing another academic year as a graduate student.

The Jafet Library at the American University of Beirut has two collections of black and white photographs of the period Shoghi Effendi was at Syrian Protestant College – the Moore and Blatchford collections. The Moore collection comprises the photographs taken by Dr Franklin T. Moore during his teaching position at this college (1892–1915), and shows views of the campus buildings.[34] The Blatchford collection covers pictures of the area including 'Akká and Haifa. These collections help us visualize the environment frequented by Shoghi Effendi during his student years.

II

Learning from the Master

3

In the Service of the Master

Autumn and Winter 1918

The miseries, sufferings and losses experienced by millions during World War I had prepared many receptive souls for the divine message which the Master had so lovingly delivered on His Western travels. The desire for peace and the prevention of war caused many of these receptive souls to investigate and embrace the Faith. The increase in the number of new believers and the opening of the channels of communication between the Holy Land and the rest of the world brought in hundreds of letters from veteran as well as new believers. Floods of mail poured in from the United States, Germany, France, India, Burma and Persia; letters carrying news of the activities of the believers and their joy at the re-establishment of communications with 'Abdu'l-Bahá. The believers wrote repeatedly to the Master giving Him news of their activities, introducing to Him new believers who had expressed their declaration of faith, asking Him questions about the Cause, seeking His advice on personal decisions and beseeching His blessings, confirmations, guidance and prayers. Such letters were referred to during this period as 'supplications'.

These supplications, many in English, needed to be translated into Persian and the replies of the Master then needed translation into English. The person ideally suited to render this important service was Shoghi Effendi.

In addition to the volume of correspondence that flowed into the Holy Land, the removal of restrictions on travel opened opportunities for visitors to journey to the World Centre. The conversations of the Master with the Western visitors also needed translation and Shoghi

PRELUDE TO THE GUARDIANSHIP

Effendi was in a position to render this important service as well.

Thus a new chapter opened in the life of Shoghi Effendi, a period of dedicated service to the Master. He saw at close quarters the way 'Abdu'l-Bahá responded to every challenge and every situation that arose; the way He showered love on all: pilgrims who had taken the long and arduous journey to attain His presence, believers from the East and the West who had written heartfelt supplications seeking His guidance, government officials who sought His counsel and advice, and military officers who wished to pay their respects. No one left His presence disappointed. He responded to each person according to his or her capacity and need, and inspired them all.

Imagine the youthful Shoghi Effendi observing these daily actions of the Centre of the Covenant! It is illuminating to see the Hand of Providence preparing the young successor of 'Abdu'l-Bahá for the high office of Guardianship he was destined to assume. Without a doubt, the example set by the Master and the experiences of memorable scenes with Him were to leave profound imprints on the future Guardian of the Cause and would sustain, cheer and comfort him 'in the thorny path' he was 'destined to pursue'.

Shoghi Effendi's service covered a period of about one and a half years, from the summer of 1918 to the spring of 1920. The type of work he performed was uniform throughout this period, consisting mainly of translations for 'Abdu'l-Bahá. However, the volume of the work, as well as the content of the material he translated, varied from month to month. This period of service was perhaps the happiest in his life.[1]

At the beginning, during the winter of 1918–19 in the aftermath of the untold suffering experienced by the masses in the World War and when communications were being restored, Shoghi Effendi translated significant Tablets of the Master in which He showered His love on each one of the believers who wrote to Him. The Tablets show the Master's perfect understanding of the questions the believers had raised as well as questions they had in their hearts but did not mention in their letters. The Master answered them all with the utmost love.

These Tablets were particularly significant because they became the magnets that drew the believers close to 'Abdu'l-Bahá, inspiring many to dedicate their lives to the Faith, striving to reach the station He was calling them to attain. Through such loving correspondence these souls increased their devotion to 'Abdu'l-Bahá and consequently rendered significant services to the Cause of God.

Shoghi Effendi, while serving the Master as a translator, became acquainted with many of these heroes and heroines of the Cause and began correspondence with several of them, correspondence which continued throughout his life. Two such believers were Dr Luṭfu'lláh Ḥakím and Dr John Esslemont.

Dr Luṭfu'lláh Ḥakím was from a distinguished Bahá'í family of medical doctors. His grandfather, Ḥakím Masíḥ, the court physician of Muḥammad Sháh, had first caught the spark of faith from Ṭáhirih and was later confirmed in the Cause by one of the Bahá'í prisoners in Tehran. His grandson, Luṭfu'lláh, was born four years before the ascension of Bahá'u'lláh. He grew up in a Bahá'í home. Like his grandfather, he decided to pursue a career in medicine and, when his secondary education was completed, he went to England in 1910 to study physiotherapy. He was an active believer who consecrated his life to the service of the Cause and towards the end of his life served as a member of the Universal House of Justice. He attained the presence of the Master many times and wrote to Him frequently.

Dr Esslemont, a medical officer at the Home Sanatorium in Bournemouth, was introduced to the Faith in 1914. His teacher, the wife of one of his associates who had met 'Abdu'l-Bahá in London in 1911, recounted her experience while in the presence of the Master and gave Dr Esslemont some pamphlets. The Word of God contained in those pamphlets touched his heart and set him on a course of search that led to his declaration of faith. Just over 12 months after his initial introduction to the Faith, he wrote an inspiring letter to a Bahá'í friend in Manchester that clearly demonstrated the depth of his knowledge and certitude in the Cause of God. While he continued his correspondence with the friends and shared his love for the Cause, Dr Esslemont felt an inner urge to write pamphlets and a book about the new revelation.[2] This intention was communicated to Dr Ḥakím.

When Dr Ḥakím attained the presence of 'Abdu'l-Bahá in Haifa and saw the Master saddened by publications in Europe attacking the Faith, he gave the news of a new believer in the Faith, Dr Esslemont, who had embraced the Cause of God with great enthusiasm. He told the Master that Dr Esslemont desired to write a book about the Faith to 'help the ready souls to reach the fountainhead of love and faith'.[3]

This news pleased the Master. Further mention of the untiring services of John Esslemont, the young doctor in Bournemouth, England, made the Master exceedingly happy. When Shoghi Effendi witnessed the joy in 'Abdu'l-Bahá's countenance, he was prompted to write to Dr Esslemont to convey the Master's pleasure and to deliver the glad tidings that the Master had 'prayed for you and asked His Heavenly Father for confirmation and help'. Shoghi Effendi continued:

> I now hasten, altho late at night, to open a correspondence with you which shall be continuous, inspiring, and regular.[4]

Shoghi Effendi began a similar correspondence with Dr Luṭfu'lláh Ḥakím, which continued throughout his student years. In one of his early letters to him, Shoghi Effendi communicates his own happiness and pleasure at being able to serve the Master:

> I am so glad and privileged to be able to attend to my Beloved's services after completing my course of Arts and Sciences in the American University at Beirut . . .
>
> The past four years have been years of untold calamity, of unprecedented oppression, of indescribable misery, of severe famine and distress, of unparalleled bloodshed and strife, but now that the dove of peace has returned to its nest and abode a golden opportunity has arisen for the promulgation of the Word of God . . . This is indeed the Era of Service.[5]

Many of the Tablets of the Master translated by Shoghi Effendi during this period of service were eventually published in *Star of the West*. For example, volume 10 of *Star of the West* reproduced Tablets of the Master translated by Shoghi Effendi for Ella Cooper and Roy Wilhelm on 12 December 1918.[6] Such Tablets were significant not only for those believers who had the bounty of receiving them but for all believers. The Tablets contained the Master's counsels and instructions for a disillusioned and confused world, counsels that were much needed at that time and are even more relevant today. The brief excerpts from some of these Tablets quoted in the next few chapters demonstrate Shoghi Effendi's developing style of English as well as convey the fragrance of the Master's words.

IN THE SERVICE OF THE MASTER, AUTUMN AND WINTER 1918

On 17 December 1918 Shoghi Effendi wrote from Haifa to Major Tudor-Pole attaching a translation of a Tablet the Master had written to Dr Esslemont in response to his supplication. Major Tudor-Pole acted as the trusted person in England who would distribute the messages from the Holy Land to the Bahá'ís. In his letter to Major Tudor-Pole Shoghi Effendi gave the news of the events of the day in the Holy Land. He described, for example, a meeting of the different religious heads of Haifa to institute relief work for the poor of the town. 'Abdu'l-Bahá had donated 50 Egyptian pounds for this work.[7] That same day Shoghi Effendi translated a Tablet of the Master for Mr and Mrs Vail to be sent to America.[8]

Shoghi Effendi was not known to the American Bahá'í community at this time. Dr Esslemont introduced Shoghi Effendi to the readers of the *Star of the West* in a letter published in volume 9 of that magazine:

> I was delighted to receive a copy of the translation of a Tablet which Abdul-Baha has written for me. The translation is by Shogi [sic], a grandson of the Master . . .[9]

Letters of Shoghi Effendi to Dr Ḥakím dated 19 November 1918 and to Major Tudor-Pole dated 17 December 1918 were also published in *Star of The West*; thus the American believers were introduced to this rising star in the Cause of God.

On 23 December 1918 Shoghi Effendi wrote to George Latimer, a friend he had made four years earlier and who was on active service in France. In this letter, Shoghi Effendi expresses his joy at the news that God had given his friend a child, and the hope of meeting this friend. He also expresses the difficulties surrounding the life of the Master since his earlier communications four years before.

> The Beloved's experiences of the past four years with the accompanied privations, danger, sickness, famine and oppression are indeed indescribable. So different and so contrasting they have been with those peaceful, quiet and serene days of 1914 that were spent with you . . .[10]

The winter of 1918 was a period of intense activity for Shoghi Effendi as he translated numerous Tablets revealed by the Master. Following the departure of Ahmad Sohrab, who had served as one of the Master's secretaries, for Cairo, Shoghi Effendi kept a diary of daily events in the form of letters typed by him on a manual typewriter. The letters convey significant information about the events that occurred during this period in the development of the Cause of God. They give us an insight into the way Shoghi Effendi spent his time during the sweetest and most cherished period in his life and provide us with a fascinating picture of what it was like to be continually in the presence of 'Abdu'l-Bahá.

We know from other sources[11] that the Holy Family woke up at dawn every morning and had breakfast in the presence of the Master after the morning devotions. The stories of the Master's attention to the needs of the poor, the sick and the orphan as part of His daily routine are well known. Brief excerpts from letters written during the last week of 1918[12] describe not only the daily routine but also the significant events that occurred each day in the presence of the Master.

23 December 1918

> ... the bitter cold and constant rain have made of to-day a depressing and monotonous one. The Master was all the time indoors, alone and pensive while I was translating and preparing for him the recently arrived supplication from America.

24 December 1918

> To-day I have spent my whole time with a dear friend of mine; a Moslem sheik, tall and imposing, an ashar scholar . . . and lastly a true, zealous and firm Bahai . . . Early this morning I was ordered by the Beloved to accompany this friend to Acca that he may visit the Holy Sites and fall on bended knees, for the first time, at the Holy Threshold. On our way to Acca as we rode off on the sandy beach, I was thrilled by the tale of the interesting incidents of his conversation . . .

These diary letters, as well as others to friends, are redolent with the excitement that surrounded his heavy workload.

25 December 1918

To-day is Christmas day – a day of festivities and merriment. Well appropriate is therefore the news we received from Japan . . . The news are promising and will undoubtedly refresh and gladden the heart of the Beloved when I shall translate to him the contents of the letters of Juzo Muchizuki, a Japanese girl of eighteen, and Mr. Tokijiro Torii, a blind brother of that land . . .

It would be incomplete if I should not close this impressive and significant account of the awakening of Japan, with some extracts of a supplication of that ablazed girl again, to the Beloved. It . . . is remarkable for being the supplication of the first woman of the Land of Japan. 'To the Holy Servant of God! O the unexhaustible Fountain of love and mercy! O the Teacher who gives new life and strength to these weak lambs in the world.

'I feel very honored, having been born in a secluded village in a corner of the Orient, Japan, to be able to write a letter to the Divine Teacher . . . My thought is your teaching; my beauty is your teaching; my courage is your teaching and my love is your teaching . . . I am studying under the care of our Bahai mother, Miss Alexander, and have your name and picture upon my writing desk, whose merciful eyes are watching over me and I can gain from them always life and strength. O my teacher! Let me cry in thanks, you are my whole life!'

Such is the breeze from Japan and such is the condition of the souls that are being awakened! I remember in this connection the remark of the Master when I reported to him the eager inquiry and seeking of some of the British and allied officers to know more about the Cause. He said:– We are tranquil and silent in this city of Acca but awakened souls are every day responding to the Trumpet call of the word of God which is sounding and resounding thruout all the world. At another instance, he intimated, our conquests and victories know no defeat and failure but are everlasting and eternal. This morning the Master, notwithstanding the rainy weather and the bitterly cold morning breeze, enveloped in his Aba, came down to the waiting room to greet his friends . . . In the afternoon He rode off in His landau to pay visits to some of the prominent Christians of the town.

I wish you a merry Christmas.

26 December 1918

Every day carries with it its fresh tidings and happy news. From the Far-Eastern land, the centre of news has shifted to-day to Persia, in the Middle East, and thence to the extreme west in the U. S. America. Many telegrams have arrived and each contributed its share of consolation and solace . . .

Early this morning I was ushered to His Holy Presence and there facing the Beloved on the sofa, enwrapped in His mantle with masses of supplications scattered around Him, I sat, the pen in my hand, putting down the words that flowed from His lips . . .[13]

Noon had drawn near and as the Master got out of His writing room and walked along, Mr. Abdul Ali Musa appeared and with a bow greeted the Master. The Beloved for his sake sat a while with him and questioned him whether he would graduate this year as a doctor in medicine to which he replied affirmatively. He then said that thank God we have sent so far some good doctors to Persia and we anticipate the results . . .

In the afternoon, I rode up to Mount Carmel . . . I was back at 3 p.m. and found the Beloved in His room . . . Few moments later, some Moslem and Christian guests arrived and the Beloved entertained them till sunset when the great and venerable archbishop of Haifa arrived. The first thing he did was to ask Him for counsel and advice for his work. He received plenty of admonitions and was overwhelmed with bounty and kindness. When at night the friends assembled, He ordered me to translate for them the contents of Miss Agnes Alexander's letter which contained the news from Japan. In conclusion he said: Undoubtedly Japan will turn ablaze and great will be its flame.

The next day Shoghi Effendi translated several Tablets revealed by the Master, two of which were addressed to Tokijiro Torii and Juyo Muchizuki in Japan and three to Marion Jack, Agnes Alexander and Beatrice Owens.[14] This example of Shoghi Effendi's translation of one of these Tablets, to Beatrice Owens, provides a glimpse of the Master's loving counsels to His devoted disciples:

Every imperfect soul is self-conceited and thinks of his own good.

But as his thoughts expand a little he will begin to think of the welfare and comfort of his family. If his ideas still more widen his concern will be the felicity of his fellow citizens; and if still they widen he will be thinking of the glory of his land and of his race. But when ideas and views reach the utmost degree of expansion and attain the stage of perfection then will he be interested in the exaltation of humankind. He will be then the well-wisher of all men and the seeker of the weal and prosperity of all lands. This is indicative of perfection.[15]

The Master's guidance to Beatrice Owens was certainly related to an inner question of hers, which this Tablet addressed, but His profound message, which is the key to the prosperity of humankind, was for all believers and for all time.

Late that evening Shoghi Effendi wrote his usual diary letter, this time from 'Akká, where he had that afternoon accompanied two believers to the Shrine of Bahá'u'lláh. Sitting round a table in the House of 'Abbúd with these friends 'both engaged in the reading of newspapers', Shoghi Effendi wrote:

27 December 1918

The night is quite advanced ... With my thoughts centering around the activities of the day, I am holding the pen and am dropping you these lines ...

The forenoon ... was spent largely in the Beloved's presence taking down what he dictated to me. Before his revealing any Tablet a certain needy and destitute person, a native of the town, came to Him. Of course he gained admittance very easily for the Beloved's doors are flung open for the high and low alike ... The Beloved listened to all his details and threw at him at times sympathetic and affectionate glances. When his tale was told, the all-generous drew out from His pocket some paper money and delivered them to him. He seized the Blessed hands of his Benefactor and approached to kiss them. But the Beloved withdrew His hands saying: Are we not both the servants of God? Are you not God's creature and servant? Am I not the same? ...

This incident is simply another clear and manifest illustration of the Master's care of the Poor, of His constant succour of the indigent, His consolation of the disconsolate, and His providing the deprived ones.

When he retired – infinitely comforted and for ever grateful – the Beloved took up His work which on that morning was mainly correspondence with the believers . . .

Having bestowed thru His words the necessary stimulae and force that will help these souls to arise in the Service of the Cause, the Beloved ordered Esfandiyar, the coachman, to prepare the carriage that He may attend the Friday mosque. 'I go that they may understand that my past attendance in the mosque was not a matter of wisdom and carefulness but was a heartfelt sincere and fervent action. Now that restrictions are removed I still attend such services for to a Bahai, a synagogue, a mosque and a church all afford a similar and equally favourable place of worship and adoration.'

Returning to Haifa the following day, 28 December,

as we reached the post-office, a bit of news from Kudai Effendi, who is as ever our punctual and assiduous post messenger was to the effect that Major Tudor Pole had despatched for the Master a big parcel post which was first thought to be some clothing. When however the Beloved opened it it was a big packet of a multitude of letters numbering almost a hundred of supplications that had been forwarded by earnest and eager Bahais from all over the world each bearing its prayers, its wish, its report and its glad-tidings. They are still scattered on His sofa and I cannot venture to fix the number of those which he shall be able to read or answer. His desire is certainly keen to read, to ponder over and to answer each and all but time is an unhappy hindrance. Even at night, with the flickering light of His room and while speaking to his friends, He sometimes takes hold of a letter, throws a glance on it and even comments upon its contents . . .

Until now I haven't been privileged to translate any one for Him . . .

On Sunday 29 December 1918, Shoghi Effendi translated Tablets of the Master to George Latimer, Shahnaz Waite and Jessie Revell,[16] as well as to Howard Colby Ives, Mr and Mrs Gregory in Washington, and Ethel Rosenberg in London. One touching letter concerned a bereavement; to Mrs Edna Ballora, who had 'been many years ago in close touch with the Holy Household and who now mourns the loss of her six-years-old child', 'Abdu'l-Bahá wrote:

> For years thou hast been in our household, and wert intimately connected with the daughters and eventually thou hast been favoured by the entrance into the kingdom. Therefore be sad of nothing for this joy no grief can overcome . . . This world is not a place wherein man should, because of death and separation, become the captive of sorrows. No soul in this world is entitled to rest and comfort for it is a world of test and trial. Hast thou seen in the course of thy life a soul who has not been grieved or depressed? If thou sayest: yes; I say look thou into thy family . . .

As the year drew to its close, fewer letters were received:

30 December 1918

> . . . the mail of this day was scanty, in fact, it amounted to nothing save a letter from our dear Letitia, who many years ago was a teacher of French and Arabic to the children of the household and who is now in Egypt . . . In reality it seemed as if we had plunged again into the dark war days of the past, isolated, separated, and lonely.
> Fortunate was I therefore in being shut up in my room for 11 consecutive hours busy in my copying, transcribing and translating the 16 Tablets that had been revealed the past two days.
> . . . To-night we had a short but exciting profitable talk by the Master. Having in His presence nearly a score of Bahais He opened the meeting by bidding me chant a few verses from the Ishrakat after which our nightingale, having performed all his ceremonies and preparation followed warbling an ode composed by the Beloved in Turkish . . .

4

In the Service of the Master

Early 1919

'This day is a memorable and glorious one', wrote Shoghi Effendi in his diary letter of 6 January 1919. It was the celebration of the Declaration of the Báb according to the lunar calendar, 'as well the anniversary of the birth of . . . the Center of the Covenant'. Shoghi Effendi continued:

> The feast which has a double significance is celebrated to-day under circumstances totally different from those of the previous years. Not only has security, peace and comfort been established, not only are the hearts appeased and satisfied, not only are the doors of communication with the distant parts of the Bahai world flung open but the very fact that this glorious anniversary is celebrated at a time when the whole world has just awakened to the principles of the Cause is itself a noteworthy if not the most important feature of the day . . . Sweets, bonbons, roses, rose-water sweeten the mouths and embalm the nostrils of these grateful souls who being privileged to be in the vicinity of the Holy Sites and near to the Center of the Covenant are sharing with their fellow-brethren in Persia, India, Europe and America the joy and triumph of this memorable day.
>
> Early this morning the friends assembled in the parlour of the Beloved's house, some on chairs, others sitting on the ground and a few others standing so crowded was the room and so attractive was the occasion. The Beloved entered and all bowed in greeting and thanksgiving. Rose-water was distributed, tea was served and sweets were presented.
>
> The Beloved's talk on that occasion was short but thrilling. Later

on he ordered Haji Nasrollah to chant the poems appropriate to the occasion after which I was privileged to chant some of the prayers revealed by Bahaollah in memory of the Supreme Declaration.

[In] the afternoon a general meeting at which men and women separately met was held at the Holy Tomb. It was a long, warm and spiritual gathering. The Beloved, unable to attend, had sent His message to the friends and had expressed His wish that the meeting should be as elaborate as possible. Accordingly three of our able singers contributed each their share to the programme after which I gave a talk on the significance of this celebration in view of the rapid progress of the Cause and the fulfilment of Bahaollah's explicit prophecies. Mr. Azizullah Khan who had come with our dear brother Abdol-Hossain Khan from Beirut to pay a short visit to the Beloved then followed and delivered a talk on the spiritual activities of the Bahai students in the Syrian Protestant College of Beirut. When we visited the Holy Shrine, it had grown dark and the visit at this silent hour of twilight was indeed imbued with a deep sense of fervour and respect. The whole day was marked with a sense of triumph, merriment and gratitude and was in accordance with the wish and recommendation of the Beloved.

A big mail of some fifty supplications from France, India, America, Egypt and England has arrived this evening.[1]

On 4 January Shoghi Effendi recorded the following in his diary letter about the visit of an Indian officer:

> The papers written in the Indian language which I had kept for distribution when such occasion should arise were quite appropriate and valuable in connection with the visit of a certain Indian officer from Lahore, Punjab, by the name of Captain Ajah Khan who having heard of the Bahai Movement had hastened to seek a personal interview with the Master. 'You are very welcome,' were the opening words of the Beloved as he took his seat, 'I am so pleased to meet a representative of India. How varied and numerous are its religions and sects at present. In a single house no less than 25 representatives of different creeds and sects were once found. How do they stand at present?' With this as a topic the Beloved treated fully the principle of the 'Fundamental unity of all Religions'. He

then emphasized the fact that the source of man's activities to-day, scientific and political, all emanate from the Divine manifestations of God. The principle of Democracy, the political constitutional machinery of Europe, the principle of arbitration and representation, all these ideals spring from the Fountain of God's Truth and [are] embodied in the teachings of His manifestations.

When our visitor departed he left with an intention to call again, to learn some more of these truths and meanwhile to read and digest the references on the Cause that had been made in some of the Indian papers which he was glad to carry with him to his camp.[2]

In a letter to Dr Luṭfu'lláh Ḥakím in London dated 7 January 1919 Shoghi Effendi explained how the Master spent His time from morning to evening:

> How pleased was the Beloved to receive your long letter which I immediately translated for him word by word. The Christian Commonwealth dated Dec. 4 was received to-day and the contents of the short article on the Cause duly presented to the Master ... These days often from morn till eve have been spent in revealing tablets – and what vigorous and enthusiastic words are revealed! for America, Persia, England, India, Russia, Japan and Egypt.[3]

On 8 and 9 January eight further Tablets were translated by Shoghi Effendi, addressed to Agnes Parsons, Mrs Rasmussen, Amy Wilkinson, Isabel Chamberlain, Genevieve Coy, Anna van Blarcom, Emma Carmichael, and Alice Ives Breed.[4] An excerpt from the Tablet to Alice Ives Breed provides another example of Shoghi Effendi's developing use of English and describes the role of women in preventing war:

> If the mass of women in Europe and all those in America had been enfranchised throughout all the states, undoubtedly they would not agree to the war. At present this war has made millions of children fatherless and millions of fathers and mothers destitute of sons; this war has snatched from pitiable sisters their brethren; this war has turned millions of women widows and destitute of husbands; this war has made cities desolate; this war has brought confusion and

chaos in millions of villages; this war has made the very foundations of mankind quake and quiver.[5]

As the volume of supplications received from all parts of the world continued to increase, the Tablets revealed by the Master kept pace and Shoghi Effendi kept up with the translations. On 10 January he translated Tablets in honour of Zia Bagdadi, Martha Root, Geraldine Luxmore, Belle Luxmore, Henrietta Wagner, David Buchanan, Alfred Lunt and Mabel Nickerson.[6] 'Today has been an active day,' he wrote in his diary letter that evening, '. . . the piles and masses of letters that had been contributed by the previous mails were greatly eliminated by the great number of Tablets that have been revealed this morning.' Commenting on these Tablets, he wrote that they:

> all center around one point, namely the Rise for teaching and for the promulgation of the word of God. All petty differences must be left behind and all thought concentrated upon the best way of delivering the Divine message. For, as the Beloved has repeatedly declared, the world of mankind which has just emerged from the sea of strife is indeed most ready and best prepared to receive the resuscitating principles . . . We hope that these repeated appeals of the Beloved will cause souls to arise and concentrate their whole life to the service of the glorious Cause.[7]

Despite the pressure of work, a high degree of care can be seen in the translation of each Tablet. Here is an example of Shoghi Effendi's translation of the Tablet for Mabel Nickerson in which the Master reiterates the promise that divine confirmation will surround any of the friends engaged in teaching and living a Bahá'í life:

> O maid-servant of His Holiness Baha'o'llah!
> Thy letter dated September 25, 1918, was received. Thou hast solicited confirmation. Know thou verily that the magnet of confirmation is the promulgation of divine teachings. Whosoever arises for the diffusion of the fragrances of God, the confirmation of the Kingdom will assuredly surround him to such an extent that he will himself remain confounded.
> However, this is conditioned upon the conformity of words

with deeds. The people of Baha must strive to diffuse the fragrances through deeds more than through words . . .[8]

Despite the burden of work on his young shoulders, Shoghi Effendi maintained an interest in what was happening at his alma mater, the Syrian Protestant College in Beirut, in the aftermath of the World War:

> The athletic field of the college is being used by the British soldiers while the preparatory dining-room has been converted into a hospital for officers.
> A school for 500 soldiers has been started . . . The soldiers are to ride in from the Pine forest of the city of Beirut to study their lessons in Fisk Hall all day and then to ride home in the afternoon. The college has greatly been interested, of late, in the work of the Red Cross Society and the students and teachers have just started a soup kitchen opposite to the college gate which will help 500 people.
> The college is running quite smoothly. Its special annual devotional meetings have just started . . . In a letter from the manager of West Hall . . . the writer expresses his keen anticipation and his profound wish to see the Beloved on its platform addressing the student body and the administration board. The same desire and wish has been expressed in a letter which I had lately from its president, Doctor Howard Bliss. We hope the day will come soon.[9]

In the remaining weeks of January Shoghi Effendi translated Tablets to the Assemblies of Cleveland, Santa Barbara, Akron and Urbana, to Luṭfu'lláh Ḥakím, Ella and Ellah Rice-Wray, Sarah Gertrude Harris, Isabella Brittingham and Claudia Stuart Coles, to the Bahá'ís of the British Isles. These were published in *Star of the West*,[10] but there were countless others. His diary letters[11] tell the story, not only of his own increasing workload and his delight in the progress of the Cause, but also of his burgeoning interest in the development of Haifa and the gardens, as Spring began. They also give us precious glimpses of 'Abdu'l-Bahá:

11 January 1919

A blind Japanese girl of twelve has sent this supplication to the Beloved:– 'I have heard from Miss A. [Agnes Alexander] of the spiritual instructor to our comfort. She wrote me about your words who am an orphan from early age and lost my sight afterwards. Thru wonderful provision I was sent to the blind school and I am quite happy now . . . As a rule we blind people like myself live in the dark world and never out into the world of light. This is my point and I feel I have now got Light, the light in spirit which can never be put away . . .'

The supplication of this child has not yet been answered materially, but in spirit she has received a convincing response. The flame of Abdul Baha's love is consuming the hearts of these young and physically destitute souls leaving behind it the gold of faith . . .

Days seem to be insufficient and the hours of the day afford no adequate amount of time for the answering of the showers of supplications that are daily pouring in . . . in India the Cause is progressing by leaps and bounds. Its appeal is specially felt among the aristocratic circles in contrast with the course the movement has assumed in Japan, where the blind, the deaf and the orphans seem to be attracted and drawn. The Maharajah has for nearly two years been reading the Holy Books which his youngest daughter places in his hands. In his speeches he repeats sentences from the Books.

The Cause is becoming more and more the world-movement which every faithful Bahai eagerly awaits to see . . .

12 January 1919

The Beloved has just left the waiting room having bid good-night . . . and has gained his room tired and fatigued by the activities of the day.

Our visitor to-day has been Mr. Safouat . . . He has spent to-day almost all of his time in the presence of the Beloved and has been favoured in accompanying the Master, who bid him sit close to him in His carriage, to the Blessed Tomb of the Bab. Badi Effendi, [it] being Sunday and consequently a day of recess for him, was also in the carriage, sitting near me, with our gardener Ismail-Agha who has so rarely been able to visit the Shrine, in front of us; all driving off on a clear, sunny but rather cold afternoon to the Makam where some thirty believers awaited us . . . we found them gathered, notwithstanding the bitter cold, outside the rooms talking with and entertaining some British soldiers who had taken a temporary leave from their camp. Tea had been offered to them and they awaited the spiritual warmth of the heart to be contributed not by tea but by the Master's interview and welcome words.

He affectionately shook hands with each and immersed them indeed in an ocean of Kindness and affection. One would think that these souls had been for a time warm and loving followers of the Master.

When they left . . . the Beloved gathered together the scattered groups of the friends and . . . gave us an original and picturesque talk on Trust and faithfulness . . . As the meeting came to a close, we were all led to visit the Blessed Shrine, at the door of which stood as usual the Beloved in the utmost of humility and respect. That spot was exceptionally cold and exposed, yet there was the Servant of Baha giving the good example to his friends and servants.

13 January 1919

Our nightingale has indeed excelled to-night. With his exceptionally harmonious melodies still ringing in my ears, I am sitting right after our evening meetings, resuming my diary . . . Indeed the tune coupled with the wonderful selections from the 'Masnavi' of the Blessed Perfection made of the song an inspiring one which has, I am sure, affected the least responsive member of the gathering. The Beloved Himself accompanied by his low murmur some of the striking stanzas of the ode and thus bestowed a special charm and breathed into it a new life . . .

In connection with the anticipated departure of two of our friends in the college on their way to Persia with whom Abdol-Hossein Shirazi may probably travel, the Master to whom this news had been reported . . . addressed him as follows: – 'Tell me now art thou a democrat or a Bahai? To what category does thou belong? Verily thou should'st identify thyself with the teachings of Bahaollah. For a Bahai has adopted a cause that is all inclusive that gathers within its folds the pure and unadulterated essence of all that is best and highest in this century . . . humanitarian principles and the object of all worldwide philanthropic movements. The Bahai Revelation is the spirit and glory of this age. It is the pure and unadulterated esscence of all that is best and highest in this century . . . Thou must be a true and zealous Bahai, so that when thou attainest to those shores of thy native land and come in contact with souls that are athirst for the news of the Holy Land, thou mayest refresh, revive and inspire and comfort them thru thy deeds and words.

Once communication with the West was restored, the Bahá'í friends began to receive much-longed-for news of 'Abdu'l-Bahá and to write letters signed by the whole local community:

14 January 1919

The first collective supplication ever received since the restoration of communications was from the Bahais of Urbana which was forwarded from Port-Said and which reached to-night just at a time when the friends were ushered to the Beloved's presence. He bid me translate its contents . . . These are the concluding sentences of this joint supplication:– 'Shall ever again American pilgrims be allowed to appear before thy Holy Presence? Thank thee, O Abdul Baha, that Thou hast taken us up among the children. Praise be to Thee! Assist us to realize more and more clearly this glorious Revelation, this unique and heavenly age . . .'

From two to three scores of signers, a great number being children of 4 to 6 who have enclosed some short longing letters in their own handwriting, this supplication is an evidence of the warmth and activity which prevail among the friends of that city.

15 January 1919

The Beloved hardly stepped out of doors to-day. Ahmad Safouat . . . was with him for a few hours. He is quite versed in civil and international law and has written books on local jurisprudence which are widely known. The Beloved exposed to him some facts concerning the comparative law among the Turks and the British and cited interesting illustrations which a specialist like him deeply appreciated.

The transference of general Headquarters has been carried out fully and the Commander in Chief of the Expeditionary Force lives not far from here, in the German colony at the house of Frank. A great part of the surrounding houses and a big portion of the colony has been appropriated by the body of staff and members of the entourage of the general and the erection of Camps has become these days a frequent and familiar matter. The rooms are well lighted, the houses and shops neatly numbered, the roads mostly named, the telephonic and telegraphic wires extended thruout all their ramifications in almost every corner of the city, the station blazes at night and has been extended, developed and enriched, the public park has been provided with 160 shrubs, the Egyptian railway cars are constantly sliding to and fro on the railroad drawn west of Mt. Carmel, the people in the city are daily increasing with every afternoon train coming directly from Kantara carrying a fresh supply of officers, staffites and visitors – in a word the signs of advancement and progress are not wanting.

What we eagerly look forward to, however, is the practical opening of ways and the removal of all travel restrictions so that pilgrims and friends may pour in, may set foot on the Holy Land, may visit the Holy Mount, may look again at the Beloved's face and may circumambulate the Holy Shrine.

This day we trust will not be indefinitely postponed.

16 January 1919

The garden immediately surrounding the Beloved's abode is blooming with verdure and flowers. The grove as well as the rose-garden have indeed turned out into a delectable Paradise. Over three thousand mandarines sparkle like unto fire from among the leaves of young trees that bend under the weight of their clusters of fruits. The alleys are adorned on each side with rain-drenched roses of varied colors. The Balustrade is almost concealed from view, so extensive and rich have become the branches and the offshoots of the ivy. The white rose bushes seem indeed to be covered with spots and masses of snow reflecting the lights of the sun so much as to dazzle the eye. The fragrance that embalms the air, the freshness that one encounters around himself, the sight of the trees that seem from afar to be set on fire, the violets, modest yet betraying by their scent their presence, the jasmine, lily, and rose all combine to make of the rose-garden a favorable place on such a sunny afternoon as the one we had to-day, for the Master to dictate the Tablets to his dear friends all over the world.

Indeed this morning, as soon as the flaming disk arose high in the heavens, flooding the air and earth with heat and light after this misty and damp weather of last week, the Beloved began revealing glorious and important Tablets to his friends in India, in Egypt and in Persia . . . Indeed to-day as perhaps never before has the tender and fresh memory kept by the Beloved for his friends in the outlying and distant portions of the globe been made manifest and evident. With what a tender care, what a fatherly solicitude, what an alluring exhortation does he surround them. His promises, conditioned upon their rise for service, are stupendous and their retribution, if at all they fulfil God's will, unbounded and invaluable.

Will such promises of the Beloved and the exposition of such a bright prospect incite every true Bahai to enroll himself in the legions of the Supreme Concourse? Will these words breathe a new and rich life in every soul? We shall wait and see.

18 January 1919

To-day has been almost wholly devoted to the friends of God in London. Out of four thrilling Tablets, three were destined for London while the fourth was the first general Tablet revealed to the Bahais collectively in Cleveland, Ohio . . .

On Nov. 30th, a unity meeting . . . was held at Miss Rosenberg's in London. The Christian Commonwealth of Dec. 4th 1918 refers to it as characterised by 'an atmosphere of great joy, being the first gathering since the signing of the armistice . . . moreover, a general letter of petition was written and signed by all present and was sent to the other cities in British Isles to be signed by the friends and then to be forwarded to the Holy Presence. In that meeting also the long-expected, direct news of the Master's health and safety were announced.'

Antecedent to these celebrations weekly regular Bahai meetings were being conducted . . . Dr. Esslemont . . . is writing a book on the Bahai Revelation . . . The other friends such as Lady Blomfield, Miss Rosenberg, Mrs. Cropper and Mrs. Stannard are engaged in service, in lecturing, in helping the poor and indigent, in organizing meetings, in publishing Bahai books and in spreading the message in every possible and effective way.

Ample reward and recompense is therefore bestowed upon these awakened souls by the revealing of these wonderful Tablets of to-day – Tablets in which the Beloved highly praises their activity and attributes it to the 'purity of their hearts and the freshness of their souls . . .'

20 January 1919

. . . a certain old and tested friend in the Cause, by the name of A. Ghaffar . . . had come from Acca a few days ago in order to catch another glance from the countenance of the Beloved, for the long and tedious months which had kept him in bed had enkindled a fire of longing in his heart . . . However, as he was still weak and infirm the Beloved out of his boundless compassion immediately penned himself a few lines to his family in Acre, assured them of the health of the convalescent father and informed them of the advisability of his remaining for a few days at the Red Cross Hospital. Having despatched the letter, he ordered me to accompany our friend to the Hospital, have him assigned a ventilated spacious room, explain his case to the Doctor and to commit him to the charge of the nurse . . .

When I returned, the Beloved later on sent Mirza Mohsen to see him and provide as much as possible for his needs and wants.

How compassionate is the Beloved! With what a fatherly care doth He surround His feeble and frail children!

This afternoon again the Beloved started on His benevolent and charitable occupation. He went and visited the poor and the lonely, gave money to the poor, and walked up long distances in some of the rocky places on the slopes of Mount Carmel in order to administer to the indigent and the helpless.

When he returned home it was dark, and tired and fatigued he sat enwrapped in his cloak in the corner of His sofa and asked for a cup of tea. He had not finished it when Khosro reported visitors were at the door. They were poor people who had been thrown out of business and had lost their job but in reality trustworthy, kind and upright men. In the time of need they turned to their benefactor and their saviour who altho' exterminated with fatigue entertained for over an hour, alleviated the burden of their anxiety, refreshed their minds and made them hopeful of the future and lastly made them sit around his table and partake of his humble supper.

21 January 1919

As the day was bright and warm and the winds that had fiercely blown during the past days had calmed down, the Beloved rode up to the Holy Tomb of the Bab alone and was back for dinner . . .

Myself, accompanied by the Holy Mother drove off to the eastern section of Haifa where a certain Bahai family was struck with a severe calamity, in the sudden and serious almost dangerous illness of one of its members . . .

At night the friends of God assembled and spent a whole hour in communion and meditation. The Beloved assumed an almost continuous silence and gave them ample time to review in their own hearts their lives and actions and estimate how far they have exemplified in their daily activities the daily heart to heart exhortations of the Master. They retired with fresh determination and a hopeful heart.

. . . Persia is practically severed from the motherland and welcome will be the breezes that shall waft from that region and the word that shall be received from its people. We realize how expectant is the heart of the eager Bahai in Persia, how thirsty is his soul . . . I shall surely let you know of the least bit of news that I may gather from any source for undoubtedly the Cause has progressed in Persia thruout these gloomy years.

22 January 1919

He said: the true Bahai must shake off the dust from his shoes when he leaves a city lest he should carry with him any acquisition from the people. 'Born in calamity, reared in calamity, grown up in calamity, attained maturity in calamity, reached old age in calamity, for seventy years, under chains and fetters, banished and exiled, incarcerated and confined, neither the absolute nor the constitutional rule secured for me rest and deliverance until in the past days the British [rule] has been extended over this Holy Land and the pavilion of security and comfort has been pitched.'

24 January 1919

Although in general, security and comfort have been amply provided for the people in these regions since the significant fall of Palestine yet still these days are days of sadness, of discouragement and of anxiety . . . people are mourning the loss of their dear ones whose blood has been shed in this awful war, others keenly realize the loss of their property, their sacred rights which have been robbed and trampled under the previous regime. A few are thrown out of work and unable to engage in commerce and industry wonder how they will be able to support their family.

In view of this sad reaction, the all-compassioned Beloved from early morn till in the afternoon started on his accustomed round among the fallen, the disconsolate and the mourning.

Streets, nay rather lanes which I myself had not traversed for seven or eight years; places which I had never gazed at before were visited by the Beloved who walked continuously long distances and ascended steep and tiring staircases only to lay some coins in the palm of an indigent, or leave with a sorrowing heart few words of comfort . . .

As the weather was calm and the sun was shining the Beloved took his afternoon tea on Mount Carmel and visited the Holy Tomb of the Bab and was back just on time for the regular evening meeting of the friends.

25 January 1919

In the afternoon as I was summoned by the Master . . . a Tablet was revealed to a friend in Port-Said wherein the postal and telegraphic addresses of the friends in India were asked for. This seems necessary for in all probability the eager friends in India are still deprived of the blessing of a direct communication with the Master. Their petitions, their cables and even their letter have arrived but their response on the part of the Beloved has been deferred due to lack of a sufficient address.

Later on a certain notable of the city called on the Beloved and still later in contrast with him gained admittance a poor, almost ragged, old laborer with hands hard and rugged denoting strenuous labor but with a broad smile and bright eyes. He greeted the Beloved and sat close to the rich man both on exactly the same level in the presence of the Master. Both of them forgot their rank and their position, absorbed by the equal treatment of the Beloved, began to talk and even to joke with one another. When they retired the Beloved was pleased for the poor old worker, being of a humorous character, had told many a pleasing tale and humorous anecdote. Often does he come to the Beloved, points to his patched garments and begs for succour. Ample is the contribution and quick is the response of the generous Lord . . .

Calls after calls of such a kind one may witness on a single day and never does a seeker or petitioner retire disappointed or dissatisfied.

26 January 1919

For four years has the annual convention of the Mashrekol-Askar of America been sitting under circumstances which isolated it from the Holy Land which deprived it of the directions and instructions of the Beloved . . . The coming convention which will be held in the days of Rizvan in this coming month of April, will undoubtedly exhibit a new power, a fresh spirit and a renewed zeal for the hand of the Master is now directly directing its activities thru his letters and telegrams. The friends who will represent the assemblies will sit as delegates who have been stimulated and refreshed by the wafting of the breeze of glad-tidings which had ceased for four years to emanate from the Holy Land. . . .

Yesterday evening (for the mail is now presented to the Beloved every evening) a joint supplication emanating from the English friends thruout the British Isles was received which was enclosed in a letter from Major Tudor Pole. Some sixty-five petitioners widely scattered thruout the United Kingdom, had issued this joint letter which opens with the following words:– 'In the name of all the Bahais in the British Isles we send loving and heartfelt greetings. It was with great joy that we learned through Capt. Tudor Pole of the health and safety of your family and yourself... We rejoice that, by the mercy of God, this terrible war is now at an end. Thruout the long conflict we have been sustained by the faith that in this day of Resurrection the whole earth is but God's Handful and that in His Hands are the reins of all things. Knowing that the war came in accordance with the clear forewarnings of Bahaollah we trust that now the most great Peace will follow, in accordance with His promise and prophecy.'

Closing with the earnest entreaty to become more zealous and more united; with the hope of seeing the whole human race become one family and all the world one home and expressing the heartfelt yearning of having Abdul Baha again visit their shores – this supplication indeed stands as a land mark in the history of the Bahai Revelation in England. Crushed and stamped out is the hope of the ill-wishers and violators who wanted to sow seeds of doubt, of error, the Cause has emerged victorious and resplendent; its call has been hearkened by individuals and assemblies and cities as Bournemouth, Manchester and Liverpool, hitherto unaware of the call have duly responded.

'The Blessed Beauty is my confirmer, sustainer and my assistant' was the comment of the Beloved as he perused the contents of this significant letter.

28 January 1919

This morning the Beloved summoned me to His writing-room and ordered me to translate for him the supplications that had arrived last night by the evening mail. The first one in order was a letter of sorrow and of mourning, yet of confidence and trust from a maid-servant of God . . . struck with a sudden calamity by the loss of her young and beloved son Corporal Erwin Noar Harris who being wounded in the battlefield of France was transferred to a hospital in England wherein he breathed his last on the 7th October 1918 with

'Ya-Baha-el-Abha' on his lips. What a trial for his poor mother whose son was so cherished, so admired and so praised by the Beloved. His life insurance goes to his mother in monthly installments and she wants to use it in his name to spread the Bahai message far and wide according to her son's desire to become a Bahai teacher when he set foot again on the American soil. The Beloved's words condensed in a brilliant Tablet will surely be her stay and solace, will be a balm for her wound and will bind her broken heart.

29 January 1919

This morning I was sent by the Beloved to the telegraph office in order to despatch the answer to another telegram from two zealous friends in the Far East, two Parsees from Bombay, Javanmard and Isfandiar. Two days ago they were mentioned by the Beloved in a Tablet . . . and lo! to-day a cable from them is at hand. They presented their humble compliments and requested his favor to which this generous response was forwarded:– 'Isfandiar, Javanmard Parsees, Bombay, entreat God ye may ever remain safe and sound.' The joy and ecstasy that will be felt by these friends when these words shall reach them will undoubtedly be unbounded and the energy that shall be breathed into their souls will be most promising. Why not when the heart and the soul of the Beloved in eager anticipation is turning toward that far distant land expecting from it a special awakening and a quick response. India's turn is soon to come and in the activity and zeal of the Parsees of India lay the great victories of the Cause.

Shoghi Effendi's work continued to increase. He produced the translations no matter how much time they took. His diligence, thoroughness and awareness of the significance of the work before him kept him at it without pause. In a letter to Dr Zia Bagdadi written on the same day, 29 January 1919, he indicated the magnitude of his work in the service of the Master. From this letter can be seen his adaptation of a rapid, almost telegraphic style suitable for communicating information and saving time.

PRELUDE TO THE GUARDIANSHIP

To Zia M. Bagdadi, Chicago.

Dear brother in El-Abha:
Greetings and salutations! Your supplications are arriving; the news of the friends of God noted. A Tablet has been revealed for you; a telegram dispatched. So far, the Beloved has revealed nearly one hundred Tablets for the friends in the United States of America. Some of them have been dispatched and others will be. Convey the glad-tidings to the friends. Beloved in perfect health. Supplications and cables are pouring in constantly from morn till eve; life-giving words are revealed. From Persia, India, Japan, France, England and Switzerland, letters and telegrams are showering.[12]

Indeed, Shoghi Effendi mentions in his diary letter for that day 'the seventy Tablets piled up before Him for correction and signature . . . These masses of Tablets . . . are being followed almost every day with a fresh supply of still more inspiring Tablets. Oh! I wish time would be at my disposal and its flight would not be so swift that I may share with you more if not all these wonderful words.'[13]

But his work of translation, as we have seen, was punctuated by the constant visits to the Master on the part of poor and rich, ordinary folk and dignitaries alike. That afternoon the following significant visit took place:

At 3 P.M. sharp, General Sir Edmund Henry Allenby motored down to the house of the Beloved, accompanied by a member of his staff and Major Nott, the assistant Military Governor. Rain was showering yet the General was punctual and faithful to his engagement. My father, Badi Effendi and myself were favored in being present at the interview. Having taken off his water proof and disposed of his hat and cane he stood at the door and begged the Beloved to gain precedence and enter first. The first statement he uttered after having firmly grasped the Beloved's hands was this:– 'Excellency! I am indeed privileged and honoured in meeting you.' Having expressed His great pleasure in meeting the gallant and confirmed General, the Beloved . . . made him sit close to Himself. To this the General replied 'I indeed appreciate fully your words and consider them most gratifying as they come from a person whom I esteem and honour more than any one else in this region.' The Beloved then answered forcibly and clearly some of the questions He was asked by the distinguished visitor referring to His early life and His 40 years incarceration in the fortress of Akka. Following that the Master having ordered Persian tea to be served began expressing vividly the peculiarities, the characteristics and the outstanding features of this land of Palestine – a land physically endowed with immense gifts, historically famous, geographically enjoying a commanding position, embodying in its plains, mounts, seas, rivers, meadows and valleys the elements of nature characteristic of different regions, its climatic preference and lastly its religious and spiritual significance being the dawning place of God's manifestations and the birth place of His Holiness Christ. Whoever extended his sovereignty over this gifted land has been able to become a world empire. The Greek, Macedonian, Persian, Roman and Arab states offer a striking example. 'I congratulate you Sir, for having conquered nay rather liberated this Holy Land having achieved your conquest by the least shedding of blood unlike the conquerors of the Past such as Nebuchadnezzar, Saladin and the like.' This was the tribute paid by our Beloved to this General whose plan once executed, has meant so much to the Bahai world. The interview was not of a long character and ending with an exchange of compliments and appreciative remarks, the General rose, begged the Beloved not to tire Himself and come out under the rain and reiterated before leaving the assurance of his regards and his joy at being honored to meet such a great personage.

30 January 1919

According to a letter from Chicago, the Blessed Tablets that were revealed during the war in 1916 for some of the American friends had recently reached their destination and had imparted great joy to the longing hearts . . . What will their joy and gladness be if they come to know at present, that nearly out of two hundred Tablets that have been revealed hundred and fifty of them are destined for the United States of America.

Some of the supplications had asked for permission to attain the court of the Beloved's Presence . . . So far nearly a dozen of such permissions have been accorded and preparation for lodging etc. are being made for these welcome and longing visitors. The Holy Mount of Carmel may serve as a residence and probably other places close and even adjacent to the Beloved's House may be designated. From the battlefield of France, American warriors are entreating to come and they shall soon start on their journey to the Holy Land for permission has been instantly granted. Some are on their way to Haifa, others shall journey in spring and many will flood next year.

During the early part of February Tablets translated for the following individuals were published in *Star of the West*: Mrs. J. Stannard, Elizabeth P. Hackley, Louise D. Boyle, Viola Kluge, Vitula Edith Whitton, and Corinne True.[14] And later that month Shoghi Effendi himself wrote to the editor of *Star of the West* enclosing a copy of a Tablet revealed by 'Abdu'l-Bahá and conveying the Master's wish that the Tablet be published in full:

Dear Sir:–
In accordance with the desire of our Beloved Master, enclosed herewith a copy of a Tablet that has recently been revealed to a friend in Persia which He wants you to publish fully in the Star of the West.
Sincerely yours,
Shoghi Rabbani
(grandson of Abdul Baha)[15]

Through *Star of the West* Shoghi Effendi was becoming increasingly known among the western Bahá'ís. He was also keeping up his diary letters, some of which were now being published in *Star of the West*.[16]

Saturday 8 February 1919

This afternoon our Indian officer, Captain Agal Khan of Lahore, Punjab, who is a devout Moslem, keenly interested in the role that the Cause will play in the future . . . called on Abdul-Baha carrying with him the article of Abbas Ali of Rangoon, published in one of the local Indian papers of Punjab, which he had translated for

Abdul-Baha into English. The article was a lucid and at the same time a striking account of the teachings of the Cause, of the early life, the declaration, the persecution and the martyrdom of the Bab and the rise of Baha'o'llah, his early trials, his exile, his declaration and his amazing power displayed in the distant fortress of Acca. Abdul-Baha entertained for over an hour this diligent scholar, told him that under chains and fetters Baha'o'llah propagated his teachings, the mutual arrangements of the rulers of Turkey and of Persia to quench his Light and the utter failure of their plans and intentions. Agal Khan was amazed to know that the remains of the Bab ... were transferred to this Holy Mount ... He resolutely decided to visit the shrine and if possible to visit the Holy Tomb in Acca.

Sunday, 9 February 1919

This morning some Tablets were revealed to the friends in the United States of America. One of them ... has written these words to Abdul-Baha: 'This humble maid-servant especially wishes to ask thee at this time, concerning the publication of two indexes. . . . If this work does not interfere with carrying out the instructions already given, this maid-servant would very much like to go on and work on a complete and scholarly index of all the writings . . .

. . . Although the answer to the supplication has not yet been revealed, yet one thing is sure, that Abdul-Baha will most deeply appreciate such services and will undoubtedly breathe into their life a new breath that will sustain them throughout their activities.

This afternoon being bright and warm, Abdul-Baha ascended the mountain and visited the Tomb of the Bab where the friends had assembled for their weekly Sunday gatherings, where he inquired regarding the spiritual activities of the SPC (Beirut) to which one of its members, Mr Bahader . . . replied that their weekly Sunday gatherings are uninterruptedly held within the college grounds. This leading to a certain statement made by the president of the college with respect to his Sunday morning Bible classes, Abdul-Baha referred to the relative standing of the Holy Books and their adaptation to their respective environment. The Old Testament, he said, is largely historical and partly states various commands and regulations. The Gospel . . . reveals a whole set of admonition and exhortation, of counsels and advice. The Koran embodies all three of these and in addition reveals abstruse, scientific and mathematical problems. He then spoke in detail of the variety of the branches in mathematics and astronomy as expounded by the Egyptian, Babylonian, Greek, Roman and Persian leaders and scientists. He then referred to the rise of Ptolemy . . . . He told us how all astronomers and philosophers believed in his system and although Pythagoras and Plato revealed contradictory facts, that the Ptolemaic system was considered the immutable and correct law. Then arose that illiterate, young, inexperienced Arab leader in the Arabian peninsula, who revealed in his Koran . . . .: 'The sun moves in a fixed place and each star moves in its own heaven.' These bodily challenged the whole Ptolemaic system and shook it down to its very foundation . . . The whole scientific world arose to the consciousness of this truth. What clearer and stronger proof may be stated for the establishment of the truth of the Mohammedan Revelation?

Monday, 10 February 1919

The misery and need of the civil population of Haifa . . . has necessitated the formation of a Haifa Relief Fund composed of the heads of the different religious denominations . . . Abdul-Baha, through the announcement made by the military governor, contributed the noble donation of £50 and inserted his name at the head of the list of contributors, which will stand as a token of his generosity, his approval of the means undertaken to alleviate the burden of the poor and his setting the noble example to the rich and leaders of the city. This morning again I was sent to the Governor and offered him a further sum for the relief of the poor. Colonel Stanton was indeed touched and, moved by this further donation, hastened to write . . . to Abdul-Baha in token of his admiration and thanks . . .

The supplications that have come today abound with refreshing news. A letter from Bombay . . . from Lausanne, Switzerland . . . from southern Palestine . . . A detailed supplication from Juanita Storch,[17] exquisitely written . . . I cannot prevent myself from sharing with you some of its charming passages:

'. . . A picture of the Master comes to me as he holds his rosary in hand out-stretched to all who heed this heavenly call. A picture of the Master comes to me as he holds his rosary, thinking of the friends both far and near as pearls of his heart. A picture of the Master comes to me as he holds his rosary, chanting in a prayerful hour, "Glory to the Most Great Power." '

To his profusion of genuine sentiments and to this authoress of tender feelings, Abdul-Baha not only spends the days in revealing his words of appreciation, but even until late at night when everything is hushed in silence and every tongue is at rest . . .

. . . As I am writing these lines, I am again moved to present myself in his presence and take down his words in response to the recently arrived supplications.

Tuesday, 11 February 1919

News as contained in letters, the first since the outbreak of the war, have reached us from Persia as well as from India. Meagre and insufficient as the news is at present, yet it assures us of the welfare of the friends. Although few have succumbed to the trials and calamities occasioned by the war . . . yet consolation lies in the safety and well-being of the mass of the friends . . . In Teheran, the most active centre of Persia, the friends associate, deal and transact as Bahais, openly declaring their faith, emphatically and fearlessly delivering the message and gathering in their flood men of every class, of every denomination and of every sect – as Abdul-Baha has already repeatedly intimated in his blessed Tablets for Persia, Russia and Egypt, the only group and the one body which is able and wields the necessary power to assure for Persia her weal and her prosperity . . . for at present amid the agitation and uproar that still prevails in Persia, the qualities of trustworthiness, truthfulness, obedience, frankness, conscientiousness and loyalty are exclusively embodied in the friends of God . . . Abdul-Baha spent the whole day indoors, with no outstanding event marking the activities of the day . . .

Wednesday, 12 February 1919

This morning, some of the recently arrived supplications were answered in the form of short yet effective Tablets. The second supplication from India is signed by a certain influential person, a khajeh, who has been recently attracted to the Movement and is craving to attain the court of Abdul-Baha's presence. As emanating from a soul that has been entangled in superstition and prejudice and immersed in a sea of imagination, his words embodied in his supplication are indeed significant: 'Thy generosity is the elixir and thy bounty the solace for the weak heart of this humble servant, and the near prospect of attaining to the holy presence sustains his breath. O most beloved Lord, look not at the failings, shortcomings and weakness of this humble beseecher and entreater, but towards the boundless ocean of thy love, mercy, bounty and grace. Grant the fervent prayer of this humble one to approach thy holy self, keep him not far away and separate from thee and confer upon him the high privilege of viewing thy beautiful, illumined face.' ... The Tablet revealed to this friend this morning is a model of the sweetest and most gentle expressions that a beloved can reveal to his loving ones.

News reaches us to the effect that the friends of God in the different parts of Persia, devastated by famine, pestilence and internecine war, have been miraculously protected and saved ... Letters have been received so far from Teheran, Shiraz, and tonight from Najafabad ... However, one thing brought gloom and depression into this lively and clear atmosphere ... A certain friend, buried with respect and ceremony by his beloved and relatives, was disinterred, his coffin was smashed to pieces, his corpse was taken out and buried directly with no wooden case ...

Thursday, 13 February 1919

The call of Abdul-Baha bidding the friends of God to arise in one accord, to fling away the garb of concealment and to deliver the divine message has resounded throughout all regions and has propagated its waves to countries hitherto the bulwark of conservatism.

... This morning he [Haji Mohammed Yazdi from Damascus] was ushered into Abdul-Baha's presence ... With a smile and a nod of appreciation Abdul-Baha greeted every bit of news and was glad to know that a reaction from the passiveness and inactivity of the past had set in. 'Deliver the divine message with prudence and wisdom', was his recommendation to the teachers who are serving in these regions. Having said this he arose, again welcomed our guest and regained his room to correct the Tablets that had been revealed . . .

Abdul-Baha remained in doors until 3 P.M., when Major Nott came and motored him to the house of the Commander-in-chief, Sir Edmund Allenby. This was the second time Abdul-Baha had called on the General and this time the conversation centred around the Cause and its progress . . . He is a very gentle, modest and striking figure, warm in affection, yet imposing in his manners.

Tonight a telegram received . . . fixing Major Tudor-Pole's arrival at Jerusalem on the 14th inst. and his departure on the 17th. We will be delighted to meet again this young and active friend who is doing what he can to bring about the comfort and the satisfaction of the Beloved.

Friday, 14 February 1919

Abdul-Baha spent the whole forenoon in correcting and signing the sixty Tablets that had been made ready during the past days and as I am dropping you these lines he is having his fortnightly hot bath which ameliorates so much his health and strengthens his physical constitution.

Tonight we had another concrete evidence of the merit and value of Major Tudor-Pole's article in the *Palestine News*. Indeed, inquirers and seekers multiply with astonishing rapidity, a keen interest is aroused and a wide demand is being pressed more and more. The contributor of the article, Miss Hiscox in Cairo and Miss Rosenberg in London, are in correspondence with many souls, most of them in active service, who desire to learn more about the Cause than this introductory article of Major Tudor-Pole presents. Abdul-Baha was weary, tired and sleepy as a result of the heat of his bath and was intending to sleep when a slight knock at the door revealed the presence of a non-commissioned officer at the door seeking an interview. Admittance was cordially granted and there was Private Sinclair, a Britisher, working as an assistant at the Red Cross Egyptian hospital in Haifa. During his sojourn in Cairo, when visiting its reading room, he had come across Bahai literature and had thereby caught the first glimpse of the Cause. The perusal of Major Tudor-Pole's article raised his interest to its highest pitch and henceforth he became an ardent inquirer. From what could be gathered from his countenance, he was so lowly, so respectful, so gentle and so modest that the first words of the Beloved were to this effect: 'I am glad to meet thee for thy face is illumined, thy brow is pure, thy heart is clear and thy purpose is right.' . . . In view of his earnest inquiry and his lack of any preconception, the Master spoke in detail of the main purpose of the Bahai teachings, the idea of peace and reconciliation, the most immediate need of mankind. He told him of the futility of men's efforts to establish a lasting peace, resting on secure foundations, through material means. Whenever such efforts have been exerted they were doomed to failure. History affords a striking illustration. 'From what I can gather from the events during my life', said Abdul-Baha, 'history clearly shows the wars that have been waged, the peace measures that were subsequently adopted, have proved inevitable failures. The Crimean war and the Treaty of Paris in 1856, the Austro-Italian war of 1859; the Danish war of 1864; the Austro-Prussian war of 1866; the Franco-Prussian war of 1870; the Russo-Turkish war of 1877; and the Congress of Berlin, the Balkan war and subsequently this world war with its present Universal Peace Conference. Wars will succeed, peace measures and pacific documents will remain dead letters unless the Word of God and His supreme power comes to exercise its influence. Not until this is attained may lasting peace be realized.'

Our attentive visitor listened and was absorbed. He was glad to listen to this remarkable talk and was furthermore grateful to receive a copy of Mr Remey's *Some Vital Bahai Principles* which Abdul-Baha put in his hands. When he retired, he was inwardly moved and outwardly satisfied and assured.

Saturday, 15 February 1919

My head is in a whirl so busy and so eventful was the day. No less than a score of callers from prince and pasha to a simple private soldier have sought interview with Abdul-Baha.

Tonight again, our attracted friend, Private Sinclair of the Red Cross hospital, called. His eyes sparkled as he shook hands with the

IN THE SERVICE OF THE MASTER, EARLY 1919

Beloved. He had read the pamphlet which had been given to him and was glad to receive another different one, published and edited by Mr Remey, entitled *The Message of Unity*. He expressed his firm intention to correspond with the different booksellers in London, as soon as he is demobilized and thus able to gather more detailed information. When he arose to take his leave, he seemed full of the spirit of Baha'o'llah, absorbed in meditation, and ablaze with His love. 'Thou art my son, my dear son, I love thee, and I pray for thee,' were the farewell words as the Beloved embraced him on his shoulders...

Letters, or rather parcels, were today received from Port Said, London and America. Enclosed in Mr Lotfullah's letter from London, were two supplications that had been received last year from Teheran. They contained good news. The Bahai school in Teheran is advancing by leaps and bounds. The Israelite Bahais have established schools which are rapidly widening. The school of Tarbiat in Teheran, Miss Kappes describes as by far the greatest establishment among the 430 schools in Teheran... In Yezd meetings of different character, each of no less than 60 to 70 attendants, were organized... In Yezd the maid-servants of God have risen and are overshadowing (or rather have foreshadowed) the men in their spiritual activities. Of Kashan, the writer relates, 'I had thought of it a mount of snow but later on I found it an active volcano. The friends were aflame with the fire of the Word of God.'

Sunday, 16 February 1919

From among the supplications recently received is one that is most significant and of particular interest as it emanates from a Greek friend who is one of the few, if not the only of her race, that has responded to the call of the Kingdom. Let me share with you its contents: '... O dear Father, how could I do otherwise than believe in you because many times my mind is so tired, but when I take your picture, and I read one of your prayers, I feel just like a bird when it rains and its feathers are wet and it cannot fly, but when the sun's rays come out, is happy and flies from tree to tree – exactly I feel every minute when I make my prayers in your name. I shall not stop all my life, until I am an apostle for your name, to my people."

... What the response of the Beloved will be, or rather how far the Lord's favour and blessing will surround her, is one that we can hardly venture to forecast, but one thing is sure, that the Tablet that will be revealed to this soul will act as a mighty impetus in awakening the Greek people to this call.

This morning Abdul-Baha went out for a long walk and returned an hour before noon, when he resumed his work which consisted mainly of the perusal of detailed supplications from Persia.

Monday, 17 February 1919

A day of jubilee is ahead of us. The arrival of a group of the Parsee friends of Adassieh, including men and women, has not been without a definite purpose. Another marriage festivity is to take place . . . Preparations are now being made for that day and everybody is looking forward to the celebration, the first of that kind since the extinction of the fire of war.

This morning Agha Ahmed Yazdi, his elder brother and Agha Mohammed Taghi Esfahani were called to the Beloved's presence. Tea was served and everybody assumed almost an uninterrupted silence for Abdul-Baha was throughout perusing supplications of the Egyptian friends, who had recently arrived. Supplications from every corner of the globe, of different length and character, written in different languages, enclosing clippings of papers, pamphlets, typewritten reports, petitions, etc., are ceaselessly pouring in and the time for their perusal is sufficient to exhaust all the time that one might possibly have at his disposal. Although the ways have not yet fully opened and communication with all parts has not yet been restored, one is baffled at the amount of letters, books and magazines that the postoffice daily delivers.

A letter from Mirza Mahmood Zarkani from Bombay to Haji Mirza Haider Ali reveals the great longing of the Parsee friends to meet Abdul-Baha, whether this takes place in the Holy Land or in India.

Tuesday, 18 February 1919

Greetings with sweetest remembrances to you . . . from this hallowed spot! From this solitary plain of Bahjeh, in this solemn solitude, away from life's tumult and bustle, I take the pen . . . The Beloved has again decided to tarry for a time at the vicinity of the tomb of his father. Here he is, in the adjoining room, sitting by the candle light, viewing from his window the solitude from afar, the silent surroundings, which nothing breaks save the distant roar of the waves which die away in the immensity of space. He is engaged in his meditations, absorbed in his prayers, thinking of his friends across the seas, remembering their prayers and their supplications and communing with his heavenly Father on behalf of such souls. What a vivid contrast does this vicinity of the Holy Tomb represent with the increasing activity of the life in Haifa. The air over there was filled with gases and vapours which steam and motor engines continuously discharge, while the atmosphere here is as pure, as clear and as fragrant as it can be. The traffic accompanied with its deafening noise and bustle, gives way here to a stillness, a calmness and a quietude which nothing interrupts but the stillness of nature. The dazzling lights of the city are gone and nothing but a flickering taper's light cheers this cold and starless night. The constant movement and circulation witnessed in the Beloved's house has stopped, and tonight everything is at a stand still, everything quiet and at rest. The morning hour of prayer is maintained and even lengthened for twice a day, the Beloved visits the holy shrine, kneels in reverence and devotion, orders communes to be chanted and often spends an hour or more in silent prayer. His attendants, friends and relatives are absent and no one save Kosro, Esfandiar and myself, the two vigilant guardians of the Tomb, and Ali Eff, a friend who will leave tomorrow for Beirut, form his small retinue.

Everything, the environment, the atmosphere, the view, the stillness, all are uplifting, elevating and inspiring. One feels to have forgotten his cares and his concerns, his mind is refreshed and his burden alleviated. No matter how long the Master will tarry in this sanctified place, no feeling of monotony, and ennui overcomes the soul. It is the Spot which so many souls crave to attain and long to visit. Particularly is it magnificent at such a time when nature is smiling, the sky above is no more gloomy and threatening with clouds but serene and blue, the plains and meadows as if covered with a multicoloured carpet, the shrubs sparkling with roses, jasmins, lilies, narcissus embalming the pure and refreshing air; the grass growing luxuriously everywhere and the breeze wafting in every direction. Often is the Beloved seen in the open air, majestically walking to and fro upon the verdant plains and amid the wild flowers that abound in this gifted region. He treads the same ground that the blessed feet of his heavenly Father have trodden, circumambulates the shrine where for many years He has lived, waters the flowers and plants, many of which have been blessed by His hands and lives and moves and has his being in an atmosphere which fully reminds him of His manners and His conduct. What a dear and blessed spot to be privileged to live in!

5

In the Service of the Master
Spring 1919

During the Spring of 1919 the pressure of work on translations decreased, allowing Shoghi Effendi to direct his attention to correspondence. This included his own correspondence, as well as letters he wrote conveying the Master's wishes to the friends throughout the world. His translation work did not, however, completely cease. On 15 March 1919 Shoghi Effendi translated Tablets of the Master for Louise Waite and Olive Couch.[1] The Tablet to Louise Waite conveys the significance of the Covenant of God and assures the friends that the damage caused by those who break the Covenant will not endure. A paragraph from the Tablet to Louise Waite describes the fortune of Covenant-breakers:

> Ere long thou shalt consider that no sign and no trace shall remain therefrom. The ocean of the Covenant shall send forth a wave and shall disperse and throw out these foams.[2]

Concurrent with the sad news of the activities of the Covenant-breakers, the news of the dedication, steadfastness and services of the believers reached the Holy Land. Corinne True, who will always be remembered for her services in furthering the construction of the Mother Temple of the West, had sent a supplication to the Master with news of the devoted services of the friends. In a letter to her dated Monday, 17 March 1919, Shoghi Effendi expresses his happiness with the news of her dedication and conveys his appreciation of her glorious services to the Cause and her keen interest in the Bahá'í temple.

In this same letter Shoghi Effendi writes of 'Abdu'l-Bahá's untiring efforts to promote Bahá'u'lláh's teachings:

> The Beloved from morn till eve, even at midnight is engaged in revealing Tablets, in sending forth his constructive, dynamic thoughts of love and principles to a sad and distracted world. In most of the Tablets he lays great stress upon unity, love and firmness in the Covenant.[3]

On the same day, Shoghi Effendi translated Tablets of the Master to Jean Masson and Dorothy Nelson.[4] A paragraph from the Tablet to Jean Masson is typical of the Master's repeated reminders to His steadfast band of followers of His earnest hopes for their spiritual advancement and provides an example of Shoghi Effendi's translation skills at this time:

> My hope is that day by day thou mayest be more confirmed and may serve to the best the world of humanity; that thou mayest adore mankind and ignite in every heart the lamp of guidance, may serve the world of morality so that human realities may be freed from the gloom of the world of nature which, in essence, is purely animal in character, and may be illumined with the light of the divine realm.[5]

With a letter to *Star of the West* written on the same day, Shoghi Effendi enclosed a Tablet of the Master revealed to the 'friends and the maidservants of the Merciful in the country of Egypt'. He indicated that it was the wish of 'Abdu'l-Bahá that the Tablet be published in *Star of the West*. This Tablet, published in both English and Arabic, expresses the Master's praise and gratitude to God for the bounties He has bestowed upon humanity through this glorious revelation. The English translation was made by Dr Zia Bagdadi.[6]

On 30 March Shoghi Effendi translated the Master's Tablets to Edna True and Mrs Brooker.[7] To Mrs Brooker the Master expressed His good pleasure at the meeting she had organized for teaching the Cause:

> Praise thou the Lord, that thou hast been ushered into the divine Kingdom as one of the chosen people of God and the light of guidance hath been reflected upon thy pure heart . . . thou hast organized a meeting and hast been engaged in the promulgation of divine teachings.

Rest thou assured that divine confirmations shall reach [thee] ...[8]

On Friday, 4 April 1919 Shoghi Effendi translated a Tablet for Juliet Thompson in which the Master calls upon her to detach herself from the world of nature and become 'God-like, Lordly, illumined and merciful'. He also asks her to convey His greetings to Kahlil Gibran.[9]

On Friday, 11 April Shoghi Effendi translated Tablets for the Cleveland Assembly, Elizabeth Herlitz and Mr and Mrs Richter.[10] This excerpt is from the Tablet to the Cleveland Assembly, addressed to 'the children of the Kingdom':

> My highest wish and desire is that ye who are my children may be educated according to the teachings of His Holiness Baha'o'llah and may receive a Bahai training; that ye may each become an ignited candle of the world of humanity, may be devoted to the service of all mankind, may give up your rest and comfort, so that ye may become the cause of the tranquillity of the world of creation.[11]

Such inspiring counsels revealed by 'Abdu'l-Bahá and translated by Shoghi Effendi continued to stream forth from the pen of the Centre of the Covenant. They covered a wide range of topics raised by the believers in the East and the West and touched the hearts of their recipients. They served as a beacon of light to a confused and distracted world, calling it to a higher plane of existence and raising aloft high standards of conduct and service to humanity.

The Master's plea to each group was directed to the situation and the needs of that group. For example, in a Tablet to Howard MacNutt translated by Shoghi Effendi on Sunday 13 April 1919, 'Abdu'l-Bahá encouraged the friends to write papers that communicate the Bahá'í teachings and to present them in meetings with brilliancy and eloquence:

> At present, like unto the morn, the lights of the Sun of Truth have been shed around. Effort must be made that the slumbering souls may be awakened, the heedless become vigilant, and the divine instructions, which constitute the spirit of this age, may reach the ears of the people of the world, may be propagated in papers and enunciated in meetings with the utmost brilliancy and eloquence.[12]

PRELUDE TO THE GUARDIANSHIP

A letter dated 25 April 1919 written by Shoghi Effendi to Dr Zia Bagdadi is a general communication to the Bahá'í world reminiscent, in retrospect, of the messages he would send to the Bahá'í world at a later period of his Guardianship, as these two paragraphs demonstrate:

> News, refreshing and inspiring, is being daily received from all over the world, from the far west in the United States of America to the middle east in Persia and the far east, Japan and India, and still beyond from the Hawaiian islands in the mid-Pacific ocean. From New Zealand even the glad tidings of the Kingdom are breaking upon us and indicate the brilliant future that is stored for the far-off continent of Australia . . .
>
> What strikes us most vividly is the good news of the welfare and safety of the friends of God. All throughout the years of war, civil as well as national, of loot and of riot and rebellion and of bloodshed, the friends have been continuously engaged in service to the Cause of God. Their meetings have not been discontinued, their fervour has not decreased and their energy has not relaxed.[13]

The next day, 26 April, Shoghi Effendi translated a Tablet for Joseph Hannen.[14] On the same day he wrote to Joseph Hannen referring to this Tablet:

> My dear brother in the love of El-Bahá!
>
> Your letter dated March 10th 1919 enclosing a supplication to the Beloved arrived & its contents exposed to the Beloved. A Tablet has been revealed for you yesterday afternoon in response to your inquiries on different questions. It will be duly forwarded.[15]

A Tablet for Roy Wilhelm was also translated that day in which the Master reiterates the futility of the efforts of the Covenant-breakers.[16] On 28 April Shoghi Effendi wrote to Ella Cooper communicating to this Bahá'í sister in California his fervent hope and highest wish, and giving news of the safety of the friends around the world.

> How glad and grateful have I become when I perused your letter

which abounded with sweet recollections & charming thoughts! My fervent hope & my highest wish is to be able to serve continuously, efficiently & whole-heartedly my Beloved Grand-Father & thus to be of service to the friends of the Merciful & the Cause of God.

. . . Multitudes of supplications are pouring in every day – each & all conveying the news of the good health & safety of the friends of God in America, Europe, Persia, India & Japan. From the distracted region of Turkestan & Caucasus news, refreshing & invigorating, are being received to the effect that amidst civil war, pillage, famine, & disease the assemblies of the friends & their Mashrekol-Azkar gatherings have not been discontinued. From the devastated land of Persia, where famine, plagues, intestinal war, & ravages made by contending armies have made it desolate, the friends of God have remained all throughout this dark period safe & protected. Foodstuffs in Esfahan reached exorbitant prices (kilo of bread costing approximately one dollar) & the death rate in Teheran on one day reached the alarming number of 1178 & yet the friends of God have not suffered & have not been in need & have not fallen victims to these calamities. From India the news we receive are very encouraging. The friends are exhibiting a general & deep interest in the spreading of the Divine teachings among the people of India who have responded, have grasped the substance of these teachings and have displayed a great deal of activity and a great zeal in teaching.

Day & night the Beloved is revealing wonderful and inspiring Tablets & often wakes up at mid-night in order to open & peruse the contents of piles of supplications that are being heaped up every week . . . [17]

On Thursday, 8 May 1919 Shoghi Effendi wrote from Haifa to Dr Luṭfu'lláh Ḥakím, giving him the news that the annual consultative Baháʼí Convention of the friends in India and Burma was being planned for the coming Christmas. He stated that the friends in India were active in the service of the Cause and were hoping that their services would draw 'Abdu'l-Bahá to their shores.[18]

The Master received a joint supplication bearing the signature of a thousand believers in the United States and Canada inviting Him to visit America again.[19] In a postcard to Joseph Hannen written on 22 May, Shoghi Effendi conveyed the joy of the Master and gave the news that a general Tablet had been revealed that morning to the friends and maidservants of God throughout the United States and Canada.

> My dear spiritual brother:-
> Your most welcome letter dated April 17, 1919 received. So far two Tablets have been revealed for you i.e. since the fall of Haifa dated Mar. 17 & Apr. 26. The Beloved is indeed very happy & quite healthy. He revealed this morning a general Tablet to all the friends & maid-servants of God throughout the U. States & Canada – a most invigorating remarkable affectionate & detailed Tablet. Piles of supplications are being received & multitudinous reports are pouring in from Persia, India, Japan, Australia, Europe & America. From morn till eve, life-giving Tablets are being revealed & Heavenly Blessings bestowed upon eager and expectant souls . . .[20]

On 22 May 1919 Shoghi Effendi wrote to Ahmad Sohrab, who had left for America on 23 December via Cairo and Liverpool. In this letter, Shoghi Effendi enclosed a Tablet from the Master for the Bahá'í friends in the United States and Canada in response to their loving supplications and invitation. Here is an excerpt from Shoghi Effendi's letter:

> The clock is striking ten, and having just returned to the Beloved's own sleeping room on the terrace of Abbas Kuli's house which lies only a few steps east of the Tomb of the Bab, I remembered my friends in the West and therefore resume at this period of the night my correspondence with them. In view of the repeated attacks of malaria that I have been subjected to, the Beloved ordered me to pass a few nights on Mount Carmel in the vicinity of the Tomb, enjoying the pure invigorating and spiritual atmosphere of Makam . . . such a lovely and silent scene would have long detained me outside had it not been for my keen desire to share with my spiritual brethren and sisters the contents of a general Tablet, the first of its kind since the resumption of communication and addressed to all the friends and maid-servants of God throughout the United States of America and Canada.[21]

In His Tablet the Master showered His love on these believers and called them to attain higher levels of unity and concord, as in this excerpt:

> Ye are inviting me to America. I am likewise longing to gaze at those illumined faces and converse and associate with those real friends. But the magnetic power which shall draw me to those shores is the union and harmony of the friends, their behaviour and conduct in accordance with the teachings of God and the firmness of all in the Covenant and the Testament.[22]

The idea of writing the supplication to 'Abdu'l-Bahá which attracted this remarkable Tablet had been born at a Feast held on 16 October 1918 in the home of Mrs Leo Perron (Arna True, daughter of Corinne True) in Chicago. The idea was discussed at the meeting of the House of Spirituality, where it was suggested that all the friends in the country could join in an act of unity and send a joint supplication to the Master. The secretary was instructed to address all the assemblies and put the matter before them. Miss Jean Masson, assisted by a committee, drafted the supplication. The signatures were received over several weeks and in the early part of January 1919 the entire document was sent to 'Akká.[23]

6

In the Service of the Master
Summer 1919

By the summer of 1919 Shoghi Effendi was a youth of 22. One year had elapsed since his graduation from the American University of Beirut and commencing his work of service to the Master. His entire learning and scholarly discipline had been channelled into the work of translation and correspondence. Yet Shoghi Effendi's contribution went far beyond these twin tasks. Looking back at this period in the history of the Faith, it is remarkable to see the two figures into whose care the Cause of God was successively entrusted – 'Abdu'l-Bahá, the Centre of the Covenant, and Shoghi Effendi, its future Guardian – working together at the centre of the Bahá'í world.

The work of Shoghi Effendi during this period continued on the same path, sometimes with a heavier concentration on translation and sometimes on correspondence. Here is a letter he wrote on 4 June 1919 to Joseph Hannen.

> Dear brother in the Cause:–
> The Beloved has recently come to Acca & enclosed diary (which I used to send through you for Ahmad and now am addressing it to you directly as Ahmad may be too busy or away from Washington) relates of the activities & whereabouts of the Beloved in that city. I hope it will interest you.
> Your letter dated April 30 has been received with its enclosures. A Tablet has been revealed for your dear mother & will be duly despatched. I shall soon secure a word of blessing from the Beloved for the new-born babe, Carl Nategh Junior whom I hope will grow to be a pure and efficient servant to the Cause.

Hereafter Tablets will be dispatched to you and to Roy Wilhelm directly. A great many are awaiting the Beloved's signature, some forty will soon be transcribed, some thirty are in the process of being translated and a great many are piled up to be posted in the near future.

They will be sent to you by small packages & I hope they will safely arrive . . .[1]

In his diary letter of Sunday, 8 June 1919, Shoghi Effendi refers to a gathering that day in the presence of the Master around the Shrine of Bahá'u'lláh at which one of the Persian friends gave a description of the Bahá'í House of Worship in 'Ishqábád. The Master referred to the uniqueness of this House of Worship, the first of its kind to be erected to the praise of God, and remarked that the 'Temple that is going to be erected in the United States will be an important and magnificent one, its influence and reaction upon the Cause will be tremendous, and the impetus it shall give to the movement, irresistible'.[2]

Such clear guidance and vision regarding the House of Worship in North America communicated that day by the Master would emerge years later in the form of repeated messages from the Guardian of the Faith encouraging the friends to complete the Mother Temple of the West.

The precious period when Shoghi Effendi served the Master was indeed filled with excitement. Letters giving news of the progress of the Cause and the devotion of the friends were pouring in every day. As mentioned above, one such letter was the joint supplication of the believers in the United States and Canada bearing over a thousand signatures. This supplication brought great joy to the heart of the Master. On Wednesday 11 June 1919 Shoghi Effendi wrote on a postcard from 'Akká to Dr Zia Bagdadi that a remarkable Tablet had been revealed by the Master 'for the friends and maid-servants of God throughout the United States and Canada'. He stated that he was enclosing the Tablet along with the supplication and the names of those who had signed it. In his note Shoghi Effendi conveys the specific instructions of the Master about the publication of these important documents:

> I am enclosing the supplication of nearly 1500 American friends, their names have been sent with the Tablet already. The Beloved

ordered me to write to you upon this important, momentous question:– 'Publish in the Persian & English columns of the Star of the West the Persian and English texts of the enclosed supplication, then publish all the names one by one & after that publish the general Tablet in Persian as well as in English, all in the same copy of the Star, no matter how voluminous it may become. Then send at least a couple of copies to every province in Persia, addressed to Bahai assemblies or individuals. Also send at least one copy of the 1919 convention photo to each province of Persia, that all the Persian Bahais may see what miracles have been wrought, what achievements have been made, what victories have been won, what a universal, & simultaneous response to the trumpet call of service has taken hold of the Western friends. This is the Beloved's command, fulfil it & power to your elbow . . .'[3]

This postcard conveys the instructions of the Master in a style intended by Him. It is clear that the decision about how much of the material to publish was made by the Master, His wishes in the matter being communicated clearly and unmistakably by Shoghi Effendi.

The American friends had been busy drafting the joint supplication to the Master during the winter and in January of 1919. Therefore many people had not sent individual letters to Him. By the summer, however, having already sent the joint supplication, the friends resumed writing their individual supplications.

In his letter of 12 June to Dr Esslemont, Shoghi Effendi refers to the increase in the volume of supplications:

Supplications are flooding and pouring out incessantly. Mighty and numerous are the Tablets revealed every day. Often I am kept working at my desk and translating Tablets till past midnight. But still I am happy and grateful . . .[4]

On 12 June Shoghi Effendi wrote to Juliet Thompson from 'Akká enclosing a Tablet revealed for her in Persian.

My dear sister in El-Baha,
    Your letter dated May 7th was received. I most heartily thank you for your kind and tender remembrances.

> The Beloved has been for few days & is still in Acca, in the vicinity of the Tomb of his Heavenly Father. In this hallowed Spot, I ever pray on your behalf & beg of God that you be confirmed in service to the glorious Cause.
> I enclose a copy of the Tablet revealed on Dec. 30. Another since dated Apr. 3 has been revealed for you. I trust you have received it. Henceforth all Tablets will be sent c/o Mr. Hannen & c/o Mr. Wilhelm & will be mailed directly from Haifa.
> I ever remember you and hope to meet you soon.
> Yours affectionately, Shoghi[5]

The Master continued to reveal Tablets in answer to these supplications. On 24 June Shoghi Effendi translated Tablets addressed to the Executive Board of Bahá'í Temple Unity, to Harlan Foster Ober and Agnes Leo.[6]

In the midst of his translation work Shoghi Effendi found time to write to Dr Esslemont, from whom he had not heard for some time, enclosing a few pages of his diary:

> It is a long time that I have been deprived of the pleasure & privilege of reading your lovely letters and I hope you will soon interrupt this silence & will assure us of your safety and welfare . . .[7]

During the month of July 1919 the volume of translations continued to increase. On Wednesday, 16 July, Shoghi Effendi translated Tablets for Jessie Revell, Maria Rebecca Robertson, and Maud Thompson.[8] The next day he wrote to Joseph Hannen enclosing important and remarkable Tablets in honour of Mr Fran Gilipac, Mrs Anna Edsel Reid, Lillian James, Aspasia Diamesis, Mrs Nadie Mirige, and Mrs Parsons,[9] and on Friday, 18 July, he translated Tablets addressed to Helen Whitney, Edgar Waite, Ollie James Watts and J.E. Gilligan, Sarah Van Winkle, Amy Williams, Ernest Walters and Norma Wilson.[10] On Sunday, 20 July, an additional ten Tablets were translated addressed to John Wolcott, Mr and Mrs Latimer, Sophie Loeding, Edward Struven, James Simpson, Elizabeth Stevens, Ferdinand Peterson, Martha Root, Ella Quant and Mr and Mrs Scheffler.[11] Two days later, on Tuesday, 22 July, again Shoghi Effendi translated ten Tablets, to Mary Lesch, Mary Morrison, the Fruitport Assembly, L. B. Nash,

Peter Maus, Emily Olsen, James Morton, the Racine Assembly, Alfred Lunt and Jean Masson.[12]

On Thursday, 23 July, Shoghi Effendi continued to undertake translations, with Tablets to Mr and Mrs Beckett, Mother Beecher and to the Bahá'ís of California.[13] The next day, 24 July 1919, he translated Tablets to Corinne True, Louis Gregory, Kokab MacCutcheon and Mr and Mrs Howard MacNutt.[14] On Friday, 25 July, two Tablets were translated, for Ruth Klos and William F. Kyle.[15] The next day, 26 July, Shoghi Effendi translated four Tablets, for Mr and Mrs Gift, Oscar Hanko, Mary Hall and Dr Pauline Barton-Peeke.[16] On 29 July Tablets for the Bahá'ís of Central States and for Gertrude Buikema were translated[17] and on Wednesday, 30 July, Shoghi Effendi translated a Tablet of the Master for Agnes Alexander.[18]

These Tablets translated during the month of July conveyed the love of the Master to His disciples and contained His response to each supplication. Some were brief, while others were quite lengthy. Some conveyed the Master's pleasure at the spiritual atmosphere of the recent Convention, as in this Tablet to Ferdinand Peterson:

> Thou hadst written that this year thou hast attended the Convention, hast been present at that illumined assemblage, hast heard those merciful addresses, hast secured a fresh spirit and hast increased in faith, assurance and firmness in the Covenant. Appreciate the value of this lordly bounty and thank God that thou art living in the dispensation of the Covenant, and art attracted to the Sun of the Reality of the Abhá Beauty – May my life be a sacrifice to His friends![19]

Another theme of the Tablets translated by Shoghi Effendi during the month of July was Covenant-breaking, in response to reports of the activities of the Covenant-breakers. While the Master's love surrounded both the friends and the enemies of the Cause, He warned the friends about the personal motives and intentions of the violators of the Covenant and made it clear that the only power that can unite the world is the power of the Covenant. Questioning the power of the Covenant is the same as questioning one's belief in the principle of oneness. In the Tablet to Martha Root of 20 July the Master referred to the Covenant-breakers as follows:

... these souls are themselves at present among the pioneers of violation. This is because of their personal motives for they had thought of securing leadership and wealth, but when they considered that in remaining firm in the Covenant their purpose would not be realized, they deviated from it. Those souls must have been either at first truthful and now disloyal or at first disloyal and now truthful. At any rate their lie is manifest. Notwithstanding this, some souls who are not aware of this fact waver when those cast the seeds of suspicion. Awaken all the people and send a copy of this letter to Mr Remey, Mrs Goodall and Mrs Cooper.[20]

Among the Tablets translated during this month by Shoghi Effendi is one to Alfred Lunt, which contained the Master's words of wisdom on another barrier that could deprive one of God's bounties – excessive wealth:

> The essence of the Bahai economic teachings is this, that immense riches far beyond what is necessary should not be accumulated. For instance, the well-known Morgan, who possessed a sum of three hundred millions, and was day and night restless and agitated, did not partake of the divine bestowals save a little broth. This wealth was for him a vicissitude and not the cause of comfort.
>
> He invited me to his library and to his home that I might visit the former and have dinner at his house. I went to the library in order to look at the Oriental books, but did not go to his house, and did not accept his invitation. In short, he eagerly desired that I should visit him in the library but meanwhile important financial problems arose which prevented him from being present, and thus he was deprived of this bounty. Now, had he not such excessive amount of wealth, he might have been able to present himself.[21]

On 1 August Shoghi Effendi wrote to Dr Zia Baghdadi giving the good news that the Beloved's health was excellent and better than the previous year. He mentioned that the Master was day and night 'engaged in perusing supplications, revealing Tablets, receiving visitors, entertaining pilgrims, and directing as ever, in a quiet yet effective and unique way the onward march' of the Faith.

In Bahjih, as he sojourned with his friends and pilgrims, within the short space of days and a half, some 150 supplications were perused and answered, 95% of them addressed to the friends and maid-servants of God in America...[22]

The next day Shoghi Effendi wrote to Mary Lesch thanking through her the Bahai Publishing Society of Chicago for their contribution to his library. He assured this friend that he had arranged the books 'in an orderly and systematic' way in his library. As a token of his appreciation, he sent six Bahá'í ringstones blessed by the hand of 'Abdu'l-Bahá with this letter.[23]

Shoghi Effendi's Diary for these early days of August records other letters too. On Friday, 1 August, Dr Luṭfu'lláh Ḥakím carried several letters with him from England and presented them to the Master. One came from Joan Fforde, the wife of a Royal Navy Commander, on behalf of herself and her husband:

Dear Master, I had a word from you when you were last in London. I was Joan Warings then and now I am married and my husband and I have heard with great joy of your safety and health from Major Tudor Pole. I think with shame of the little I have done for the Cause and pray that we may be helped to serve it. With love and reverent greetings from us both.[24]

Another letter, from that 'devoted soul' E. T. Hall in Manchester, opened as follows:

Dear Master, I have been suffering from great weakness of body and sometimes dullness of mind, but the spirit has been preserved by the goodness of Baha'u'llah, through it all, and I have asked him for strength and light continually. The mercy of God is wonderful. God forgives and re-builds and loves everlastingly and I am making another effort to spread the Cause in Manchester and district... My longing is to be of use to the Cause of Baha'u'llah and Abdul Baha...[25]

Shoghi Effendi states that he looks forward to the Tablets that are to be revealed in response, 'Tablets that shall inspire and guide these earnest

IN THE SERVICE OF THE MASTER, SUMMER 1919

souls and will direct their steps toward the sublime aim that they have set for themselves'.[26]

On Saturday, 2 August, a supplication from Burma turned the Master's attention to the friends in that region, and particularly to India. The believers in this region had made sacrificial contributions to the building of the House of Worship in America despite their poverty, and by so doing had demonstrated their love for the American friends.

On this day three pilgrims who had been the guest of the Master for two months were dismissed, to return to their homelands in the Caucasus and Mazindaran. These friends, ablaze with the love of God, were leaving the Holy Land determined to diffuse the divine fragrances in their homelands. When they received 'the word of dismissal that fell so intolerably hard from His lips', they fell at the Master's feet with tearful eyes and were assured by Him of His love, His prayers, and His intercession for them.

Meeting with Officials

On Sunday, 3 August the Master made several significant statements to officials who had come to visit Him. Consul Abella, who had been in charge of British interests in Haifa before the war, came to visit Him. The Master spoke to this visitor about the oppression and misery in the region during the war. He also revealed a Tablet for the ex-governor of New York City in which He presented the basic teachings of the Faith and praised the humanitarian actions of the government officials.

Before noon more visitors, the deputy governor of 'Akká and his wife, came to see 'Abdu'l-Bahá. The conversation centred on topics that interested the deputy governor including social reconstruction, the industrial crisis, the spread of Bolshevism and so on. He and his wife had lunch with the Master, during which 'Abdu'l-Bahá spoke of the sacredness of Mount Carmel and the unique position of the Shrine of the Báb. At two o'clock the deputy governor and the Master were driven to the Shrine. There, near the middle gate facing 'Akká, they sat and discussed the spiritual significance of Carmel.

In the afternoon, after the deputy governor and his wife had gone, Mrs Stannard, the friends and pilgrims arrived. They sat in the presence of the Master and listened to His important discourse. Mrs Stannard said to the Master that she was happy to see Him at rest and comfortable. In response, the Master said:

> I have always felt at rest. Hast thou ever seen me uncomfortable? It does not make any difference to me. Do you want me to tell you the truth? At a time when I was confined, I felt much more comfortable and was much happier . . .[27]

During the next few days, 4–9 August, owing to the pressure of work comprising the transcription, translation and dispatch of Tablets as well as the perusal of a great number of supplications addressed to the Master from Europe and America, Shoghi Effendi had to discontinue his daily notes and summarize the events of the week. He wrote:

> Piles of supplications await His immediate consideration while His communications and Tablets which have reached the proportion of booklets have to be immediately revised, translated and transcribed. Telegrams are pouring in every day from different parts of the globe and newspaper reports and clippings, books and pamphlets add a great deal to the amount of mail that is being conveyed every day.

Major Moore, a British officer and correspondent for the *Times of Teheran*, came to see 'Abdu'l-Bahá. This officer, an ardent proponent of the League of Nations, received the Master's vision for the future of this body and its evolution towards an effective world organization. The Master spoke further about how the war had shown the need for peace. War, He said, is not a means for acquiring power. Far greater results are possible through unity: scientific achievements employed for war can be used for peace and human faculties can serve to accelerate the movement towards peace.

Major Moore came again on Sunday morning, 10 August, to see 'Abdu'l-Bahá and to ask two questions. First, he wanted to know what effect prayer and concentration have on those who are the subject of concentration and how one acquires the condition of prayer – the state of ecstasy. Second, he wished to know the nature and text of Bahá'u'lláh's prophecies.

The Master's answer to the first question was that man cannot stimulate and awaken others if he is speechless and inactive. His prayer can only bring a change through divine power. However, as soon as the person puts his thoughts into action his hearers can be inspired.

Shoghi Effendi in the service of the Master, circa 1919

Shoghi Effendi, seated second from the right, with the Master and Bahá'ís in the Holy Land

Shoghi Effendi is introduced to the American Baháʼí community, photo published in *Star of the West*

Shoghi Effendi with the Master, February 1919

Shoghi Effendi, seated third from the right, among the believers in Alexandria in 1920, prior to his departure for Europe

Shoghi Effendi, standing to the left of 'Abdu'l-Bahá, in Haifa, 2 October 1919

Shoghi Effendi in the oriental dress he often wore before leaving the Holy Land to study in England

Shoghi Effendi's letter of application to Balliol College, Oxford

Neuilly-sur-Seine,
6 Bd. du Château,
11ᵗʰ June 1920.

Dear Sir;

My esteemed friend, Sir Herbert Samuel, advises me to write you inquiring about admission as a non-collegiate student at Balliol College or any other college at Oxford University.

My sole aim is to perfect my English, to acquire the literary ability to write it well & translate correctly & fluently from Persian & Arabic into English. My aim is to concentrate for two years upon this object & to acquire it through the help of a tutor, by attending lectures, by associating with cultured & refined literary circles & by receiving entrances in Phonetics.

It would be much sought if you could help me along this line;

Yours very sincerely,
Shoghi Rabbani.

Regarding the condition of prayer, the Master said that the best time for prayer is at dawn and dusk. The power of will draws one to the condition of prayer. When one is not in a receptive mood and is rather immersed in one's worldly affairs, he can pull himself into the condition of prayer by an act of will:

> By a force of will and an effort of mind, man turns his attention to God, to His knowledge, His wonderful creation, His wisdom and His Omnipotence, and then by thinking frequently and deeply of Him, attains the state of Love, of desire for prayer, of supreme ecstasy. But sometimes one finds that Divine power and not human effort transports man into that condition.

Regarding Major Moore's second question, the Master said that Bahá'u'lláh's prophecies had been published some 30 years earlier in India, Persia and Egypt. He asked for a copy of two books to be brought to Him, from which He read in a thrilling voice. From the Kitáb-i-Aqdas He read prophecies referring to:

> ... the fall of Abdul-Hamid, the oppression and misrule that raised high their head in Constantinople, the cry of the Owl which is heard from the people of Turkey, the collapse of Germany, the sudden fall of the King of Berlin, the lamentations again of Berlin and the promising and bright future that lies ahead of Teheran particularly and the whole of Persia generally.

A copy of a set of diary letters was sent to Dr Esslemont on Monday, 11 August. In the cover letter Shoghi Effendi wrote of his anticipation of Esslemont's visit in October:

> My dear, dear Dr Esslemont:
> Your kind letter enclosing your most welcomed portrait was received. Dear Lotfullah who arrived safely delivered it to me and I was glad to hear your news and those of the friends in England. As soon as your supplication & photograph was presented by dear Lotfullah, a lovely Tablet was revealed for you which shall be duly forwarded. The Beloved is in the best health & pilgrims are pouring in from the four distant corners of the globe. Now we all look

forward to meet you, safe & healthy this coming October! As I have no good single picture of my own, I send you a grey picture taken recently in the vicinity of the tomb of the Bab, wherein I am marked with a cross on the sleeves.

I enclose for you some recent copies of my diary which include some of the interesting talks & remarkable declarations of the Beloved. I must gladden your heart, as I know how anxious you are, of the good health & happiness of the Master. He is feeling indeed very well and is exceedingly busy.

I am well and glad to have met Lotfullah, whom I meet daily and with whom yesterday I had a lovely walk in moonlight on Carmel. I hope to meet you there in October & pass with you a long time in perfect joy & fragrance.

I am ever your friend,
Shoghi

Welcoming the Pilgrims

In his diary for the period 11–14 August, Shoghi Effendi describes the five-month journey of a newly arrived group of 19 pilgrims from Persia, a group that included four men, five women, two youth and a baby from the family of the well-known Ḥájí Muḥammad Ismá'íl-i-Zabíh, whose name was mentioned by Bahá'u'lláh in the Epistle to the Sultan.

The journey of these pilgrims had been truly arduous. In their longing to meet their beloved, they had faced hardships, obstacles and dangers. They had experienced successive delays and severe restrictions, paid exorbitant fees and were lodged in poor accommodations. During four days of their 20-day voyage on tumultuous seas, they had no sustenance but a glass of water and a cup of coffee. And when finally their ship approached within sight of Carmel, instead of anchoring at the port of Haifa it suddenly changed its course and took the direction of Beirut, to be held in quarantine for four days.

Despite all this hardship, when this group of pilgrims saw the sight of Carmel again, tears of joy flooded their eyes. The Master welcomed them with infinite love and enquired how they had passed the journey. To this question they responded that they had undertaken the journey in extreme joy and fragrance. The Master remarked:

Although outwardly the monsoon storm was violent and travel restrictions were severe, yet that hardship was comfort, that affliction was gladness, that trouble was mercy, and that woe was a blessing.[28]

The group of pilgrims had brought news of the firmness of the friends in their hometowns. The women had brought gifts – carpets they had woven with their own hands and with genuine love. Each of these beautiful carpets bore the name of one of the ladies of the Holy Family. They stretched the carpets on the floor and were happy when the ladies of the Holy Family walked on them.

During the evening of 15 August the Master spent hours with the group of friends and pilgrims in the garden adjoining His house, wrote Shoghi Effendi, 'along a beautiful alley under the tresses of vine from which hang many a cluster of grapes and round which are scattered flowers of different variety, fragrance and colour. In such a still, fragrant and cool spot the Beloved spends with his friends his evening hours.' At an early hour next morning the female pilgrims and the ladies of the household attained His presence. The children chanted prayers in this gathering. Then the Master went out to His garden to meet the other pilgrims; the newly arrived group was scheduled to go by train that day to 'Akká, returning the same day. 'Abdu'l-Bahá helped them understand the significance of their pilgrimage to the Sacred Shrine of Bahá'u'lláh. Here is Shoghi Effendi's translation of the Master's words:

> Ye are now on your way to the Sacred Shrine. Ye must visit that Shrine first on behalf of the far-away friends in Persia, and then on my behalf. Those souls who visit the Sacred Tomb are totally transformed, a new spirit is breathed in them. Their case is like unto a man who endowed with a keen sense of smell enters into a garden and thus inhales from every direction a refreshing odour. An extraordinary pleasure and vigour are felt and extreme joy and gladness are realized. Some visit this spot but are impressed only by its verdure and greenness and they are like unto a man who being afflicted with a severe cold enjoys only the verdancy and freshness of the garden.
>
> At present, God willing, as ye attain unto that Shrine ye shall secure a fresh spirit and a new light. The bounties of God are not appreciated by those who are devoid of understanding . . . The

Divine bounties are enjoyed when man is conscious and aware and he who is endowed with this consciousness secures a new spirit by visiting this Sacred Spot . . .

Man must approach the Holy sites with the utmost humility and lowliness. His Holiness the Supreme One would never enter into the interior of the sanctuary of the Prince of the Martyrs. He stood at the door with the utmost reverence and lowliness and there would address the visitation prayer. Likewise, the Blessed Beauty when a group of us would accompany Him to Kazemayn assumed the same attitude. On the anniversary of the great martyrdom day at Kerbala some 10–15 thousand souls gathered at that spot. Not one among this great concourse could be seen in as humble and lowly attitude as the one assumed by the Blessed Beauty on that occasion. Ye must be the same and must approach the Spot with the same degree of reverence. As ye start from this place ye must be constantly absorbed in prayer and supplication. May ye rest under God's protection![29]

The day after the pilgrims had returned from 'Akká, the Master met with them and showered them with His love. Among them was a devoted believer whose brother and son had both been martyred in Yazd. His son's name was 'Abdu'l-Wahhab, who at the age of six had been surrounded in the street by a group of mischievous children belonging to a fanatical sect of Islam and was asked to tell them his name. Falteringly, he had pronounced ' 'Abdu'l-Bahá' instead of ''Abdu'l-Wahhab'. Having heard the word 'Bahá', the wicked children had stoned the child to death.

Shoghi Effendi describes the words of the Master to this devoted pilgrim who had suffered affliction in the path of God.

You have indeed undergone severe calamities and afflictions. You have been greatly vexed, agitated and have suffered by successive trials. But afflictions and calamities are, when examined closely, the Bestowals of God. In the last analysis, taking consequence into consideration these incidents although outwardly seem to be calamitous, yet in reality they constitute a supreme favour. Verily thou hast been severely tried and hast fallen in great distress. First thou hast experienced the martyrdom of thy brother and later on that of thy dear son. Praise thou the Lord that thou hast been made the recipient of such bestowals. These relatives of thine have been confirmed and assisted to attain unto the station of martyrdom. These confirmations are beyond any description and in reality they are the cause of everlasting life.[30]

These devoted pilgrims were anxious to meet the Western believers, who were also looking forward to being with their fellow pilgrims from the East. The Master encouraged the meeting of East and West. Mrs Stannard describes this meeting, which Shoghi Effendi recorded in his diary:

> The faces of these women shine with the spiritual joy of their convictions, and their bearing express[es] the serenity of a noble faith. With them as with all true Bahais, faith and knowledge are sure and inseparable factors in their lives. It was one morning during busy household hours, that I came upon them with the members of the Beloved Family, seated on mats on the ground in an outer courtyard. They surrounded a low circular wooden table covered by heaped up corn. On this grain they worked, each on her separate share sifting and sorting out impurities or stones from the wheat. Typically oriental and cheery was the scene as heads draped in glistening white muslin that fell over the shoulder they bent over their work conversing in low tones. As I seated myself near by watching the play of deft fingers, my eyes fell on a young mother and her newly-born babe. The wee chap was gaily swaddled in vivid silk of hand woven texture and sat on his mother's left arm as her right busied itself with the grain sorting. Absorbed in watching them both, I heard someone say to me, 'He was born on the way,' and then I heard the story of how little 'Rahbar', the 'guided' (as Abdul Baha has wonderfully named him) came and lived to make his first pilgrimage with his parents and attain the Holy Threshold. Little 'guided' was compelled to make his entry into the world of men when our company had reached a day's march beyond Shiraz in a sparsely inhabited country and where conditions were none too promising.
>
> It had not been foreseen when the travellers started that the going would take months and not so many calculated weeks; so now little Rahbar's mother had to be carried in a special basket, a 'kajaveh', on the back of mules till her hour should come. When this became evident our pilgrims halted the caravan and consulted

PRELUDE TO THE GUARDIANSHIP

how to settle this matter for the best. A small habitation being seen in the distance some walked to make enquiries and found a woman at the door who after hearing their request opened it and offered accommodation. But on viewing the interior quarters it was decided to be neither sufficiently clean nor convenient and hearing that something better might be procurable, further on, they walked to a house of better aspect where again a woman came forward who to their great joy declared herewith to be an expert mid-wife. These surroundings were suitable, a running stream passed close by, trees were near, all seemed providentially ready. Thankfully they dismounted while an adjacent chamber of canvas was specially rigged up for the reception of the coming guests.

One remaining obstacle however had still to be overcome, viz, the head mule owner of the caravan, who when he heard that a three days halt was intended flew into a rage, declaring he could not consent and demanding extortionate terms for every hour of unnecessary delay. No arrangements apparently prevailing, he left them to round up his animals while they debated with perplexity together. To their surprise he did not return soon and when at last a highly crestfallen man appeared it was to say that his best mule had run away, how or when he declared was a mystery. With apologies he begged to go and resume his search, for search he must till the beast was found. Our modern Mary and her babe were left in grateful peace and gladly enjoyed the repose they so much needed. Anxiety and fear were now allayed as they thanked the Blessed One who had sent such timely help in their distress. Pleasing indeed is it to relate that three full days elapsed during which the pilgrims rested, ere the irate muleteer returned with his missing animal. It was he who begged forgiveness and expressed regret.

Although by no means a robust woman, Rahbar's mother felt sufficiently recovered to resume the travelling though it was another day or two ere they reached a stage where milk and other comforts were procurable.

Consider then ye western mothers how great was the spirit of love and faith which upheld this young Persian woman to bear without fear or suffering a frail babe, under such primitive conditions, through Monsoon storms, and on turbulent seas, till they arrived at the gate of the Beloved's house and rested weary heads under the shadow of his roof. No wonder little Rahbar felt elated as he blinked sleepy eyes at me on that memorable morning, for had he not done his best too to make things easier all around? His mother had looked at him with quiet certainty as she smiled at me. He and she understood one another for they knew that God had guided them through perilous ways to the 'Door of Hope' and to His 'green pastures' in safety and all was well with the little flock.³¹

Visit with British Officials

On 23 August 1919 Major-General Watson met the Master at the house of the Military Governor, Colonel Stanton, in the German colony of Haifa. This General, who was visiting with his wife, two daughters and staff, was the newly-appointed chief administrator of the southern section of the occupied territory, headquartered in Jerusalem. During the conversation he expressed his amazement and admiration at 'Abdu'l-Bahá's endurance during forty years of incarceration in the forlorn and ruined city of 'Akká. The Master, however, expressed His happiness during those years. Shoghi Effendi translated the words of the Master to this officer of the British Empire.

> All throughout this period, I was happy and thankful, my heart was at rest for I was happy, submissive and resigned. During those days of confinement, I imagined the condition of the grave, to which eventually and inevitably man shall be confined, a dark subterranean place, narrow, solitary and gloomy. When I pictured to myself that condition, I felt that I was in a wide and spacious region, flooded with light and surrounded by companions and friends. To me the fortress – this penal colony – was indeed when compared to the eternal abode of man a palatial residence. Once I was informed of my soon being thrown into the sea. At this report, I rejoiced for instead of being confined to a dark and narrow grave, I would secure a resting place, the wide and spacious sea. My trust was in God and this kept me ever happy, tranquil and grateful.³²

Referring to the victory of the British forces in Palestine and Syria, the Master remarked, 'God hath wished it to be so, it was His Divine aid and assistance that made it possible.' The General said that it was God's help and the wish of the oppressed people. The Master reiterated that the essential factor was God's assistance and confirmation. 'It was God that helped you from every standpoint.'³³

General Watson remarked that he had heard a great deal about the Baháʼí Faith, and listened intently to the Master's words, Shoghi Effendi recounts. When 'Abdu'l-Bahá stood up to leave, the General and his wife expressed their satisfaction at meeting Him and were deeply impressed by His charm and dignity during the interview.

Tablets to European Friends

On 24 August Shoghi Effendi recorded in his diary 'some remarkable Tablets' addressed to 'the group of friends gathered in Stuttgart, Hamburg and a few other cities' in Germany, some to individuals and others collectively. One of these was Johanna Hoff, who had entered the Cause of God two years earlier, had taught her mother and sisters, and was constantly engaged in service by translating the sacred texts and delivering Baháʼí talks in factories and workshops in Germany. The Master revealed a Tablet in her honour referring to her as 'a leaf upon the Tree of Life'.³⁴

In addition to individual Tablets, a general Tablet was revealed for the friends in Germany, reminding them of the glad-tidings of this day of Revelation.³⁵

> O ye the chosen ones in the Abha Kingdom! Offer ye thanks unto the Lord of Hosts that He hath descended, riding upon the clouds, from the Invisible Plane to the nether world and hath flooded with the light of the Sun of Truth the East as well as the West. The call of the Kingdom has been raised and the Divine heralds with the melody of the Supreme Concourse have declared the glad-tidings of the day of Revelation . . .
>
> . . . In short the doors of Bounty are wide open and the signs of God are manifest; the light of truth is shining and the Divine Bestowals are boundless. Realize how precious is this time and strive with heart and soul that this gloomy world may become illumined, this dark and narrow realm may be expanded, this mortal dust heap may become a mirror that reflects the everlasting rose-garden, this material world may obtain a share and portion from the Merciful Bounties . . .

Later that week, Shoghi Effendi recorded in his diary 'a promising letter from Holland, disclosing the good news of the possibility of the promotion of the Cause in that land', and quoting from the letter:

> Since long I am trying to find the uplifting and liberation of humanity from the material slavery. In that respect I cannot see anything neither in Socialism, or anarchism or Bolshevism that is satisfying me . . . Since 1914, I have held meetings in Holland about the Bahai Movement . . . My speeches have been received favourably but I always felt that I was dealing with the surface of the matter. The reason is that I cannot read foreign languages very well and that I have no nearer connection with Bahais in the other countries – this being a result of war.
>
> I will be very delighted if I may receive a letter from you telling me . . . what I can do to get hold of a better knowledge of the matter . . .[36]

'Abdu'l-Bahá revealed this reply, as recorded by Shoghi Effendi in his diary:

> O thou who art attracted to the Kingdom of God! Thy letter was received. Its contents were conducive to the utmost joy. Praise be to God, that respected personage stands athirst at the fountain of Life and a seeker after the path of salvation. He investigates Truth and is wholly detached from prejudice. This age is the age of Truth and the outgrown antiquated ideas are discarded by the wise and active learned men. In this remarkable century all the antiquated and old principles are totally discarded and in every respect new thoughts have arisen. For instance, old scientific conceptions are done away with and new conceptions and principles have taken their place; old policies have been rejected and more modern ones have been adopted; old sciences have been totally laid aside and a new and up-to-date conception has been formed; old customs and habits have been forgotten and have given way to more modern ones; new achievements, new discoveries, new investigations and new inventions have amazed and bewildered the minds of men and in short all things have been renewed.
>
> Consequently the reality of the religion of God must also be

renewed, imitations must be dissipated, the light of Truth must shine resplendently and those Teachings that constitute the spirit of this age must be promulgated – the Teachings of His Holiness Bahaullah that are spread broadcast throughout all regions and constitute the breaths of the Holy Spirit . . . Everything has been renewed and undoubtedly religious precepts must be also renewed.[37]

Dispersal of Shoghi Effendi's College Friends

During the month of August Shoghi Effendi was separated from his college friends from the American University of Beirut. The group of Persian students who had attended the University was dispersing. Many were now leaving for Europe. On 24 August 1919 Shoghi Effendi wrote about the scattering of this group:

> This week has been, viewed from one aspect, a sad and depressing one. It has witnessed the scattering of friends who during the war and prior to it have been for years held closely and affectionately together by bonds of fellowship and common interest. The student Bahai group at the American University – that company of young, brilliant, active and upright men, which has all throughout the war retained, notwithstanding its vicissitudes and blows, its cohesion, is now splitting up, its numbers mostly graduates of that university departing from that common centre . . .[38]

The paths many of these young men were about to pursue are described in the diary:

> Dr. Seyed Ghasem Ghani has left for his home at Sabzevar in Persia, while previously two of his fellow Bahai students have left, one for Baghdad in Mesopotamia and the other to the United States of America. Few days ago, Mssrs. Kamal and Jalal Bakeroff, respectively an M.A. and an undergraduate of the School of Arts and Sciences, have with the full authority of the Beloved gone to America, in order to complete their studies at Leland Stanford University, in San Francisco, California. Yesterday evening another split occurred by the parting of another group of four, three of them

IN THE SERVICE OF THE MASTER, SUMMER 1919

being Mssrs. Bahadur, Abdul Hossein Khan and Ali Mohammed Khan, who after few months tour in Europe will return to Persia, while the fourth, Mirza Ali Mohammed Afnan is going via Egypt to the United States to study the course of agricultural engineering. He carries with him also an autographic recommendation from the Beloved. One or two are tarrying a while at Haifa and then will proceed to Egypt and thence wherever circumstances will direct their path and assure their future, while another one, Mr. Ali Yazdi, is just starting from Damascus to Haifa where after meeting the Beloved, he will proceed to Berlin to engage in higher studies.[39]

Ali Yazdi, mentioned in this passage, was one of the closest friends of Shoghi Effendi. He left Haifa by train to go to Port Said where he was to take the ship to Switzerland and Germany. Shoghi Effendi saw him off at the station in Haifa. They sat in the compartment until the train was ready to leave; then Shoghi Effendi said good-bye and asked Ali Yazdi to write to him. In his diary he wrote:

> Sad has been the farewell that we bade them this week, but the idea that these young men, enlightened and active as they are, may one day each in his own sphere of action render a service to the Cause, affords sufficient consolation for the hearts of those that remain behind.[40]

7

In the Service of the Master
Autumn 1919

Shoghi Effendi remained in Haifa while his school friends were dispersing. His own turn would come to leave the Holy Land, but for now he was where he longed to be, in the presence of his beloved Master. He had significant contributions to make and much to learn at the feet of the Beloved.

The *Star of the West* contains no Tablets translated by Shoghi Effendi in September, but correspondence continued unabated: on 16 September Shoghi Effendi wrote to Mrs Arthur Platt of Los Angeles acknowledging the receipt of a postcard and told her that he had presented it to the Greatest Holy Leaf.

> My dear Bahai sister!
> I am so grateful for the beautiful post-cards that you have twice sent me – all indicating your warm Baháʾí love. The Beloved is in the best of health & is always engaged in praise of the friends & prayer for them. I always remember you at the Holy Shrine and beg for you as well as the maid-servants of God in that land the confirmations and assistance of God.
> Yours in His Name,
> Shoghi[1]

Shoghi Effendi wrote a postcard on this day to another maid-servant of God, Mrs Louise Waite.

> My dear Bahai sister:-
> Your letters and supplications have all arrived. I have the great

pleasure of announcing to you that a most beautiful Tablet has been revealed to your respected husband, wherein you are most affectionately mentioned. A similar Tablet has been revealed to Mssrs Ollie Watts & Joe Gilligan. My aunt Monever Khanum has also written you a letter & it has been recently despatched. Mrs Stannard is here & is feeling very well indeed, both physically and spiritually. The magnificent sunshine of Syria & the still more magnificent & resplendent light that radiates from the Orb of the Covenant, sustain and enliven her. The Beloved is so busy and so active that one can hardly believe. Pilgrims are constantly arriving & supplications from all parts of the world are pouring in without interruptions. You will excuse me therefore if I have sent you on this card this hurried note . . .[2]

On 22 September Shoghi Effendi wrote a postcard to Mrs Ella Cooper answering correspondence from her in which she had enquired about the book of addresses of the Master in California. Shoghi Effendi stated that despite having searched and re-searched, this document had not been found and that the search would continue.[3]

Thanks to his diary letters, we have a glimpse of what took place during these precious months, although, as he writes in a letter in mid-October to Joseph Hannen, 'pressure of work has forced me to discontinue it during the month of Sept., but with the first of this month I have taken it up again.'[4] The themes Shoghi Effendi describes in these diary letters, so varied and so uplifting, will forever inspire generations of believers. Three significant events took place in the first week of October: the observance of the births of the Báb and Bahá'u'lláh, the Master's words concerning the condition of the friends in the aftermath of the World War, and His visit to a British battleship.[5]

Observance of the Twin Anniversaries

The twin anniversaries of the Birth of the Báb and Bahá'u'lláh fall on two successive days, the 1st and 2nd of Moharram according to the lunar calendar. On October 1st, Shoghi Effendi records in his diary that the anniversary of the birth of Bahá'u'lláh, on the 2nd of Moharram, was celebrated in the presence of the Master

PRELUDE TO THE GUARDIANSHIP

... the large number of pilgrims, including men, women and children, representatives of Persia, India, England and Egypt, that had flocked during past months to Haifa, were all summoned by their Master to come and celebrate this anniversary day in the vicinity of the Sacred Shrine. A concourse of sixty to seventy souls, pilgrims as well as residents of Haifa filled almost all the compartments of the morning train that left on that day for Acca. When they reached their destination the friends of Acca, likewise men and women, who had gathered in that same Spot in anticipation of their arrival, raised the number of the participators in the great jubilee to well nigh a hundred. Although the night before they had hardly slept a wink, so eager and impatient were they to catch the early morning train, yet when at last they found themselves on their way to the Sacred Spot, they manifested by their songs, exclamations, clamour and movements, a joy that amazed everyone even the conductor of the train. Not a minute did elapse in quiet and calmness from the time the train pulled away from the station of Haifa to the time it stopped at Acca. Amid the uproar and the jubilant songs that rent the air, the chief of the train was seen as if carried by an irresistible torrent, clapping, applauding and cheering. All the day was spent in the demonstration of such fervid and unbounded emotions, displaying thereby a scene that exerted its clear effect upon a group of British officers, who in that hour of stir and animation, had motored from Haifa to meet specially the Master of whom they had heard so much. It was indeed a picturesque as well as imposing and significant scene, to witness again after these dreadful and perilous years of war, in the close vicinity of the Tomb of Bahaullah, the Beloved sitting with majesty and confidence with British officers in His presence and His faraway devoted friends sitting side by side on the ground or crowding the adjoining hall and corridors – all beaming with thanksgiving and joy at this happy and sudden turn of events. When twilight had set in and all outsiders had gone and nature seemed to present the opportune moment for prayer, the Beloved dressed in white, came out and proceeded with reverence and majesty toward the Sacred Shrine, followed by a long retinue of friends, marching all with a look on their faces and an expression in their countenance, that are exclusively attributed to the ablazed and steadfast believers of Persia. In the interior of the Sacred enclosure, all fell prostrate on the ground and then with their supplicant and tearful eyes directed toward the interior of the Tomb, plunged all into a moment of silent prayer.

This fervent meditation was broken by a most excellent and thrilling melody, sung by the well-known poet Kabil, a believer of Abadeh, who was bidden by the Beloved to address the opening prayer at the Sacred Threshold. This was followed by the chanting of the prayer of visitation, after which all retired to receive from the hands of the Beloved the various sweetmeats and fruits that were prepared for this remarkable occasion.

After that with hearts refreshed, with souls inspired and with mouths sweetened, they sat in the open air and gave vent as never before to their intense feeling of joy and of gratitude. Their leader who at every turn stirred and animated them had composed a poem in honour and memory of these two consecutive feasts, with a most charming chorus and a lovely tune and in the chanting of which all participators, young and old, heartily joined and swelled the chorus with the clapping of their hands and the tramping of their feet.

Joy was indeed unconfined . . . At dawn they awoke and in a mood of prayer hastened to the garden encircling the Tomb, plucked its flowers, circumambulated the shrine and visited again its interior.

Having partaken of the morning tea in the presence of the Beloved, and having received His blessings and favours they returned to their pilgrim-house on Mount Carmel . . .[6]

The Condition of the Friends in the Aftermath of the World War

The First World War had ended a few months earlier, yet the prevalent mood of 'unrest, of anxiety, of revenge and of terror' lingered. Concerns for 'the great crises in industrial, political, financial and social circles, the threatening advance of Bolshevism, local disturbances . . . the continuation of active warfare on so many different fronts, the slow progress of affairs and all the many thorny questions that are still unsettled and are perplexing the minds, the prevalence of bitter racial animosities' – these occupied the thoughts of the friends as they assembled on the evening of 3 October and listened, 'intent upon the words that might fall from the lips of the Beloved with respect to the numerous startling and repeated reports that abound in the local press'. Shoghi Effendi wrote in his diary that 'the Master's words tonight are highly significant':

> The world is astir and regions are in commotion. However, the friends of God at every spot are in the utmost joy and fragrance, in tranquility and repose. This oppressed group, this wronged party, at a time when all peoples, nations and communities of the world were in a state of comfort and of rest, was then threatened, molested and attacked from every side. At present, contrariwise, the leaf has turned and when all peoples and nations are entangled, restless and afflicted, this group is free from every concern, from every fetter and from every care. Through the blessings of the Blessed Beauty during this tumult and carnage, the friends have been miraculously protected. Praise be unto God! Many are the souls that have been killed! Huge is the amount of property that has been sacked and plundered! Enormous is the loss that has been inflicted! Innumerable are the villages, towns and cities that have been razed to the ground! Notwithstanding this heavy toll, every single abode that pertained to the friends of God has been preserved and kept intact. This is verily attributed to the bounty and favor of my Lord!
>
> We have taken only one step in this path and if at all we rise to live and act in accordance with the admonitions of Bahaullah, there is no doubt that all that dwell on earth would unmistakably gather under the shade of the Cause. There is no doubt about this.
>
> 'Our wine, adulterated though it be, does intoxicate us all; what then will its effect be if it happens to be pure and clear?'
>
> Our relationship to the Cause and the fact that we pertain to it has achieved such wonders and has wrought such marvels, what will happen therefore if we live and act in accordance with the precepts and Teachings of His Holiness Bahaullah? Let us arise and act accordingly.[7]

In this discourse the beloved Master was calling the believers to a new level of action where they would show to the world by their deeds the transforming effect of the Abhá Revelation. Detachment from the love of this world, living in conformity with the divine teachings, purifying the hearts, and striving for the Kingdom of God – these were the standards He was calling them to attain.

These admonitions assumed deeper meaning each day through the example He Himself set for the believers. What He expected from them was to be as He was, to follow His example.

The Master's Visit to a Battleship

An example of the Master's involvement in the events of the world, yet providing those around Him with spiritual perspective, is his visit to a huge battleship of the British Navy, the man-of-war *S. S. Marlborough*. In this example we see how He treated those whose orientation was opposite to His own. The ship, launched in 1914, had played an important role in the Battle of Jutland and was now anchored in the port of Haifa for a few days. On 4 October the British naval commander requested the Master to 'give him the honour of visiting the battleship in person'. The Master accepted the invitation and accompanied by a number of attendants went on board and was greeted by a group of British officials as well as local notables including the Bishop of the city and the Mufti of 'Akká. After welcoming the Master, the Captain ordered some naval officers to conduct a guided tour of the ship for Him – the turret, the interior, the command centre and the place where the 13.5 inch guns were located. When the tour was over, the Master joined the Commander and the military governors of Haifa and 'Akká for afternoon tea at the officers' mess. After a brief conversation, during which the Master jokingly compared the weather in London to the 'clear blue sky of the Holy Land', He uplifted the vision of the officers to a higher purpose:

> It is the first time that I have come on board of a man-of-war. I hope and trust that all these implements and means of warfare will be turned into factors that shall promote peace and industrial prosperity, that these men-of-war will be turned one day into merchant ships, stimulating thereby trade and industry. This is my hope.

'When the picket-boat was made ready,' writes Shoghi Effendi, 'the Commander of the ship grasping the hand of the Beloved thanked Him heartily . . . to which the Beloved expressed his satisfaction of this visit, His gratitude for the hospitality and His prayers for the Commander's success and safety.' The Master also shook hands with the acting military governor of the city and the deputy governor of 'Akká, 'both of whom expressed their deep satisfaction and appreciation for the visit of the Master to the battleship'.⁸

* * *

On 8 October 1919 Shoghi Effendi wrote a letter to Louis Gregory expressing his love and admiration for this devoted servant of God. Here is the text of this letter:

> My Bahá'í brother: –
> Your admirable letter has thrilled us all & I am so grateful to you for your kindness in imparting to me these glad tidings. I in turn send you some recent copies of my diary that you may be acquainted with the whereabouts & words of the Beloved.
> The Beloved is well & happy. He is always busy in revealing Tablets & meeting friends & I too am always kept busy & occupied.
> The days we spent at Ramleh, your shining face, and the affection & love which the Beloved unmistakably showed towards you are things that have left an indelible mark on my memory.
> Wishing you success in your noble undertaking & with best greetings to Mrs. Gregory whom I will remember when she was in Acca & on board the 'Cedric'.
> I am your Bahá'í brother,
> Shoghi⁹

Next day, two ships coming from opposite directions anchored simultaneously in the bay of Haifa, providing a contrast to the huge battleship. They were Italian liners, not warships, and they were transporting the loved ones of God – devoted pilgrims, precious souls, who had travelled with longing anticipation to reach the land of their desire.

'From the southern route crossing the Indian Ocean', wrote Shoghi Effendi, one of the ships brought 'an old and active teacher, Mirza Mahmood Zarqani, accompanying an elderly, influential and promising Bahai teacher Indian by origin and high in social standing, by the name of Set Yousef who with his daughter, Ashraf, have journeyed for the first time to the Holy Land.' The other ship brought seven believers from Persia including two distinguished believers: the Hand of the Cause of God Ibn-i-Aṣdaq, who had been referred to by Bahá'u'lláh

IN THE SERVICE OF THE MASTER, AUTUMN 1919

as Shahíd-ibn-i-Shahíd (martyr, son of the martyr), and Faḍíl-i-Mazandarání, 'the erudite from Mazandarán'.[10]

The story of the pilgrimage of these two groups of pilgrims totalling eleven souls is inspiring indeed, and adds to the precious record Shoghi Effendi has left of this period. When they were ushered into the presence of the Master, tears and sobs expressed the joy and exultation in their hearts. They fell on their knees before their Beloved and heard these loving words of welcome:

> Ye are welcome! Ye are most welcome! Long and extensive has been the period of expectation and long have we anticipated your arrival, and eagerly have we looked forward to meet you. I hope you have had no difficulties on your way and I trust you accomplished the journey with comfort, with joy and fragrance . . .

Addressing the Persian pilgrims, the Master praised the services of several believers from Persia including Hakím Báshí, the late Ibn-i-Abhar, Jináb-i-Adíb and Samandar. He then turned to the friends coming from India who had sustained great difficulties prior to this pilgrimage. The Master comforted them as they sat at His feet and listened to His words of wisdom. He assured them that whatever hardship had transpired in the path of God was acceptable and welcome, and counselled them that reward is in direct proportion with the difficulties endured and the hardships sustained. These are His words, as translated by Shoghi Effendi:

> Difficulty under such circumstances was turned into happiness and ease and alarm converted into tranquility and contentment. Viewed from the standpoint of consequences, both are the same and if the object is attained without experiencing any hardship, it is undoubtedly preferable. This world is likened to a general market, 'bazar', in which one man is seen tranquil and restful while another is restless and active. Towards the end of the day the former as a result of his inactivity and rest is deprived of any gain and is thus gloomy and disheartened, whilst the latter in view of his toil and labor has gained and is as a result hopeful and glad.[11]

During the two weeks that this group of pilgrims enjoyed nearness to the

Centre of the Covenant, the Master composed three significant Tablets – to believers in India who had begged Him to bless their country with His presence; to the Honourable James Barr, the director of the Congresses at the Panama Pacific International Exposition held in San Francisco in 1915, regarding his assistance to the First International Bahá'í Congress held during the Exposition; and to a young believer in China, regarding teaching the Cause in that vast country. Excerpts from Shoghi Effendi's translations of these Tablets are included below.

To the friends in India He wrote:

O Thou who art firm in the Covenant!
The letter dated August 19th 1919 has been received and its contents sweetened the soul for it was a manifest sign of fidelity and a clear evidence of perseverance in servitude to the Abha Beauty... Today is the day of Teaching and this act is confirmed. Whoever engages in it the legions of the Abha Kingdom shall secure for him the victory. The cause of Teaching has got a clear charge and command from the Abha Kingdom. In fine, arouse all the friends and encourage them to exalt the Word of God and diffuse the Divine Fragrances, so that thereby that country may be animated and quickened...[12]

To James Barr He wrote:

O thou noble personage! In the past, particularly during the 19th and 20th centuries, numerous congresses have been instituted in the great cities and capitals of the world; important personages have attended them; vital questions have been discussed and firm decisions have been reached... But, consider! As these congresses of the past pertained to the nether world, no trace of them has been left behind and their results have disappeared... This is because every worldly cause is transitory... every heavenly Cause in everlasting.

Consequently the results of this First International Bahai Congress that has been instituted shall be remarkable. Do not consider the present but rather take the future into consideration.

Briefly, this Congress is like unto a seed that has been planted into a pure soil and which grows and thrives through the outpourings of the vernal rain, through the heat of the celestial sun and through the wafting of the breezes of spring, until it becomes a flourishing tree.

Rest assured that this Bahai Congress is like unto this seed which shall grow into an imposing tree. The Supreme Concourse praises and extols this Congress and the call of the Abha kingdom declaring 'well done, well done' strikes the ears of the inner soul.

Praise God that this Congress has been established through your efforts and the effect of this endeavour shall eternally remain, nay rather its fame shall be perpetuated throughout all ages and cycles and every one shall praise your efforts . . .[13]

A Tablet was revealed in honour of Chen Ting Mo, who had translated 'some leaflets on the Cause' into Mandarin Chinese. This young man, upon receiving the news of the Convention in New York and the campaign for the worldwide expansion of the Cause, had written to an American friend requesting him to translate and distribute among the Chinese people in the States thousands of copies of the extract from the words of 'Abdu'l-Bahá published in 1917 in *Star of the West*: 'China, China, China, China-ward the Cause of Baha'o'llah must march! Where is that holy, sanctified Bahai to become the teacher of China?'[14] To this devoted young man, the Master wrote:

O thou herald of God! The letter thou hadst written to ... was forwarded by him to the Holy Land and has been perused. Call it not a letter but rather a rose-garden wherein the flowers of significance were blooming and from which the sweet scent of the Love of God was inhaled. Verily thou hast the capacity and the merit for such a supreme bounty that the light of guidance should be enkindled in the globe of thy heart and should set aglow thy soul and thy body. Thy tongue has become eloquent and thy ear responsive and thou hast inhaled the perfume of the Abha Paradise.

In the land of China, the capacity of souls to comprehend the new Teachings is remarkable . . . in order to bring about regeneration, progress, the prosperity of the people, the exaltation of souls, the development of the country and the abundance of wealth, religion must be renewed...

Consolidate the assembly thou hast established at Shanghai as well as the one instituted at Peking. Engage in the promulgation of the Cause of God. The greatest means for progress lies in the propagation of the Divine Instructions and action in accordance with these precepts; for mere utterance and the exposition of principles will bear no fruit. What is needed is actual performance. Rest thou assured that the invisible confirmations of God shall encompass thee for this is explicitly recorded in the Sacred Epistle 'We shall with the help of the cohorts of the Supreme Concourse and a legion of the favored angels assure the victory to whomsoever will arise to exalt my Cause and render it triumphant.'[15]

Recalling His travel to America and His numerous talks to diverse audiences, the Master continued this Tablet by referring to the evidence of divine confirmations He had received in His own efforts in the path of His Beloved. Here is how He described the extraordinary reception shown Him in the West:

> During my travel to America it was seen that in the great assemblies and temples, as soon as a word was spoken the spirit of confirmation like unto a sea would surge and were it not for this assistance, it would have been impossible for me to utter a single word for the audience with eyes and ears wide open were ready and had purposed to criticize and raise a point of objection. Notwithstanding this readiness on their part in all these gatherings during the address and after its delivery, not a single person did object, although whatever was declared had been contrary to their opinions and thoughts.
>
> For instance, at the Jewish Synagogue, it was asserted and proved that His Holiness Christ is the 'Word of God' and His Spirit and His Holiness 'The Messenger' (Muhammad) 'The Chosen of God' and the essence of all the contingent beings. It is evident how contrary these statements are to the conviction of the Jews but in spite of this fact not even a Jew did raise any objection. When I was coming out from this Synagogue, the great Jewish Rabbi expressed his gratitude and told me: 'The Jews desire to shake hands with you." In answer I told him that I am in a feverish state and feel extremely weak, how could it be possible for me to shake hands with all these people? He said 'only with a few of the select'. Some of the prominent ones then came forward, shook hands with me and expressed their gratitude. One of them as he was embracing me cried out that 'henceforth I am not a Jew'.
>
> The purpose is to show that all this is to be attributed to the

confirmations of the Blessed Beauty and to heavenly assistance; otherwise they would have prevented me from uttering a single word. At present rest thou assured that the confirmations of the Abha Kingdom shall reach thee. Let loose the noble steed and urge it to rush forward that thou mayest witness a remarkable achievement...[16]

Two more Tablets translated by Shoghi Effendi in October were published in *Star of the West*, one for Flora Clark on 13 October and the other for H. De Boer on 14 October.[17] And on 15 October Shoghi Effendi wrote to Joseph Hannen conveying the following instruction of the Master:

> Exercise toward the Persian minister and the Persians of whom you have written in your letter the utmost love and kindness, and in order to please them do all you can to help them. But be vigilant and awake lest one of these should be a follower of Ezel (Ezelis) or a covenant-breaker! The instant you feel that a person among these Persians is an Ezeli or a covenant-breaker, assuredly and immediately avoid his company for he is the essence of evil...[18]

Shoghi Effendi added to his letter that personal touch which would later come to be so prized by the believers during his ministry as Guardian when he signed himself 'your true brother':

> Well, my dear and indefatigable friend! If you realize how much the Beloved appreciates your manifold services! How tenderly he loves you and with what a smile he mentions your name! May God ever keep you and Pauline under the shadow of his protection and bounty!... Pray for me, just as I pray for you and dear Pauline at the Sacred Spots, for I know your prayers are answered as they emanate from a pure & empty heart. Your brother in His Love,
>   Shoghi[19]

The next day, Shoghi Effendi wrote to Ella Cooper telling her about the two Tablets that had been revealed by the Master concerning the First International Bahá'í Congress in 1915, the one for Mr Barr (quoted above) and the other for the members of the Congress. Despite his heavy workload, Shoghi Effendi found the time to send Mrs Cooper a short note: 'As I realize how glad you will be to receive them I hasten to inform you of this good news.'[20]

Between 20 and 22 October the Master received visits from several Muslim Indian soldiers of the 20th Deccan Horse Cavalry. Two soldiers who had heard about the Master in their native town of Hyderabad and had read about Him in the European and local press were eager to see Him. They had gone to Mecca and now 'considered it their first and sacred duty to visit the Beloved'. After walking a long distance from their camp they arrived at the House of the Master and requested to meet Him. 'Abdu'l-Bahá welcomed them 'in a warm and fatherly manner' and told them:

> You are most welcome. I am so glad to meet you and look at your faces. I like the people of India and have many friends there. The people of India have a wonderful capacity to become spiritual. They are naturally inclined toward God and religion. Their hearts are empty and void of that which pertains to this world. They are pure and God-fearing . . . I have been greatly pleased by your meeting. Most of the people of the world have lost their faith but the people of India retain it and are firm in their belief. They are both people of faith and intelligence. They are lovable and kind. Love has vanished from this world and is to be found only with the people of God . . .[21]

Shoghi Effendi then describes how 'Abdu'l-Bahá drove to the Shrine of the Báb, followed by the two soldiers, who met the friends and pilgrims at that sacred spot, 'listened to the words of prayer, drank tea in His presence and then led by the Beloved, visited the Tomb with all the friends and pilgrims who had assembled at that Spot'. The following day one of the soldiers came again, and walked with the friends to 'the slopes of Carmel where once the pavilion of Bahaullah had been pitched':

> At that very Spot another pavilion has been raised to-day, a square tent . . . spacious and beautiful in shape and without any center pole. This imposing and splendid canopy offered by the friends in India has been submitted to His presence by the last group of the Parsee friends and has been pitched to-day at the very Spot where once the pavilion of Bahaullah had been raised. The Beloved followed by

his friends and this Indian soldier entered this afternoon the tent, distributed sweets and bonbons that had been bought for that occasion by a friend from Kasvin on behalf of the Bahai school in that city and ordered some of the pilgrims to chant prayers and address communes that thereby the tent may be blessed by the mention and praise of Bahaullah.

It was indeed a picturesque and striking scene to witness when the Beloved clothed in white sat on the blue carpet that covered the base of the tent with all the friends, representative of India, Persia, Kurdistan, Egypt and England all sitting on the ground around Him, some dressed in military suits, others wearing turbans, Indian caps and fezs and all receiving from His hands sweetmeats and bonbons which were placed before Him in three large dishes.[22]

On 22 October an Indian captain and a lieutenant from the same regiment attained the presence of the Master to receive His blessings. Showing the utmost respect, they would not drink water or tea before 'Abdu'l-Bahá had taken his own tea. The Master addressed these officers in these words:

> Although this war was terrible and fearful yet it led to our interview and made possible this meeting. I hope ye will return in safety to India and there having laid down your arms ye will engage in another warfare – a war that ye will wage against self and passion. Waging war against human beings is an easy matter, what is difficult is resistance and a successful war against the evil passions of the heart. He who gains victory over his self and over Satan is the real conqueror, has proved his power and will become the recipient of God's blessings. I hope that ye will secure such a victory and such a crown . . . Ye have visited the Kaaba. I trust ye will through His power and guidance attain to the visit of the Heavenly Kaaba. India is endowed with a brilliant capacity. The people are drawn towards God, inclined to religion, God-fearing, loving and faithful . . .

Shoghi Effendi states that the Master 'expressed the hope that they will one day illumine that region, guide it to the Truth, revive the movement of Islam, unite all those different multitudinous castes in India, harmonize the various religions and bestow upon their fellow countrymen a full share of the bounty of Guidance'.[23]

The two officers were happy with their visit. They had acquired a fuller understanding of the teachings of the Master and had received answers to their questions.

* * *

During this same period, 22–24 October, the group of pilgrims who had been galvanized through their experience of being in the Master's company was leaving. Shoghi Effendi describes the moving scene of their departure in these words:

> . . . these ablazed pilgrims men and women fell on their knees, some prostrate on the ground and shedding abundant tears upon the Threshold of their Beloved and others seizing the Master's feet and covering it with their repeated kisses and flowing tears. The children moved by the sight seized with trembling hands the hem of the Beloved's garments and kissed it while passing their tearful eyes upon it. Others sobbing and wailing embraced the Beloved, some laying their foreheads upon his shoulders, others taking Him in their arms . . . One of them crying as a little child exclaimed, 'Oh Abdul Baha, my dear Abdul Baha! How can I leave thee? how can I bear Thy separation?' The Beloved encircled by these grieving souls, some lying prostrate before Him, others falling on His feet, some taking Him in their open arms, and few grasping His hands could hardly move and as He stood, pale yet with a loving fatherly expression on His radiant yet sorrowful face, spoke these words of consolation and assurance:–
>
> 'Do not grieve, do not weep and do not wail. I am always with you, you are always in my heart, wherever ye go and in whatever place ye may stay. Ye must be glad and cheerful, ye must be thankful to God, ye must carry with joy the glad tidings of the Holy Land, ye must inflame the souls in those distant regions, ye must be cheerful and active. Grieve not and be not disturbed. Rest assured in God's blessings. Ye have attained unto such a Sacred Shrine and have secured His good pleasure. Be encouraged, be glad and arise in His service. I shall ever pray on your behalf and beg for ye assistance, confirmation and protection.'[24]

IN THE SERVICE OF THE MASTER, AUTUMN 1919

Following the departure of these pilgrims, Shoghi Effendi's diary for 25–29 October covers exclusively the teaching trip to South America of that remarkable American believer, Martha Root. He mentions how this teacher of the Cause had started out aboard a ship in New York despite a strike that threatened to cancel her trip, and how she travelled to Pará (now Belém) and other cities in Brazil, and to Argentina, teaching the Cause, distributing Bahá'í literature, writing articles for the press, and making friends for the Cause. The passion for teaching of this remarkable and dauntless maid-servant of God was immense. It derived from her vision of the advance of the Cause of God, and the fruition of the seeds she was sowing. Shoghi Effendi quotes her words:

> Within a century there will be Mashrekul-Askars in Brazil. The wonderful souls, the good articles in the newspapers, the books in the libraries, will be enveloped in the clouds of the Holy Spirit and the Bab, Bahaullah and Abdul Baha, the Center of the Covenant will be known in every city and hamlet. 'Verily He is the Powerful over all that He wisheth. There is no God but He, the Dear and the Bestower.[25]

Shoghi Effendi wrote a postcard from Haifa to Alfred Lunt on 26 October acknowledging the receipt of the addresses sent to him, as well as the supplications, and assuring him of the health of the beloved Master.

> My dear Bahá'í brother,
> Pressure of work prevents me from writing you a detailed letter giving you the news of our Beloved Master but I hope that you have read by this time some of my diary letters which I have sent to America and which expose in details the whereabouts and talks of the Master. Your letter date Sept 17 has been received and I hasten to assure you that the copies of your addresses with all your supplications have been received and a tablet for you in answer to them has been dispatched. c/o Mr. Wilhelm on Sept 27, 1919. Their contents have been submitted to the Beloved and you may rest assured the Beloved is in the best of health and is day and night occupied. Convey please my Bahá'í love to all the active friends in those regions.
> Shoghi[26]

PRELUDE TO THE GUARDIANSHIP

In this postcard we see the signature of Shoghi Effendi in the form 'Shoghi', the spelling that would prevail during his ministry as Guardian of the Bahá'í Faith.

8
Last Months with the Master

The time of separation of Shoghi Effendi from the Master was fast approaching. The five-month period between mid-November 1919 and early spring 1920 comprised the last fleeting months he was in the presence of 'Abdu'l-Bahá. During these months Shoghi Effendi witnessed the Master's continuing example of love, compassion, and counsels for His loved ones. He saw how the Beloved welcomed and inspired the pilgrims, bestowed His loving-kindness upon each soul, and how He communicated His soul-stirring exhortations through them to all believers. He saw how the Master treated the officials, and how He concluded life-changing lessons from each event and on each occasion.

Two American pilgrims, Corinne True and 'her brave daughter' Edna,[1] arrived unexpectedly in the morning of 2 November. Despite the hardship of the travel that had included delays in transport, tedious formalities of permits and passports, restrictions in travel, and repeated strikes at sea causing their ship to come to a standstill for hours in mid-ocean, all that faded away when they 'attained the presence of the Master, gazed at His radiant countenance, heard His resonant voice, saw His beautiful smile, sat beside Him at His table and partook of material as well as heavenly blessings'.[2] These pilgrims shared the news that several more pilgrims from the United States were on their way.

In the afternoon, while the Master was speaking to a group of believers gathered near the Shrine of the Báb, two Indian soldiers arrived and greeted the Master with a low bow and a glance that showed their respect and eagerness to see Him. The Master welcomed them with loving words. Shoghi Effendi describes the Master's response to their 'eager desire to be acquainted with the Principles' of the Faith:

The Master told them that at a time when the mists of ignorance and of prejudice had plunged the East in general and Persia in particular into a sea of impenetrable darkness, His Holiness Bahaullah, like unto a Divine Effulgent Star rose from the horizon of Persia, dispelled the fearful obscurity that prevailed and flooded the purified atmosphere with the resplendent light of His Teachings. His principles are based upon this two-fold foundation, the Unity of God and the truth underlying the mission of the Prophets of God – His Divine Messengers. These are the real Educators of mankind, the reformers of the world, the deliverers of man from the bondage of self, the leaders of the souls to the path of eternal glory, of everlasting salvation. Man must not follow blindly his forefathers and ancestors. Each should investigate the Truth independently for Truth is indivisible and is subject to no change. It becomes veiled, it must be freed from every limitation and fetter and must be made to appear fully and in all its splendour.[3]

Then the Master led them into the Shrine where they stood with reverence listening to the chanting of the Tablet of Visitation. The experience had intensified their interest in the Cause.

That night many distinguished believers from Persia, India and Egypt gathered at the Master's dinner table, including Ibn-i-Aṣdaq, Mírzá Azíz'u'lláh Varqá, Mírzá Maḥmúd Zarqání from Bombay, and Sheikh Faraj'u'lláh Zakí, a learned Bahá'í from Kurdistan.

On 3 November the pilgrims from the West heard a talk by Hand of the Cause Ibn-i-Aṣdaq that 'revealed the character and the conduct of the early Bahais, the pillars of the Cause who have sown the seeds and have watered it abundantly with their blood'. Shoghi Effendi writes that these subjects would be 'of great value to those who are engaged in teaching the Cause' in America,[4] and devotes most of his diary for this day to the moving account of the life of Mullá Ṣádiq-i-Muqaddas, the father of Ibn-i-Aṣdaq.

Ibn-i-Aṣdaq told of his father's search for the Promised One that had caused him to leave his native land of Khurasan and journey to the city of Karbila. There he saw the youthful merchant of Shiraz. Subsequently, his search led him to Isfahan where he encountered Mullá Ḥusayn Bushrui, the first Letter of the Living, and was led to the recognition of the Báb as the Promised One. This recognition set a course of sacrifice in his life where every minute was subjected to persecution. Ibn-i-Aṣdaq recounted how his father endured all his trials with joy. His suffering in the path of God started in Shiraz where he and Quddús were dragged through the city; their beards were burned, halters were put upon them, their faces were blackened and they were led through the streets and bazaars. He described how when the two blackened faces looked at one another, they smiled gloriously and thanked their Lord.

Ibn-i-Aṣdaq recounted that the Blessed Báb had showered his father with the utmost love and affection and had promised him that he would see the day of 'Him Whom God will make manifest'. He recounted that he himself at the age of 12, with his father, had attained the presence of Bahá'u'lláh in Baghdad before His declaration, when 'Abdu'l-Bahá was 18 years old.

Having shared these stories from the past, this eminent believer, a Hand of the Cause of God appointed by Bahá'u'lláh, turned to Corinne True, who was serving as the financial secretary of the Executive Board of the Mother Temple of the West, and told her stories of the sacrifices that were being made by poverty-stricken believers in Persia in order to contribute to the Temple Fund. Here are the words of Shoghi Effendi:

> he said that in the furthest corners of Persia, in the outlying province of Khorassan, there is a village consisting of some 30 families who have been all converted to the Cause and who are wonderfully enkindled. They live in extreme poverty to such an extent that a single rug is owned by a group of families and whenever a guest that is a travelling Bahai teacher arrives this rug is passed around that it may be used by that teacher and secure for him a partial comfort. Another village, the Bahai inhabitants of which live simply on barley bread, the father of each family gathers every day one or two handfuls of wheat and stores them to be used for the bread of a Bahai teacher who when passing by his village is affectionately entertained and kept few days in his humble abode, to teach the people who flock to his house in order to listen to the glad-tidings of the Cause and thus secure a new and fresh spirit. From such villages, within a radius of two miles, the songs, hymns and prayers of its Bahai inhabitants and children are heard. In spite of their need and poverty, they are happy, satisfied and contented.

When one talks to them they seem so glad as if they were owning all the riches of this world. They hardly live more than 50 years and of this they are glad and grateful for they believe that to live more than this would be a burden to one's fellow men, as old age makes one dependent upon others. Notwithstanding this misery and need and although their bread is made out of barley and their food is hardly sufficient, yet they manage to gather a cent or half a cent every day and send their humble contribution every now and then for the Mashrekul Azkar in America. If they own 2 piasters, one of it they reserve for the Temple. If they secure a monthly pay of 5 dollars they buy with it woollen material and weave it into clothes with their own hands, selling it for 10 dollars and reserving half of it as their capital and means of subsistence while the rest is divided between the price of their bread and their contribution to the Mashrekul Azkar.[5]

Two days later, on 5 November, a group of Persian pilgrims departed. They were to travel home to Hemat Abad, a suburb of Shiraz, and were all 'aglow with the fire of love for their Master. Shoghi Effendi writes that their farewell 'was indeed pathetic'. One young boy was tearful, he 'could hardly contain his sobs and kept weeping all throughout the farewell meeting'. The beloved Master consoled them, saying, 'Be not sad and despondent. Weep not and do not lament. Praise be to God ye have been for a long time in this Sacred Surroundings and now ye must return glad and triumphant carrying the glad-tidings of this Land . . .'[6]

The Master helped the pilgrims grasp the significance of carrying glad-tidings from the Holy Land to the friends upon their return by recounting for them an experience from His own childhood in Tehran, in the presence of the immortal Váḥid, the learned and devoted follower of the Báb. Here is the Master's story as recorded by Shoghi Effendi:

> I was a child, in the arms of Esfandiar, the loyal and faithful servant of Bahaullah. With us were sitting a group of people when a Dervish with dishevelled hair, dusty face and bare feet all covered and plunged in mud arrived in our midst. When examined closely he was found to be Agha Aly named Sayyah who declared to have come from the presence of His Highness the Supreme One, the

Bab. Immediately Jenabeh Vahid fell on the traveller's feet, plunged and stained his beard, his hair and mustaches into the mud that covered his bare feet and cried loudly:– 'Thou hast come from the presence of my Friends of my Beloved!' They tried to raise him up but he would not and remained for a time kissing and wiping his face and beard on his muddy feet . . .[7]

After tea was served, the Master rose to bid them farewell. The pilgrims fell at the feet of the Master, seized the hem of His garment and implored His protection and confirmation. The Master raised them, passed His hands over their faces, embraced them, and assured them of His love.

Earlier that day 'a new enthusiastic enlightened Bahai' had arrived – Dr John Esslemont of Bournemouth, England. Because of quarantine restrictions he was being detained at a hotel in the city and so was unable to meet the Master that day. Shoghi Effendi writes that he was 'burning with anxiety to present himself and fall at the feet of the Master':

> Confined in a room with his fellow traveller from Egypt . . . they are at present spending their quiet expectant hours in writing letters, in teaching one another Persian and English, in prayer and in meditation – numbering every now and then the flying minutes and counting the hours that separate them from that long desired moment of meeting.[8]

When Dr Esslemont was at last ushered into the presence of a loving Master the following day, the difficulties he had experienced were put into proper perspective when the Master explained that reward is directly proportional to the difficulty endured. He said, 'The more strenuous are one's efforts, severe one's tests, and trying the circumstances he lives in, the nobler and fuller will be his reward at the end.'[9]

The Master enquired about the activities of the friends in England, and emphasized the need of cooperation among them. He said that the divine Manifestations have come to promote love and unity and to encourage cooperation. To demonstrate the extent of cooperation He expected from the believers, He gave an example of how the believers in Persia were caring for each other. He told the story of a man who had taken shelter in the home of a Bahá'í friend. When the police came to the door looking for this person, the host introduced himself as the person they were looking for and gave his life for the sake of his friend.

The Master then gave another example to demonstrate the need for love and caring among the friends. During the war in Persia, the friends had established relief centres and committees to care for the believers at a time when the price of wheat had soared and 120,000 people had died in one year from disease and starvation. As a result of these relief centres not a single Bahá'í starved or was even in need. They took care of the Bahá'ís and many non-Bahá'ís and satisfied the needs of the poor and the indigent.

* * *

In his diary entry for 10 November 1919, Shoghi Effendi gives the news of the progress of the Cause in Arabia reported by Ḥusayn Effendi Rúḥí, a pilgrim. There were about thirty believers in the region, of whom twenty-five lived in Jeddah. The friends were gathering on Fridays for their regular devotions and were actively proclaiming the Faith to receptive souls. Even the Sultan of Hijaz had been approached and informed of the Cause, and had replied that such a man [Bahá'u'lláh] 'must have had an inspiration from God, and must have had a special Divine Mission, to give to humanity'. Among the believers was the learned Sheikh Sanad, an Egyptian, whose entire family were Bahá'ís. Having previously served as the Imam of the Khedive for twelve years, he was now the inspector of the Charity Asylum (Takkieh). For this soul the beloved Master revealed a Tablet, quoted here as translated by Shoghi Effendi:

> O thou honourable Seyid and erudite soul! May God confirm thee in this world and the next! His honor, Hossein Effendi Ruhy has highly praised thee and has said that thou art learned in the knowledge of the Divine and art of those souls who have become assured through the commemoration of their Lord, have resigned themselves to the will of their Creator, have entered the concourse of the servants of God, have made their abode in the Supreme Paradise . . .[10]

Corinne and Edna True had spent eleven days in pilgrimage, and it was now time for them to depart. On 12 November the Master spoke to them and through them sent a message 'to the friends in New York particularly and to all the friends and maid-servants of God in the United States generally':[11]

> My message to them is that they must be united, must remain firm and steadfast, must be always turning to the Kingdom and must be the manifestations of truthfulness, of faith, of harmony and self-sacrifice.
>
> They must co-operate and serve one another with sincerity and goodwill, with devotion and with humility. They must be pure in heart, purer than this water at table. Their hearts must be always directed toward God and turned away from man. They must seek His Divine Good-pleasure and should be wholly detached from this ephemeral world, for attachment to it will plunge man into an intense darkness. The love of this world is the fountain head of every vice and sin. It is the first sin that a soul can commit. No sin is greater than this. Whoever is detached from this world is assuredly near unto God, is a real and sincere Bahai, and whoever is attached to it know well that he is not a real Bahai, for a real Bahai cannot love this world and cannot possibly be attached to it. At most it is this that man lives a few days in this world, sleeps, eats, drinks and then passes away, is confined into a subterranean dungeon and goes to the lowest of the low, leaving no trace and no name behind him.
>
> But if on the other hand he turns during the days of his life to the Divine Kingdom, acquires human perfections and the excellent attributes of the world of humanity, his life will be a fruitful one, he will pertain to the Kingdom and will become heavenly and illumined. He will never feel inclined to this world and if he at all occupies himself with it, it is simply to acquire the means of subsistence. The two most essential requisites are harmony and severance from this world. Attachment to this world is a hindrance to union. If attachment is decreased, union and harmony will be gradually realized.
>
> Good tidings and refreshing news must be received from you when you reach the West – tidings which when I become informed with them, I may be gladdened and rejoiced. I trust that when ye reach America ye may be in the utmost degree of enkindlement, that ye may stir and quicken the souls. I pray that ye may bestow

such a joy and fragrance that when ye attend a gathering of friends and when ye address them ye may transform and stir and vivify the souls of your hearers.

Rest assured that the confirmations of the Blessed Beauty will ever come to your assistance and will ever encompass you. On your behalf I pray at these Sacred Spots and beg for ye assistance and confirmation. Rest ye assured that ye are under His sheltering protection.[12]

As the Trues were on the point of leaving, with Corinne True already in the carriage,

> Shoghi Effendi came hastening across the road to tell Edna that the Master wanted to see her. In a few minutes she was in His reception room where He was seated in a chair. He motioned to Edna to sit next to Him, on the divan, and Shoghi Effendi sat down on her other side. 'Abdu'l-Bahá looked into her eyes; she began to sob uncontrollably. Lovingly, He patted her arm and said, 'You are My daughter.' When Edna rejoined her mother, Corinne knew that something profoundly good had happened to her, that she would never be the same again.[13]

Just a few days later, on 16 November, the Master warmly welcomed a group of pilgrims from the West that included William (Harry) and Ruth Randall and their daughter Margaret from Boston,[14] Albert Vail from Chicago, Arthur Hathaway from Boston, George Latimer from Portland and Saichiro Fujita, the Japanese Bahá'í from Chicago who had at last succeeded in his long-held wish to go to Haifa and serve 'Abdu'l-Bahá there. An American Colonel who was interested in the Cause had also come with them. The Master spoke to them of the power of the Word of God and its influence in bringing together representatives from the East and the West. Referring to the newly-formed League of Nations, He said, as reported by Shoghi Effendi in his diary, that

> it should be representative of all peoples and nations – each nation sending a certain number of representatives that shall be elected by the people represented in Parliament, ratified by the organ of

the Executive, i.e. the Cabinet and confirmed by the head of the nation, whether he be a monarch or a president. Coming together they shall solve all international and inter-racial problems and shall enforce their plans and decisions and in the case of a recalcitrant nation, all the rest must unanimously rise through military pressure, force it to accede to their decision and abide by their will.[15]

Later that evening, while the pilgrims gathered around Him, the Master gave them this counsel:

> It is now 6000 years that the world of humanity has been in darkness, there has been struggle and fighting, there has been war and conflict, enmity and hatred. Now it is sufficient and something must be done to abolish this . . .[16]

The Master closed His talk with the following words:

> We pray that all these might pass away. God willing the world of humanity will find rest, the existing competition between Powers might pass away. Thank God we are free from all these questions. His Holiness Bahaullah has emancipated us. With us all are the same. All countries are one. We have no conflict with any one. Any government which is based on Justice is appreciated. Whatever government it may be as long as it is just it is acceptable. Any country is our country. Wherever we go that is our country. He says the world is one home. We are free and apart from all these questions. 'Glory is not his who loves his country but glory is his who loves his kind.'[17]

Next day the Western pilgrims were sitting at the Master's table around noon. Dr Esslemont referred to the words of Bahá'u'lláh in the Glad-Tidings (Tablet of Bishárát): 'Although a republican form of government profiteth all the peoples of the world, yet the majesty of kingship is one of the signs of God. We do not wish that the countries of the world should remain deprived of it.'[18]

'Does this mean that a hereditary monarchy such as England is preferable to a form of government whose head is elected for a period of years as in U.S.A.?' he asked. The Master replied:

Actual despotic government is unadvisable. A republican form of government is good but a constitutional monarchy is better, because it combines both kingship and republic. It is a form of government with a distinctive head, hereditary but subject to forced abdication if his rule proves unwise.[19]

Shoghi Effendi summarized further remarks of the Master on this subject:

> The Beloved then stated the advantage in having a permanent ruler referring particularly to the quarrels and dissensions preceding and accompanying the election days – quarrels that involved all classes of society even churches and ministers. He then declared that the parliament has the power to remove him and the parliament is the real ruler while the king is nothing but a nominal ruler, – a figurehead. As to the election of the premier, who is the active de facto ruler of the country, the Beloved said that his appointment is by the king subject to the veto of the parliament. The Premier shall be responsible to the parliament of the nation which can dispose of him whenever deemed advisable.
>
> As to the kingship itself the Master said that it has a particular dignity and majesty and pomp attached to it, its policy is steadier and its prestige more marked. But as to the hereditary princes and nobility, the Beloved remarked that he who serves his country and government is a noble and is entitled to the privileges and prerogatives and not the man whose father or ancestor has been of a royal blood or even has served the country. Yet such a person will be respected because of the services of his father. So far as offices are concerned, he will be given no preference but he who serves must have the mark of distinction. Were it not so no one would care to serve.[20]

The Western pilgrims continued to receive loving attention from their Master. He helped them appreciate the bounty of coming on pilgrimage by describing to them while they were seated around His table the restrictions encountered by earlier pilgrims during the time of Bahá'u'lláh. Those early pilgrims, He reminded them, were not allowed in the presence of the Blessed Beauty. To gaze at His countenance they would go to a location from which they could see their Lord. The Master gave an example of a sincere and devoted believer who had come on foot all the way from his native town of Yazd to 'Akká – a two-month journey – to attain the presence of his Lord. After gazing on the room of Blessed Beauty from a distance, he wept a great deal and then returned to his native town. On his return to Persia he was martyred. He had endured trials on the way there, and had proved his love once back at home.

This example showed the pilgrims how the friends endured tests in the path of their love for their Lord. The Master remarked that the tests that had been sent to the believers in the East had not yet come to the West. He said that there were some Bahá'ís in America who were 'very good souls' and He knew them all. They served the world of humanity, loved mankind and had no enmity; they sacrificed their life for the world. Yet the tests had not yet come to them, not to the extent of the Eastern believers whose property was pillaged, who were persecuted and abused and in the end martyred. Never knowing at what moment ten or twenty persons with swords would arrive in their homes, they endured the trials with courage and without fear. They did not defend themselves, although each one of them 'was courageous enough to overcome 10 persons'.[21]

The Master shared the story of the steadfastness of the believers in Yazd. One day, He told them, two hundred were killed, all their property was pillaged, and even the women and children were martyred. These believers did not defend themselves, not because of their inability, but because of their obedience to the divine teachings. This theme prompted Him to clarify that in the early days of the Cause the believers had defended themselves bravely because they were not aware of the teachings:

> One of them would overcome 20 or 30. Then when they understood the Teachings they no longer defended themselves . . . They did not know the Teachings. It was in the beginning of the Cause and the Teachings were not spread and they were not aware of them. They used to defend themselves bravely. 110 were in the fortress of Tabarsi . . . They were surrounded in the fortress by the army with their cannons and guns. They had nothing but swords. Yet they always defeated the army. One night they attacked the army

entrenched in a series of seven fortifications each with troops and guns. The 110 arrived at the first fortification, broke through and routed them. The soldiers at the 1st fortification fled to the second. The night being dark they were taken for enemies and so the soldiers killed their own companions. Each garrison would capitulate to the next one. They defeated all the 7 garrisons . . . They were so brave. Now if a Bahai wishes to attack he can overcome ten. He is fearless. But the Teachings forbid them to defend themselves . . . This is why the people of Yazd killed 200 people. They offered no resistance . . .[22]

Through these stories the Master was preparing the pilgrims for their services upon their departure. On 18 November He gave these instructions to the Western pilgrims: 'I want you to stop in Paris on your return. I want you to illumine Paris . . . There are some friends there and I will give you their address. Tell those friends that all the world has become illumined and you are leaving Paris in the dark.'

Loulie Mathews, Harry Randall's cousin, was planning to work in Paris, and the Master sent her this message:

> Very good. When she establishes a center the first thing to do is to gather the friends in Paris and with these gathered encourage them to start meetings. Every evening, in Paris they should meet and discuss means for teaching the Cause.[23]

Nine days later Shoghi Effendi recorded in his diary that 'recently a Tablet has been revealed by Abdul Baha wherein He refers to Paris', and quotes a part of his translation of it 'in view of the remarkable declarations recorded therein':

> . . . at present travel to the West and go to Paris and there inquire about the friends of God and convey to each and all of them on behalf of Abdul Baha His love, kindness and extreme longing. Tell them: – 'In all regions of the world the Trumpet Call of Ya Baha'il Abha has been loudly sounded and my fervent hope is that in Paris, too, this vivifying melody, this call of the Abha Kingdom may be raised. Paris in all matters is astir and active. My prayer to God is that the hymns of praise and glorification may be voiced with such

a vigor by the friends of God as to shake Paris to its very foundations. I am eagerly expecting refreshing news from the friends of Paris and assuredly in future this call shall be raised in that city. I wish it however that it be raised during the days of the Covenant and the Testament and that ye may be minstrels in that chorus and sweet singing nightingales in that country.' Upon thee be Baha'il Abha.[24]

On 18 November the Master also gave instructions to Harry Randall and Albert Vail, who had spoken about the Cause to a Japanese journalist on the boat, regarding the teaching work in Japan:

> If a delegation of Bahais should go to Japan they will do splendid work because the Japanese think their own religion out of date. Even the Mikado realized it and so he invited representatives from the different religions to Tokyo from the Moslems, Christians and Jews. But he did not like what these representatives presented. He intended to select one of the existing religions and promulgate it but he liked none of them. It was at that time that we were living at Acca under the most severe restrictions and thus it was impossible for us to send a Baha'í there. He would have done splendid work.[25]

On 21 November a flood of supplications arrived from India. The friends in those regions, aware of the fact that their unity and service would alone attract the beloved Master to their shores, had made a concerted effort to come together in unity and earn the Master's visit. They had sent supplications to 'Abdu'l-Bahá from believers throughout the country – from Burma (then an annex to British India) to Calcutta and Bombay – some in Persian, others in Arabic and one in Urdu. A petition from Calcutta arrived with 16 signatures:

> O thou dear Abdul Baha. May our lives be sacrificed to Thy love! The eyes of these longing souls are with the utmost eagerness entreating to look upon Thy face and to gaze on the countenance of their Lord. For years have we the Bahais in India offered our eyelashes to be a covering for the path that thou shalt tread on thy way to India. With all our hearts we yearningly beseech and supplicate that the soil of India may be made fragrant, purified and blessed

by the dust of thy feet and that these thirsty fishes may drink deep from the fountain head of thy meeting. The longing which our souls and the yearning which our hearts cherish for meeting thee are known by none save our burning hearts and ourselves.[26]

A similar supplication from Mandalay, Rangoon, and Kunjangoon arrived, bearing 641 signatures conveying the devotion of the ardent lovers of the Centre of the Covenant and inviting Him travel to their country. It opened as follows:

> In the name of the Beloved one! O Abdul Baha come thou to our assistance and bestow upon us thy infinite bounty! After having kissed and bowed before thy sanctified threshold, we the undersigned, thy most insignificant servants and maid-servants who have clung to the strong rope of the Testament and the Covenant entered into by God, the Almighty and the Compassionate, the inhabitants of Mandalay, Rangoon and Kunjangoon in the province of Burmah while confessing our inability and feebleness, our shortcomings and our sins, laying our heads with prayer and supplication upon the Threshold of Servitude, grasping with hopeful hearts the hem of Divine Pardon of Forgiveness and of His infinite Divine Bestowals submit unanimously the following to thee. Although until the present day we have not been confirmed in a service that is worthy of thy Supreme Threshold and in accordance with thy blessed will and are not thereby worthy of having our entreaty and supplications granted; yet as our trust in thee is unshakable and our grasp of the hem of the garment of thy bounty and mercy is firm we hope that thou wilt not take into consideration the incapability, unworthiness and the insignificance of this handful of feeble souls who are poor without support and without resources . . . May thou bestow a share and portion upon the land of India and the province of Burmah . . .[27]

A week later Shoghi Effendi recorded in his diary the Master's response:

> O ye friends of God and the maid-servants of the Merciful! Your letter has been received. Its contents were indicative of a deep sense of yearning for the journey of Abdul Baha to those climes and

regions. I, too, long to be amidst you for in the world of existence no deeper joy can be conceived than the one occasioned by the meeting of friends. In this lies our happiness and on this depends the satisfaction of our hearts. However at present the obstacles are numerous but in future it is hoped that through the assistance and bounty of His Holiness Bahaullah the means for travel will be provided. Whenever it is possible I shall immediately start for India but provided that such a voyage be made possible for it is a long journey and the Holy Land occupies a central position. Uninterruptedly from all regions letters and papers are showering and at least one in every ten should be answered. Furthermore pilgrims and visitors to the Kaaba of the Friends are incessantly arriving and with them I must associate and keep company. I must serve them for Abdul Baha is the servant of the friends and is proud of such a station. How can I give up such a bounty? Moreover other numerous hindrances are in the way but notwithstanding all this I hope to undertake this journey. Although I am at heart and soul present in the gatherings of the friends and share with them in their prayers and supplications yet physical sight must have its own share and portion.

In fine during these days India is astir and wakened. From different localities letters and reports are being received and thus in the utmost joy I supplicate and entreat at the Abha Kingdom and beg at every instance for the friends of God a fresh confirmation and assistance. Likewise in the utmost humility and lowliness I beseech and pray to the Kingdom of Light and solicit for the friends infinite glory. His Holiness Bahaullah – may my life be a sacrifice to His friends – has placed a crown of everlasting glory upon the heads of His friends – a crown the glittering gems of which ever shine from the eternal Horizon upon ages and generations . . .[28]

The pilgrims attaining His presence each day received the Master's love and attention. By observing His example, listening to His words of wisdom and counsel, receiving instructions and just being in His presence, their faith was deepened and their determination for service was strengthened.

Two Stories from the Early Days

To further deepen this group of pilgrims the Master recounted stories from the early days of the Faith. On 22 November He shared the following story from the time of Bahá'u'lláh, as recorded by Shoghi Effendi:

> For nine years Bahaullah was incarcerated in the penal colony of Acca, two years in the barracks and 7 years in a house in the city. Toward the end of the two first years confinement in the barracks, as mobilization set in [and] the barracks being needed, Bahaullah and His companions of exile were permitted by the local government to evacuate it and live in a house in the city. When Bahaullah went into the house, He did not come out of the doors of the house for seven years. Conditions in the barracks were very difficult and the companions of Bahaullah were not even allowed to go to the public bath. Every morning four gendarmes with four friends went to the market to buy food and provisions. When we came out to the barracks the friends were all sent to the Khan, caravansaray, while Bahaullah and His family were all in one house. Bahaullah was for seven years in one room. In an adjoining room thirteen persons slept. It was very narrow and therein thirteen persons lived for seven consecutive years. Once a guest came from Persia. She slept in the room we slept in. There was a big trunk and she made it her bed, and slept there. At midnight she fell off. We all woke up and laughed till morning.
>
> When things were very gloomy in the barracks, Bahaullah revealed some Tablets wherein He said:– 'Do not grieve. These doors will be opened and I shall get out from the city and go to the country and the utmost joy will be realized!' This was a great source of consolation.[29]

The Master then described how doors were opened and how He rented a palace – the Mansion of Bahjí – about three miles from the city and how He succeeded with the help of the Mufti of 'Akká in persuading the Blessed Beauty to leave the prison city and go to Bahjí. The Master explained that Bahá'u'lláh's life at this time in Bahjí and 'Akká was princely; the local Pashas would ask to meet Him and He would not accept. The miracle was that although a prisoner under drastic firmans, He lived in the utmost majesty.

The second story is about the early days of His own life as He witnessed how the friends joyfully embraced trials and martyrdom in the path of God, and the spirituality that surrounded those days despite the trials.

> There was not really the last ray of hope. Every one from his place of concealment hastened joyfully to the field of martyrdom. As soon as the bugle was sounded, all the people would gather to witness the scene that would ensue. There prevailed intense spirituality and there was a great stir and commotion in the hearts. Indeed these faithful friends of God were not walking upon the ground but were soaring in the Supreme Concourse. There was a certain Mohammad Tabrizi who took us, my mother, my sister and myself to Sangelak where he rented a house paying one Karan (9 cents) a month for its rent. We occupied that house and no one knew where we lived and thus we were safe from the attacks of the people who used to stone us and maltreat us every now and then. This Mirza Mohammad Tabrizi would inform us of the arrival of any one. Once at midnight some one knocked at the door. I got up and opened it. It was Mirza Mohammad. He came in and sat down and then began to chant and sing. After singing for a time he got up and danced until morning. He had lost control of himself so intense was the state of his ecstasy. He then left the house. Two days later he was arrested and suffered martyrdom. No one felt the least security, the least hope and no one expected to live for an hour. Under such circumstances a strange spirituality pervaded us all. It was a marvellous condition. During those times every day a new report was circulated, a new message was brought, a new soul was taken to the execution pole and was there hung.[30]

These stories served to convey the influence of the Revelation of God on the early believers and remind the Western friends of the love Bahá'u'lláh had kindled in the hearts of His devoted servants. They called the friends to new levels of understanding of the significance of this glorious Cause. After recounting these stories on this November day the Master turned to the Western believers gathered in His presence and said:

> I am talking in Persian and ye do not understand it. But Persian and English are not to be taken into consideration. Hearts are attracted by the Fragrances of God. We are discussing this matter, at present, that various calls have been raised in this world. One is the call of war, another the call of peace, and there is the call of politics, a fourth is the call of trade and commerce, still another call is that of the Churches, Temples and Synagogues. In brief the calls are varied and numerous. But none of these calls exert any influence. The call which sounds and reverberates in the heart of the Universe is the call of Ya Baha il Abha! This is the pulsating artery in the body of the world! This call ever throbs and ever pulsates, ever stirs and ever vivifies and ever bestows immortal life.[31]

The call of Ya Bahá'u'l-Abhá was what the Master wished to hear from the friends in the West. On 27 November, He expressed His hope and expectation about the raising of this call to the group of departing pilgrims – Harry and Ruth Randall and their daughter (to whom he had given the name Bahiyyih), Albert Vail, George Latimer, and Arthur Hathaway. Each one had been transformed and deepened in that holy spot. Each had heard stories of consecration recounted by the loving Master. Having listened to the story of the martyrdom of the two hundred believers in Yazd, including women and children, each had heard the Master's words of wisdom stressing the heroism and obedience of these martyrs despite the fact that they were capable of defending themselves. They had heard stories of sacrifice from the early history of the Faith worthy of emulation. Shoghi Effendi saw the transformative effect of these words on the pilgrims. He translated the parting instructions of the Master:

> ... My hope is that immediately after your arrival to America ye may convene such blessed and spiritual gatherings – gatherings that proclaim loudly the Love of God and declare His spirit. Then I shall inhale the fragrances that emanate from those gatherings and shall in spirit hear the loud call of Ya Baha'il Abha and shall listen to the sweet melody that will be raised from those gatherings. I am always

with you and although I am far, far from you in body, yet in spirit I am ever near and present amidst you all. At heart I am attached to you and the connecting waves of my emotions and sensations are never interrupted. I ever pray on your behalf and beg for you assistance and confirmations. May ye all rest and abide under His sheltering protection.[32]

The returning pilgrims communicated the wishes of the beloved Master with such excitement that the friends could not but feel the warmth of the love He had kindled in their hearts. The accounts of their pilgrimage, together with the power of the Tablets they carried, fanned the fire of love in the hearts of the friends – a love that was already evident in the letters and supplications pouring in to His holy threshold.

One such letter came from Ella Cooper, prompting Shoghi Effendi to write her a postcard on 25 November:

> My Dear Spiritual sister!
> Your most welcome letter of Oct 14, 1919 is at hand. Your letters are always received affectionately by the Master and a smile passes over His radiant face when the mail conveys your letters, to me they are a constant source of joy & gladness. So, you must realize my dear Baha'i sister that I do not feel the least disturbed when your letters reach me no matter how numerous your requests or messages may be . . .[33]

The believers saw in the Master a loving father who could advise them on important decisions in their lives. They wrote to Him about personal issues and sought His advice and prayers. One example can be found in a letter written by George Latimer in which he had sought advice about the health of his mother. On 6 December Shoghi Effendi wrote to him conveying the Master's instructions:

> I ever pray on her behalf & beg from God His divine remedy and healing. As in this Dispensation consultation with expert doctors is highly advisable and acting in accordance with their prescriptions obligatory, it is well for her to undergo an operation if deemed necessary by such doctors . . .[34]

On 8 December Dr Esslemont joined Shoghi Effendi on a visit to 'Akká together with Dr Ḥakím and Isfandíyár, 'Abdu'l-Bahá's servant. The close relationship between Shoghi Effendi and Dr Esslemont was consolidated during this pilgrimage.[35]

On Tuesday, 9 December Shoghi Effendi wrote to Ali Yazdi to develop further the friendship that had evolved from childhood:

> My dearest 'Alí
> For a long time have I awaited your letters as I was in the dark as to your whereabouts. But now that your father has come for a few days from Damascus, I secured your address and am sending you herewith some news of the Holy Land. The Beloved is in the best health and so are the friends and pilgrims. Your dear and devoted father is as ever warmhearted, loving, rosy-cheeked, and in full bloom. Your brother is studying at SPC and all runs smoothly. I was told last night that he is growing wonderfully in height and his studies above par.
> As to myself, the same work and the same room.
> So please write me and forget me not as I do not and cannot forget the dear Sheikh!
> Yours affectionately
> Shoghi[36]

Shoghi Effendi wrote again to Ali Yazdi on Wednesday, 17 December enclosing a Tablet of the Master addressed to the German friends:

> Dearest 'Alí!
> Your letter from Stuttgart dated Nov. 27 is at hand. I exposed its content to the Master, and I secured this Tablet for you in his own handwriting addressed to the German friends. I herewith enclose it.
> Your dear father is here, and we exchange the news of your letters to me and to him. He is well and happy. I trust you have received my letter to you dated Dec. 8, which I sent to the Technische Hochschule and in which I enclosed some diary letters of mine which I thought might interest you.
> We are exceedingly busy here. Some fifty pilgrims, Arabs, Kurds, Persians, Americans, Europeans, and Japanese.[37]

On 17 December 1919 we see the beginning of collaborative translations of Shoghi Effendi, translations where he secured the assistance of several individuals. A significant Tablet, revealed by the Master to the people of the world, was translated jointly by Shoghi Effendi, Dr Zia Bagdadi, Luṭfu'lláh Ḥakim and Dr Esslemont:

> O people of the World!
> The dawn of the Sun of Reality is assuredly for the illumination of the world and for the manifestation of mercy. In the assemblage of the family of Adam results and fruits are praiseworthy, and the holy bestowals of every bounty are abundant . . .
> Then, O ye friends of God! Appreciate the value of this precious Revelation, move and act in accordance with it and walk in the straight path and the right way. Show it to the people. Raise the melody of the Kingdom and spread abroad the teachings and ordinances of the loving Lord so that the world may become another world, the darkened earth may become illumined and the dead body of the people may obtain new life . . .[38]

On 24 December Shoghi Effendi translated Tablets for Charles Mason Remey and Marie Watson,[39] and on Thursday, 25 December, as a token of his friendship with Dr Esslemont, Shoghi Effendi presented him with a precious gift and this message:

> The rarest, dearest, & most precious treasure that Shoghie [sic] could give to his unforgettable friend Dr Esslemont – a drop of the coagulated & sacred blood of Baha'ullah . . .[40]

On 30 December Shoghi Effendi wrote to an American believer (probably Corinne True), referring to a car that had been acquired for the Master:

> The military Governor has secured for the Master a very cheap and new Ford for 216 pounds. Now I remember you & especially Edna when Fugita drives it while the Master is in it. Our Cunningham car will reach in few days Port-Said & will be soon here.[41]

A letter from Shoghi Effendi to Mrs Parsons dated 29 February 1920 shows the attention the beloved Master paid to serving the believers, including even writing a letter of recommendation for them. Here, Shoghi Effendi gives the news of a letter of recommendation written for Mrs Parsons' son Jeffery, whom the Master had met during his visit to Washington when Jeffery was a young boy. In this letter, he also conveys the news of the departure of Faḍíl-i-Mazandáráni for New York. This letter is among the last that Shoghi Effendi sent from Haifa while serving the Master.

> My dear Mrs. Parsons: –
> I am so glad to enclose in my letter to you such a warm and affectionate letter of recommendation from the Master for his 'son', Jeffrey. I am confident that you will greatly rejoice at the perusal of these effective and fatherly words which the Beloved has revealed for Jeffery and I am likewise sure that they will prove to be greatly valuable and helpful.
> The Beloved Master is feeling indeed very well and is intensely occupied. He often remembers you and wished you in His prayers success in our great work for the Cause.
> Mirza Asadullah Fazel Mazendarany and Mirza Manouchehr Khan have proceeded yesterday with great haste by a luggage train to Port-Said in order to make connection with a steamer leaving on March 1st direct to New-York. All this has been minutely and hastily arranged by the Military Authorities in Egypt and Jerusalem. You will undoubtedly meet them in America and I do hope that with your collaboration they will be enabled through the Divine Confirmations to achieve wonderful results in that part of the world.[42]

As early as 23 January 1920 the translations published in *Star of the West* were rendered by Azizullah Bahadur and other individuals such as Luṭfu'lláh Ḥakím and Ahmad Sohrab. However, Shoghi Effendi would continue to translate Tablets of the Master for the friends in Britain.

III
France and England

9

Recuperation in Paris

Shoghi Effendi's strong desire and determination to serve the Cause, and his sense of the urgency of the hour imposed on him a discipline that ignored his comfort and health. While at the Syrian Protestant College he had endeavoured to excel by learning as much as he could in preparation for his service. When he began his service to the Master he put the work of the Cause before his own rest and comfort, working well into the night with little rest during this entire period. The two spells of intense translation activity caused by increases in 'Abdu'l-Bahá's correspondence just after the end of the war and after the 1919 American Convention put much pressure upon the youthful figure of Shoghi Effendi and weakened his health. He was also subjected to repeated attacks of malaria in the spring of 1919. The effect of this illness and his lack of rest on the one hand and his intense desire to do his utmost to render a worthy service to the Master on the other damaged his health to the extent that he needed rest and treatment.

'Abdu'l-Bahá, concerned about the health of His beloved grandson, insisted that Shoghi Effendi spend some time in rest and recuperation. He chose a sanatorium in Neuilly, a suburb of Paris, for this purpose and arranged for Shoghi Effendi to go there accompanied by Dr Luṭfu'lláh Ḥakím.[1] Shoghi Effendi entered the *Maison d'Hydrothérapie et de convalescence du Parc de Neuilly*, located at 6 Boulevard du Château, in Neuilly-sur-Seine, in April 1920.

In an undated letter written from Neuilly to Ali Kuli Khan in Paris, Shoghi Effendi stated that his physical health was improving and his nerves were consolidated, although still under treatment. He hoped that he would soon completely recover, as this would bring joy and assurance to the heart of the beloved Master. He asked Ali Kuli Khan to please inform him of any news from the Holy Land, as such news brought tranquillity to his heart. Shoghi Effendi stated that he would miss seeing Ali Kuli Khan that evening when he planned to visit his family.²

Ali Kuli Khan was a devoted believer who had served the Master as interpreter during His visit to the United States and had arranged interviews for the Master when he served as Chief Diplomatic Representative and Chargé d'Affaires at the Persian Embassy in Washington. After the war he was sent to Paris as a member of the Persian Delegation to the Versailles Peace Conference and was living in Paris.³

On Sunday, 25 April 1920 Shoghi Effendi wrote another letter from Neuilly to Ali Kuli Khan, who was on a visit to London, sending him his most joyous and fondest Bahá'í greetings and thanking him for his letter that was filled with kindness, faithfulness, devotion and love. He gave Ali Kuli Khan the good news that, by the grace of God, the blessings of the beloved Master and the loving care that Ali Kuli Khan had provided him, his health had ameliorated and with divine assistance he would soon recover completely. He hoped to visit Ali Kuli Khan's home within one or two weeks and spend some time with him in an atmosphere of spiritual companionship. Meanwhile, in accordance with the wishes of the Master and the instructions of the doctor, he was spending the mornings till noon in his room, sometimes sitting in bed and other times busily writing and copying certain Tablets. In the afternoons he went for walks outside the sanatorium. It was the wish of 'Abdu'l-Bahá, he said, that he should wear a hat, and since his hat was worn out, he sought Ali Kuli Khan's guidance in acquiring a Persian hat in Paris.⁴

On Saturday, 8 May 1920 Shoghi Effendi sent a postcard from Neuilly to Ali Yazdi in which he described his state of health:

Dearest 'Alí!

I have not forgotten you, but do you know and realize what crisis I have passed and into what state of health I have fallen! For a month I have stayed and am still staying in this 'maison de convalescence' away from Paris and its clamour in bed until noon, receiving . . . treatment and following the Master's instructions not to open a book during my stay in this place. Be sure, dear friend, that your place in my heart is ever reserved and warm! I wish, when I recovered, I could come to see you. But I am afraid this is not possible. Your dear father had gone to Port Said for a time when

I left Haifa. The Master is in splendid health. Fourteen American pilgrims have arrived. The Holy Land is astir!⁵

On Monday, 17 May 1920 Shoghi Effendi wrote to Ali Kuli Khan from Neuilly. In this letter he expressed his disappointment at having missed the unannounced visit of Ali Kuli Khan and his family during the weekend. Shoghi Effendi said he wished that Ali Kuli Khan would inform him of his intended visits so that he might postpone his stroll to receive him. During the previous few days, he said, he had not been feeling well and his appetite had completely faded. The physician intended to prescribe him some medicine and keep him in bed for one whole day. Shoghi Effendi commented that it had been a long time since a spiritual breeze had wafted from the Holy Land and the absence of news had affected his health and caused him sorrow. He hoped that soon a sign would appear from 'Abdu'l-Bahá which would breathe a new life into him. At the conclusion of the letter, Shoghi Effendi states his intention to visit Ali Kuli Khan before the end of the week.⁶

Soon after this Shoghi Effendi felt well enough to visit the friends. He accepted an invitation to dinner at the home of Ali Kuli Khan although Khan himself was away. On the day of his visit Shoghi Effendi wrote to him saying how much he was missed and assuring him of his prayers. In this letter Shoghi Effendi reported on his progress, stating that his physical health was improving although he was still undergoing treatment. He repeated that he had not received any news from the Holy Land and was therefore overcome with considerable sorrow, which aggravated his ill health. He asked Ali Kuli Khan to please inform him of any news he might receive from the Master, as such news was balm to the heart of one who was away from the land of his Beloved.⁷

Application to Oxford

Having translated so many Tablets of the Master, Shoghi Effendi was aware of the challenge presented by the task of translation. He did not feel that his rendering of the Master's Tablets in English conveyed the charm and beauty of the originals. Furthermore, he had read the translations of the sacred writings of Bahá'u'lláh by other believers and was not happy with them. Translation of the holy words required someone with proficiency in three languages: Arabic, Persian and English. To communicate the beauty of the creative words in his English translations, Shoghi Effendi needed to perfect his command of the English language. Several of the English friends and admirers of the Master had recommended Oxford University as the environment where he might pursue this goal. The Master also wished that Shoghi Effendi receive further education in England, although a definite decision had not been made.

On Friday, 11 June 1920 Shoghi Effendi sent a letter of application from Neuilly to Oxford University seeking admission to that great centre of learning and describing clearly his intended course of study:

> Dear Sir:–
> My esteemed friend Sir Herbert Samuel advises me to write you inquiring about admission as a non-collegiate student at Balliol College or any other college at Oxford University. My sole aim is to perfect my English, to acquire the literary ability to write it well, speak it well & translate correctly & eloquently from Persian & Arabic into English. My aim is to concentrate for two years upon this object & to acquire it through the help of a tutor, by attending lectures, by associating with cultured & refined literary circles & by receiving exercises in Phonetics. I would be much obliged if you could help me along that line.
> Yours very sincerely,
> Shoghi Rabbani[8]

On Thursday, 24 June 1920 Shoghi Effendi wrote to Frank Edwin Scott, an American Impressionist painter residing in Paris, and a devoted believer. By this time Shoghi Effendi's health had improved enough to enable him to visit the French countryside and to participate in Bahá'í activities.

> My dear brother!
> Your letter has been read with great joy but how much I miss you & we miss you all! Our meetings are expanding, gaining in spirit & becoming more & more elaborate. We had a splendid meeting last Tuesday at Akbar's – Mirza Gholam Ali had returned from Berlin & Dr Mirza had come from Mesopotamia & India. Some twenty were present at the meeting, including the Dreyfuses & Lotfullah.

As to my health, I have fully recovered but deplore the fact that no news reaches me from home. Ever since your departure I have received no letter & no cable except a letter from Edith Sanderson from Vevey. I am afraid the post is not properly forwarding my letters. I have been to the concierge & no letters. I shall go again to-day. I hope something will put an end to my eager anticipation. I shall send you the photographs we took of the Holy Sites in Paris as soon as they are ready. Meanwhile I hope you will send me the picture we took together at your home. Oh! your lovely blessed abode! What a cluster of sweet memories & associations cling around it! I shall never forget our last interview under its roof.[9]

On Monday, 28 June 1920 Shoghi Effendi wrote to Ali Yazdi from Neuilly responding to a letter he had received from his friend:

My dear unforgettable 'Alí!

Your letter and the good news of you imparted by Ghulám-'Alí made me wish or yearn to come to you and see you for a few days now that I am better and almost fully recovered! I shall wait and see the turn of events before I decide to pass a sojourn with you in Berlin. Now that I have recovered . . . I am impatient to plunge again in a valuable, profitable work, to build the structure for my future and whether I shall resume my work in Haifa or go to England for two years study – it all depends upon the Master's will, which shall be communicated to me within a fortnight.

I have deplored the hard financial situation you are in, and I really feel with you. I have just written home and exposed your situation to the Holy Mother, and I trust something will be done to remedy the situation. Dr Mírzá has lately arrived here from Baghdad . . . Who knows? Perhaps we may both come and see you for some days in Berlin! It is a long time I have received no news from home, and I am growing impatient . . . President Bliss has died in America. A great blow indeed to the college! I do not like Paris. People are so superficial, empty, pleasure-seeking, and frivolous. Life bores me here, and I hope I will have soon a change for the better.

Your loving brother
Shoghi[10]

PRELUDE TO THE GUARDIANSHIP

The reference made in this letter to Ali Yazdi's financial condition shows the compassion of Shoghi Effendi for a friend in need. Ali Yazdi had left the Holy Land hoping to earn his living as a draughtsman. However, owing to the economic condition of post-war Germany with its high inflation and scarcity of jobs, he found it difficult to manage financially and save money for his college course, which the Master had instructed him to pursue. His only reserve was the one hundred English pounds that 'Abdu'l-Bahá had given him.

On Friday, 2 July 1920 Dr Esslemont received a letter from Shoghi Effendi stating that he was awaiting the Master's decision about whether he should return to Haifa or go to England.[11]

Mrs Sheybání, one of the believers residing in Paris, had invited Shoghi Effendi to visit Versailles. Shoghi Effendi accepted her invitation and planned the visit for Sunday, 4 July 1920. On this day, Shoghi Effendi was setting out on his trip when he received a telephone message from Mme Dreyfus that at last a message had been received from the Holy Land that everyone was well. This joyous news was what Shoghi Effendi had been waiting for. It made him so happy that all the events of that day were pleasing to him. It was a perfect beginning to a perfect day.[12]

When he returned from Versailles another blessing awaited him. Shoghi Effendi describes his joy on this day in a letter the wife of Ali Kuli Khan, closing the letter with his thanks to Mrs Sheybání.

My dear & affectionate Bahá'í sister:
A thousand thanks for your invitation to Versailles which has proved to be pregnant with many good results. Would such an invitation on your part necessarily entail such pleasing consequences & usher in such a brilliant morn of joy, satisfaction & assurance, I undoubtedly would have sought it every day from you for you can't imagine with what refreshing news yesterday's trip to Versailles opened & with what an event it ended. The whole day has been a remarkable one, as I & my friend have reiterated it over and over again to Mr Sheybany, who did a great deal to please & satisfy us – what a great impression the 'grandes eaux' . . . made upon me and to what magnificent, sumptuous & historically remarkable apartments we were led! Our lunch was even unexpectedly delightful & most palatable. I do not think that the big concourse of people around

us had such a fine lunch. The day in spite of its sombre look in the morning was a perfect one. In the midst of the gloom and the dreariness of the morning, just at the moment I was stepping out to meet Sheybani, I got a telephone message from Mme Dreyfus that at last a message has been received from the Holy Land to the effect that <u>all</u> are well! What a happy beginning to a splendid day! When I returned, another blessing & joy awaited me as if to crown this great day:– letters for me directly from Haifa which had been only 10 days en route with a note from the post informing me of a registered letter in my name! Oh! how my joy would be complete & how it would overflow! I mention these simply to tell you that in the coming days & years this first visit to Versailles will be closely associated with such delightful experiences & lively recollections . . .[13]

The communication Shoghi Effendi received from the Holy Land helped him to make his decision about his future. The Master not only wished him to continue his education in England but had also given him instructions on how to pursue admission into Oxford University. Despite the great love the Master had for Shoghi Effendi and His desire to be with him during the last years of His life on this physical plane, He knew the great destiny of His beloved grandson and wished him to continue his preparation for his destined mission.

Shoghi Effendi's education at Oxford was not only an important stage in his life but also a stage in the unfoldment of a Divine Plan for humankind. The Master had communicated His intention to send His grandson to England while Shoghi Effendi was still in high school. Rúḥíyyih Khánum records the recollections of a German woman physician, Dr J. Fallscheer, some eleven years after her visit to attend the ladies of 'Abdu'l-Bahá's household. Dr Fallscheer's account indicates the Master's desire to send Shoghi Effendi to Oxford:

> At this moment the son-in-law [the husband of the eldest daughter of 'Abdu'l-Bahá] entered the room . . . At first I did not notice that behind the tall, dignified man his eldest son, Shoghi Effendi, had entered the room and greeted his venerable grandfather . . . I had already seen the child fleetingly on a few other occasions . . . I never removed my eyes from the still very youthful grandson of Abbas Effendi . . . The boy remained motionless in his place and

submissive in his attitude. After his father and the man with him had taken their leave of the Master, his father whispered something to him as he went out, whereupon the youth, in a slow and measured manner, like a grown up person, approached his beloved grandfather, waited to be addressed, answered distinctly in Persian and was laughingly dismissed . . .

Abbas Effendi rose and came over to us . . . 'Now my daughter,' He began, 'How do you like my future Elisha?' 'Master, if I may speak openly, I must say that in his boy's face are the dark eyes of a sufferer, one who will suffer a great deal!' Thoughtfully the Master looked beyond us into space and after a long time turned His gaze back to us and said: 'My grandson does not have the eyes of a trailblazer, a fighter or a victor, but in his eyes one sees deep loyalty, perseverance and conscientiousness. And do you know why, my daughter, he will fall heir to the heavy inheritance of being my Vazir?' Without waiting for my reply, looking more at His dear sister than at me, as if He had forgotten my presence, He went on: 'Bahá'u'lláh, the Great Perfection – blessed be His words – in the past, the present and forever – chose this insignificant one to be His successor, not because I was the first born, but because His inner eye had already discerned on my brow the seal of God.

'Before His ascension into eternal Light the blessed Manifestation reminded me that I too – irrespective of primogeniture or age – must observe among my sons and grandsons whom God would indicate for His office. My sons passed to eternity in their tenderest years, in my line, among my relatives, only little Shoghi has the shadow of a great calling in the depths of his eyes.' There followed another long pause, then the Master turned again to me and said: 'At the present time the British Empire is the greatest and is still expanding and its language is a world language. My future Vazir shall receive the preparation for his weighty office in England itself, after he has obtained here in Palestine a fundamental knowledge of the oriental languages and the wisdom of the East.' Whereupon I ventured to interject: 'Will not the western education, the English training, remould his nature, confine his versatile mind in the rigid bonds of intellectualism, stifle through dogma and convention his oriental irrationality and intuition so that he will no longer be a servant of the Almighty but rather a slave to the rationality of western opportunism and the shallowness of every day life?' Long pause! Then Abbas Effendi 'Abdu'l-Bahá rose and in a strong and solemn voice said: 'I am not giving my Elisha to the British to educate. I dedicate and give him to the Almighty. God's eyes watch over my child in Oxford as well – Inshallah!'[14]

Thus, the hand of destiny propelled Shoghi Effendi to turn his attention to England. Unaware that his sojourn in that country would keep him separated from his beloved grandfather and would prevent him from ever again attaining His presence on this physical plane, Shoghi Effendi proceeded to London in conformity with the will of 'Abdu'l-Bahá. His departure from Paris took place within two weeks of receiving the Master's communication.

10

Arrival in England

Shoghi Effendi arrived in the United Kingdom in mid-July 1920 and was welcomed by a community of devoted believers and admirers of the Faith who had been nurtured by their loving Master. Prominent among them were Lady Blomfield, Major Tudor-Pole and Lord Lamington.

Lady Blomfield, one of the pillars of the Cause in England, had been among the first to recognize the new revelation.[1] She was a woman whose considerable influence traced back to her father-in-law, Dr Charles James Blomfield (1786–1857), the Bishop of London and the tutor of Queen Victoria. Lady Blomfield and her daughter Mary had been introduced to the Faith at a reception in Paris in 1907. Their teacher was Miss Bertha Herbert. Both had embraced the Faith upon their return to England and were nurtured by a Bahá'í community comprising two people: an American believer living in London, Mrs Thornburgh-Cropper, and Miss Ethel Rosenberg, the first British woman to accept the new Faith of God.

Major Wellesley Tudor-Pole had heard about 'Abdu'l-Bahá on a visit to Constantinople prior to the Young Turk Revolution in 1908. He had met the Master in Cairo and Alexandria in November 1910, and had been of service to Him during His visit to London. During the World War, he had served in the Directorate of Military Intelligence in the Middle East. When he discovered in the spring of 1918 from Lady Blomfield that 'Abdu'l-Bahá was in danger in the Holy Land, he attempted to alert the British Foreign Office explaining the danger facing the Master and the importance of His work for peace. As his initial efforts failed to arouse interest in 'Abdu'l-Bahá among those responsible for intelligence activities, he set out to make a direct approach to the British Cabinet by evading the very strict censorship in place, and at the risk of a courtmartial. Bypassing his military superiors, and with the help of influential figures, he succeeded in getting a letter about the Master's imminent danger to Lord Plymouth.

Lady Blomfield too was exerting every influence she had to draw attention of the British Government to the danger the Master was in. She contacted Lord Lamington, one-time Governor of the Bombay Presidency, who was another admirer of 'Abdu'l-Bahá. On Christmas Day 1912 the Master had visited Lord Lamington in London. During that visit Lord Lamington had been deeply touched by the message of peace and goodwill that flowed through the words and example of the Master. Exerting his influence, he made sure that Lord Balfour, Secretary of State for Foreign Affairs, was informed of the situation. Lord Balfour then placed the matter on the agenda of the meeting of the War Cabinet.

It was these interventions, largely through the efforts of Tudor-Pole and Lord Lamington, that produced the instruction to General Allenby to extend every protection necessary to 'Abdu'l-Bahá. Later, in 1919, when Lamington was directing the Syrian Relief work from his headquarters in Damascus, he called on 'Abdu'l-Bahá to receive His blessings and visited Him again to bid farewell. It was on this occasion that he received a ring from the Master.[2]

When Shoghi Effendi arrived in England he was carrying with him Tablets from the Master to Lady Blomfield, Lord Lamington and Major Tudor-Pole which expressed the Master's wish for the education of His grandson. During the one week Shoghi Effendi stayed in London, he delivered the Master's Tablets to these individuals and secured introductions to eminent professors and orientalists at Oxford and London Universities, including Sir Denison Ross and Professor Ker.[3]

Sir Denison Ross, the Director of Oriental Studies at the London School of Oriental Studies since 1916, was an eminent scholar who had studied oriental languages in Paris and Strasbourg and had held the position of Professor of Persian at University College, London.[4]

Professor William Ker was Professor of English Literature at University College, London. He later became a Fellow of All Souls College, Oxford.[5]

Visit with the Bahá'ís in London

The Bahá'í community of London had grown considerably since its inception in 1899. The Master's first visit to Britain in 1911, lasting one month, had nurtured this community and prepared it for its great destiny in the service of the Cause. London and Bristol were the two cities blessed by His presence during this first visit. It was in London that He addressed large gatherings of people of the West for the first time. He stayed as the guest of Lady Blomfield in London for the entire period, except for three days in Bristol.[6]

By the time the Master visited Britain for the second time in 1913, the community had grown. Receptions and large public gatherings were organized for Him in several cities, including Liverpool and Edinburgh. After this second visit activities had multiplied everywhere in England. At the end of the war the Bahá'ís of London began to hold regular meetings at Lindsay Hall in Notting Hill Gate.[7]

Upon his arrival in England in 1920, Shoghi Effendi visited the believers in Lindsay Hall. On Wednesday, 21 July Dr Esslemont met Shoghi Effendi there and later described this visit in a letter to Dr Luṭfu'lláh Ḥakím:

> I was delighted to see him and we embraced in true oriental fashion. Then shortly Mr and Mrs Ober turned up too, so we had a real Bahai meeting with both East and West well represented. I spoke shortly, then both of the Obers, and then Shoghi spoke and chanted. Miss Rosenberg was in the chair and seemed very happy. The hall was full and all seemed to enjoy the meeting greatly.[8]

The next day Dr Esslemont called on Shoghi Effendi at his hotel and went with him to Miss Grand's home where the Obers were staying. On Friday, 23 July Dr Esslemont met Shoghi Effendi again after lunch at Miss Rosenberg's. Together they went to Miss Grand's home that evening where 17 people, many of whom had never heard of the Cause before, were present.

Elizabeth Herrick had hoped a unity meeting could be arranged while Shoghi Effendi was in London. She had felt the need for some organization and cooperation among the friends and had tried hard to arrange such a meeting, but found it impossible and was much

Shoghi Effendi with Dr John Esslemont in Bournemouth, England

Nº 14

University of Oxford.
SCHOLARES NON ASCRIPTI.

Mr. _Shawgi Rabbâni_ entered by Matriculation as a Non-Collegiate Student _23 October_ 1920 and has kept by residence _one_ Term*.

Michaelmas 1920
19__
19__
19__

His name has been on the Books of the Students' Delegacy for _one_ Term*. He is of good character and has the permission of the Delegates to migrate to _Balliol College_

15 Jan'y. 1921

J. Bernard Baker
Censor.

Shoghi Effendi's Certificate of Matriculation

Shoghi Effendi during his stay in England

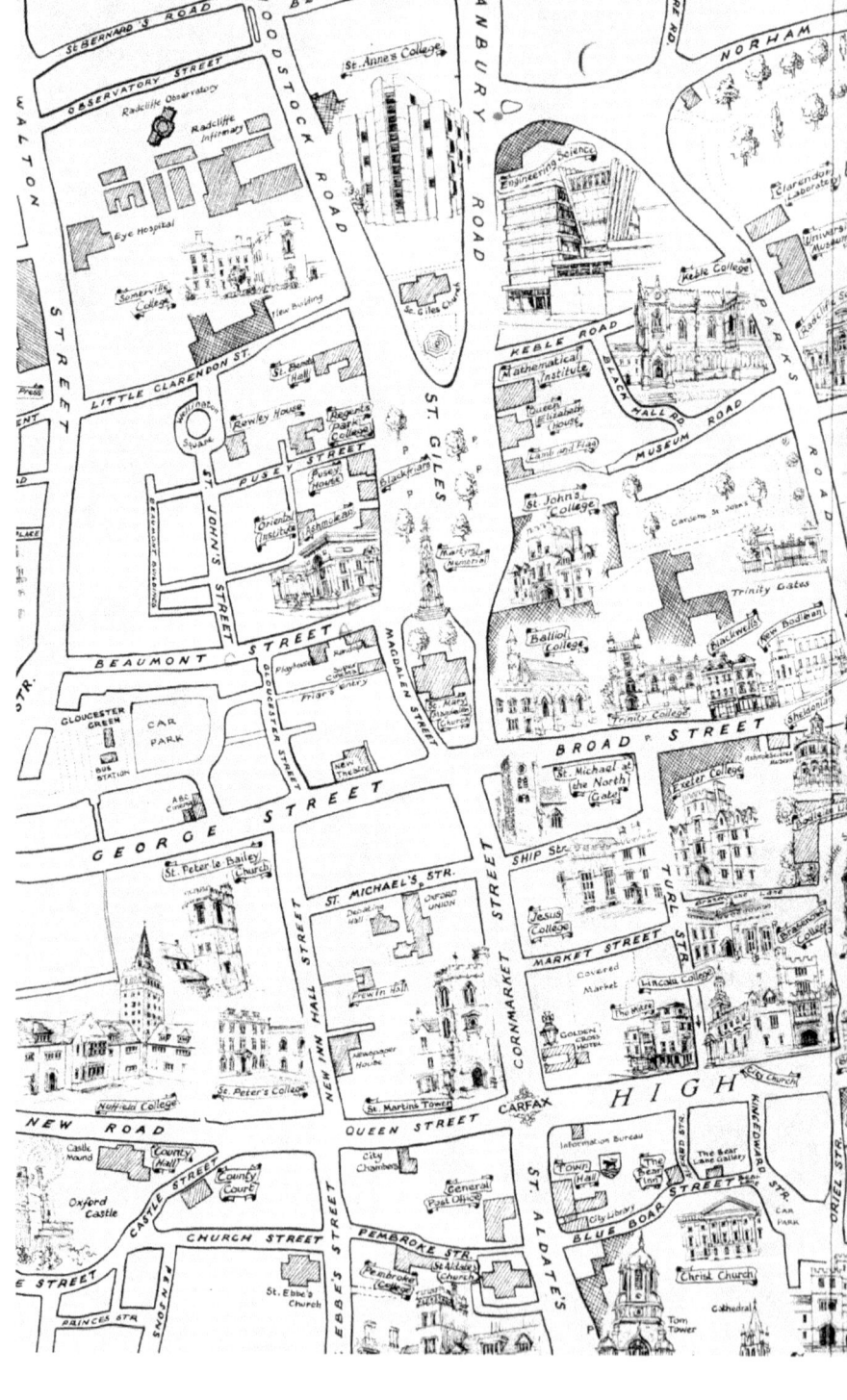

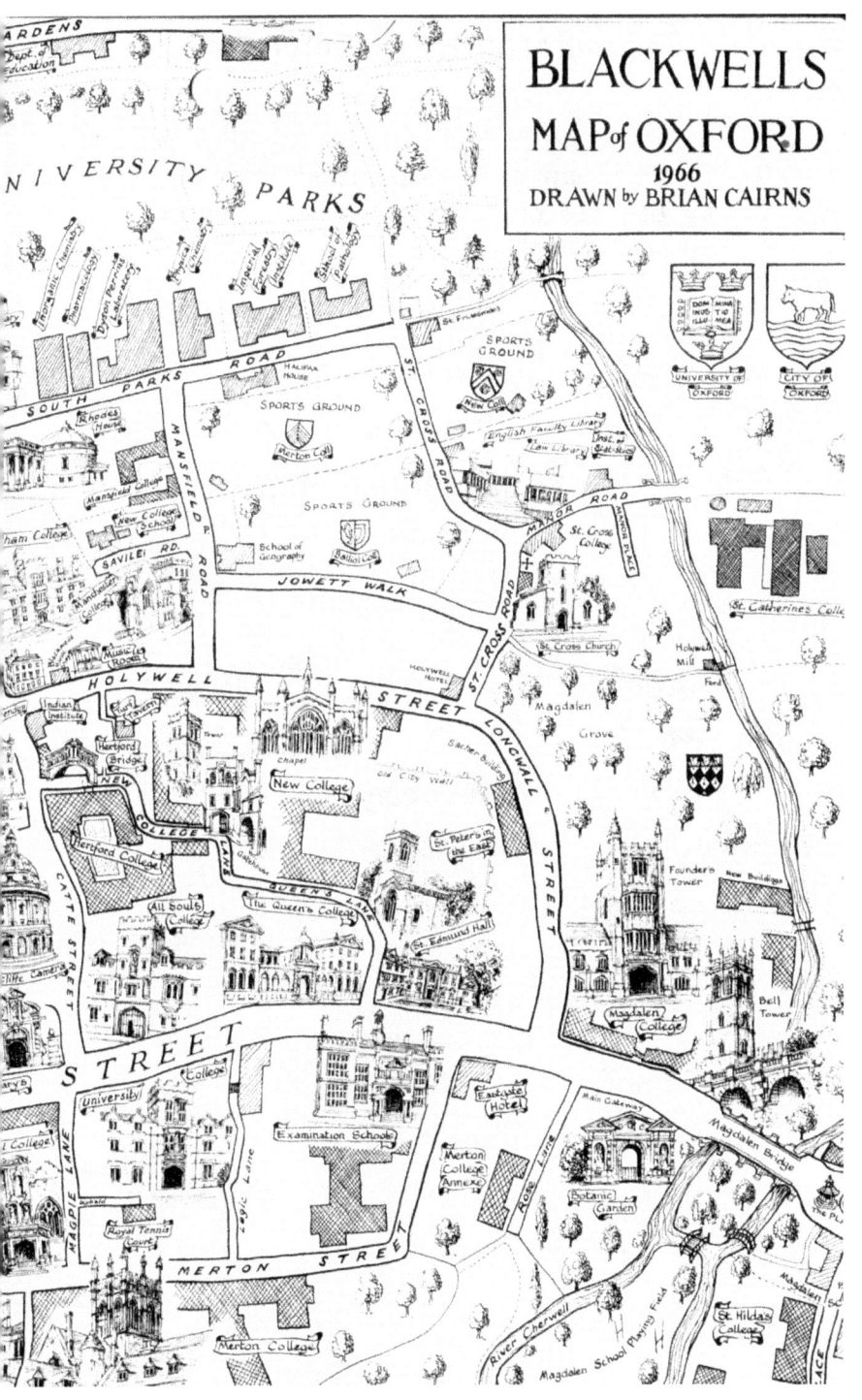

Blackwell's Map of Oxford (1966) drawn by Brian Cairns

Non-Collegiate Delegacy.

To be filled up and transmitted to the Office by the end of the first week of Term.

Michaelmas Term, 192

Name Sh. Rabbani

Course proposed Economics & Social Sciences

Lectures
Master of Balliol: Soc. & Pol. Questions
Rev. Carlyle   Soc. & Ind. Questions
Cousson   Elem. Economics
Carlyle   Pol. Science

Tutor Mr. Lindsay

Shoghi Effendi's course proposal

University of Oxford.
Certificate of Migration.

The Proctors have seen the testimonial of Mr. S. Rabbani and his permission to migrate from New Coll. and know of no reason why he should not be allowed to migrate to Ball: Coll:

G.B. Allen } Proctors.
Y. J. Fa Gm

Date Jan 17 1921.

Certificate of Migration

Letter written by Shoghi Effendi from Balliol College, 28 January 1921

disappointed. On Saturday morning Dr Esslemont came to London to meet Shoghi Effendi, and as he had no prior engagement, they both went to see Miss Herrick. Esslemont states:

> We had a fine talk together, and she became much happier. When it came near lunch-time I proposed that she should come and lunch with us somewhere, but we were sitting in the garden where it was nice and sunny. So Shoghi suggested that it would be much nicer to have a picnic lunch, so the three of us sallied forth with a basket to buy some fruit and things for lunch, and we had a jolly little lunch in the garden. We decided that Miss Herrick should see Miss Rosenberg and some of the others to try to arrange a Unity meeting for Tuesday. The Obers and I both had to leave London yesterday, but Shoghi hoped to attend the meetings on both Tuesday and Wednesday next. Shoghi suggested that a meeting of the Council of the London Group should be held at a time when as many of the members as possible could attend, when some more definite arrangements could be agreed upon with regard to the holding of feasts for the year, and a committee appointed to see to the details.[9]

After meeting the Bahá'ís in London, Shoghi Effendi's next destination was Oxford. He wished to follow up on the letter of application to Oxford University, which he had sent to Balliol College from Paris.

City of Oxford

The city of Oxford, once a walled medieval city and the scene of significant events in British history, including its selection by Charles I as his headquarters (1642–46) during the Civil War, had become recognized by the 18th century as one of Europe's great intellectual centres.

Balliol College[10]

Balliol, one of the two oldest colleges in Oxford, is part of a unique English collegiate system with origins in 12th-century France. Hotel Dieu in Paris, established through the endowment of an English pilgrim in 1180, was initially an experiment. It was later imitated and improved upon in France and gradually evolved into the collegiate system in

England.[11] In the 13th century, Oxford colleges were founded after the French models by individual benefactors.

The founding of Balliol emerged from a dispute between the secular and ecclesiastical powers over the rights to the possession of lands. The Balliols of Barnard Castle were among the highest ranking of the northern nobility. John Balliol, the head of the house of Balliol, vastly expanded his properties through his marriage to Lady Dervorguilla. He ruled over his vast estate as a petty sovereign. Yet, despite his powers, he faced bitter opposition directed by the Bishop of Durham, Walter Kirkham.

The story of Balliol College begins in the year 1255 when the bishop excommunicated some of the Balliol retainers over disputed lands. Balliol laid an ambush for the bishop and subjected him to various indignities. The bishop put his complaint before the king and obtained a writ condemning Balliol and demanding instant reparation.

Balliol lost some of his possessions as a result of this dispute. He was forced by the bishop to crown the settlement with a substantial act of charity. In obedience to the mandate, John Balliol hired a house in the suburbs of Oxford and made it a hostel for the reception of 16 poor scholars, to whom he gave an allowance of eight pence a day. This house, located in Horsemonger Street, which is today's Broad Street, became known as Old Balliol Hall or Sparrow Hall.

The credit for completing what John Balliol had begun belongs to his wife, Lady Dervorguilla of Galloway, who after her husband's death continued to be the champion of his hostel until her own death in the year 1289. She spent her money and her energies serving the scholars of Balliol.

The Old Balliol Hall survived the ecclesiastical disputes of the next centuries. In the mid-16th century the College, a staunch supporter of Rome, tried to resist Henry VIII's demand that his supremacy be acknowledged and escaped the king's wrath. Later, on the accession of Mary in 1553, James Brookes, the Master of Balliol, was appointed Bishop of Gloucester and became one of the judges who condemned the Protestant Bishops Latimer, Ridley and Cranmer to be burned in Broad Street.[12] The Martyrs' Memorial, which Shoghi Effendi is reported to have viewed from his room in college,[13] was erected in 1843 near the back gate of the college close to the spot outside the Master's lodging where the bishops perished.

By 1920 Balliol College had become one of the finest centres of learning in the world. The number of students studying there had increased over the years from the original 16 to more than a hundred in the 18th century and about two hundred in 1920. The numbers enrolled had picked up after a sharp decrease during the World War.[14]

During Shoghi Effendi's stay at Balliol, two key personages at the college were A. L. Smith and A. D. Lindsay.

A. L. Smith

Smith, the Master of Balliol in 1920, had succeeded J. L. Strachan in 1916 at the age of 66. He was known among the students for his ability to draw attention to some aspect or interpretation of facts that had not occurred to them.[15]

Smith showed great interest in the people he met. He was keen to hear about their lives, activities and problems, and was always interested in helping them.[16]

A. D. Lindsay

Alexander Dunlop Lindsay was Fellow and classical tutor of the college from 1906. He was one of the chief pioneers in the establishment of Modern Greats. In 1907 he published a translation of Plato's *Republic*. He was one of the promoters of the course 'Philosophy, Politics and Economics' (PPE) at Oxford. He later introduced the Science Greats, combining philosophy with the principles of natural science, for which he had failed to win acceptance.[17]

Lindsay had the reputation of being an outstanding tutor who had an exceptional human sympathy and was ready to help an undergraduate student needing his support. He had clear views of his own; however, he was open to fresh ideas. He believed that it was the business of the college to make the students find out what their own views were and to impress upon them their duty to think seriously and with knowledge. Lindsay influenced the students without attempting to convert them to his opinions. His aim was to raise the discussion of a problem to a higher level.[18]

Arrival in Oxford

The city of Oxford had been blessed by the footsteps of the Master and was about to receive His grandson, Shoghi Effendi, who arrived during the week of 26 July 1920. He stayed at the Randolph Hotel. He had already met Sir Denison Ross and Professor William Ker, from whom he had received introductions to Professor Margoliouth and Sir Walter Raleigh.

Sir Walter Raleigh had been Professor of English at Liverpool and Glasgow before his appointment in 1904 as the first Professor of English Literature at the University of Oxford. He was a Fellow of Merton College.[19]

Professor Margoliouth was an Arabic scholar and orientalist who had been the Laudian Professor of Arabic in Oxford since 1889 and became a Fellow of the British Academy in 1915. During the years 1919–22 he was Professor of Arabic at New College. He had the reputation of being a great Arabist and had lectured in Arabic in Cairo during the War.[20]

It was through these professors, and particularly Sir Walter Raleigh, that Shoghi Effendi was introduced to the Master of Balliol College, A. L. Smith. In a letter Shoghi Effendi wrote from the Randolph Hotel on Wednesday, 28 July 1920 to Mrs Ali Kuli Khan in Paris, he states:

> . . . before leaving for Oxford, I had a letter from Margoliouth saying that he would do all in his power to be of help to a relative of 'Abdu'l-Bahá. With this man and the Master of Balliol College – a College from which great men such as Lord Grey, Earl Curzon, Lord Milner, Mr Asquith, Swinburne and Sir Herbert Samuel have graduated – I had the opportunity of speaking about the Cause and clearing up some points that to these busy scholars had hitherto been uncertain and confused.
>
> Do pray for me, as I have requested you on the eve of my departure, that in this great intellectual centre I may attain my object and achieve my end . . .[21]

A few days later, on 8 August 1920, Lord Lamington wrote to 'Abdu'l-Bahá describing his visit with Shoghi Effendi and telling the Master that he was again impressed by Shoghi Effendi's 'intelligence and open honest manner'. He said that Shoghi Effendi had visited the House of Lords two or three times.²²

On the same day, 8 August, Shoghi Effendi wrote a postcard to Luṭfu'lláh Ḥakím in Haifa reporting his progress in the previous two weeks and indicating that he had found a tutor, a professor of philosophy:

> . . . I have settled at Oxford, have taken hold of a tutor who is professor of philosophy at Balliol . . . Lady Blomfield, Mrs Cropper, Miss Rosenberg, Lord Lamington, Tudor Pole and particularly Mrs Whyte have been of great help. I met Dr Esslemont and Miss Herrick and have addressed the meeting at Lindsay Hall. I have promised to address another meeting at Miss Herrick's, but presently I am absorbed in arranging for my immediate studies and my entering for the academic year. I am keeping well and fresh. I feel rather lonely but the immense Bodleian library, the different summer schools at the various colleges . . . keep me busy.
> Shoghi²³

Mrs Whyte, an admirer of 'Abdu'l-Bahá, was the wife of Dr Alexander Whyte, an eminent member of the Free Church of Scotland. She had visited 'Akká in 1906 and had written an account of her visit, which appears in volume 4 of *The Bahá'í World*. While in 'Akká she had seen the young Shoghi Effendi and had been moved when she observed the devotion and reverence of the child in the Shrine of Bahá'u'lláh. She had wondered then what destiny lay before this boy of tender years.²⁴ That memory was vivid in her mind when she and her husband met Shoghi Effendi in 1920.

The academic term would not start until October. Many students were in Oxford visiting the university before the term to arrange their accommodation and then return home for the remainder of the long vacation. Shoghi Effendi, however, could not wait for the term to begin. He was anxious to get started and did not wish to waste any time. He immediately commenced his work with the assistance of a tutor. He spent his time both with this tutor and in the Bodleian Library.

On Friday, 10 September, having already spent a few concentrated weeks of study in Oxford, Shoghi Effendi accepted the invitation of Dr Esslemont to visit him in Bournemouth for a few days and stay in the sanatorium where Dr Esslemont practised. Shoghi Effendi's sister Rúhangíz joined him the next day. A Persian believer, Aflátún, joined this group.

Dr Esslemont refers to Shoghi Effendi's visit in a letter he wrote to Dr Luṭfu'lláh Ḥakím at the conclusion of the visit, on Wednesday, 15 September, the day Shoghi Effendi left Bournemouth to return to Oxford:

> Shoghi Effendi is very well. He seems to be in better health and spirits than when I was at Haifa . . . Shoghi Effendi seems to be very keen on his studies and to be making very satisfactory progress.[25]

Upon his return to Oxford Shoghi Effendi answered the correspondence he had received and on Friday, 17 September 1920 he wrote a letter to Mr and Mrs Scott in Paris:

> My dear Bahai brother & sister:
> I have received your kind & affectionate letter enclosing the photographs you have so kindly sent me. I have been so busy & am still so absorbed in my studies that I have scarcely found any time to have my films developed but I shall send you the pictures I took . . . as soon as they are ready.
> I have been immersed in my studies – all having as an end a better ability in translating the words of Bahá'u'lláh and a fuller knowledge & better expression in expounding its principles.
> I have come, in the course of my readings at the University Bodleian library, across some rare & authoritative books, written by eminent statesmen & touching the Bahai Movement. Among them is Earl Curzon's (Secretary of State for Foreign Affairs) book on Persia written in 1892 wherein he writes the following:–
> 'The lowest estimate places them (the Bábís) in Persia at half a million. I am disposed to think that the total (in Persia) is nearer one million . . . Tales of magnificent heroism illumine the blood-stained pages of Bábí history. Ignorant & unlettered as many of its votaries are & have been, they are yet prepared to die for their religion & the fires of Smithfield did not kindle a nobler courage than has met & defied the more-refined torture-mongers of Ṭihrán. Of no small account, then, must be the tenets of a creed that can

ARRIVAL IN ENGLAND

awaken in its followers so rare & beautiful a spirit of self-sacrifice . . . Beauty & the female sex also lent their consecration to the new creed & the heroism of the lovely but ill-fated poetess of Kazvín, Kurratu'l-'Ayn, who throwing off the veil, carried the missionary torch far & wide, is one of the most affecting episodes in modern history . . .'

This is a sample of the work I am plunging in & I always seek your prayers that I may one day, fully-equipped, render a distinguished service to the threshold of Bahá'u'lláh.

Yours very affectionately,
Shoghi[26]

11
Matriculation and Student Life at Oxford

Sir Walter Raleigh's introduction was instrumental in the warm reception accorded to Shoghi Effendi by the Master of Balliol College, A. L. Smith. Through Smith, Shoghi Effendi was introduced to A. D. Lindsay, a Fellow of the college who held the position of classical tutor and Jowett Lecturer in Philosophy. Lindsay was very impressed with Shoghi Effendi and accepted to be his tutor. However, with the college admissions already announced, he felt he could not immediately admit Shoghi Effendi to Balliol.

Lindsay was aware that there might be a vacancy in Balliol because it was possible a Japanese student was not going to turn up. However, he did not disclose this fact to Shoghi Effendi. He wanted to be sure that the Japanese student was not coming and he wanted to be sure the college would officially accept Shoghi Effendi. He felt Shoghi Effendi should wait until the first college meeting after the completion of the first term, when admissions were considered. This would be the Monday after the beginning of term.

Lindsay therefore decided, early in October, that rather than admit Shoghi Effendi to Balliol, he would have him registered in a non-college institution affiliated with Oxford University known as the Non-Collegiate Delegacy.[1]

Background on the Non-Collegiate Delegacy

From the year 1868 young men were permitted under certain conditions to become students and members of Oxford University without being members of any College or Hall. Such persons kept their residence in houses or licensed lodgings within the limit of a circle a mile and a half in radius from Carfax.[2]

The admission of students into the University and the supervision of their work during their residence in Oxford were the responsibility of a Delegacy consisting of a Vice Chancellor, Proctors, a Censor, a Controller of Lodging Houses, and six Members of Convocation holding office for six years. The Censor, nominated by the Vice Chancellor and Proctors, supervised the students and was charged with the care of their conduct and studies. The Censor of the Non-Collegiate Delegacy in 1920 was James Bernard Baker.

The Non-Collegiate Delegacy adopted the name St Catherine's Society in 1930 and occupied permanent buildings in 1936. Members of the Society were required to keep their statutable residence in Oxford in houses approved by the Delegacy of Lodgings. They were considered members of the University and enjoyed the same privileges as other students. In 1962 St Catherine's Society received college status and became known as St Catherine's College.[3]

Shoghi Effendi in the Non-Collegiate Delegacy

On 7 October 1920 Lindsay wrote to J. B. Baker introducing Shoghi Effendi. As Censor, Baker would be required to look after Shoghi Effendi and be his tutor.

Expressing his very high opinion of Shoghi Effendi, Lindsay suggested that Baker should matriculate Shoghi Effendi in the Non-Collegiate Delegacy. He indicated that if Baker had difficulty in giving tuition to Shoghi Effendi, he himself would 'look after him in the meantime'. Lindsay ended the letter by saying, 'He is a quite exceptional young man.'[4]

In his letter to Baker, Lindsay mentioned that at one time he hoped there would be a vacancy in Balliol that could be filled by Shoghi Effendi, but that 'the prospect was not fulfilled'. Later correspondence shows that the Japanese student never came, and Shoghi Effendi could have been admitted to begin his work in Balliol during the first term.

Lindsay's decision meant that Shoghi Effendi would not be able to move to Balliol or 'migrate into college' during the first term. Postponing the decision to the 'Monday after full term' meant that Shoghi Effendi would not be able to move into Balliol in the second term either, inasmuch as according to the rules, notice for migration or movement into college must be given in the sixth week of the previous term.[5]

This caused tremendous inconvenience and disappointment for Shoghi Effendi, who was confident that Balliol was where he was meant to study. He 'had made up his mind' he would be admitted and had been counting on moving into Balliol during the first term. Shoghi Effendi was not pleased with the prospect of having to matriculate in the Non-Collegiate Delegacy. He was keen to settle into his room in college and concentrate his energies on his work.

In a letter to Ali Yazdi dated 5 October 1920 Shoghi Effendi shares his painful disappointments and anxieties regarding entrance into Balliol college.

Dear 'Alí: –

Your letter reached me at a time I was immersed heart and soul in my manifold preparations for entrance at Balliol College, Oxford. I am fearfully anxious and occupied but your letter absorbed my interest and diverted it from this phase for a time. I am glad and extremely sad in receiving your letter – glad at the knowledge that at last my efforts have proved partially successful and *some* pecuniary help has been extended to you.[6] I wished, dear 'Alí, to have had enough money at my disposal to share it with you! I immediately wrote to Mrs. George and exposed the case fully. I hope you will soon and easily sail. I am so grieved at the sudden turn of events and the complications and cost of travel have only marred the brightness caused by the knowledge that some financial help has been finally extended . . .

I assure you, dear friend, that if some are free from pecuniary anxieties, they are nevertheless subject to another set of various physical, intellectual and social drawbacks and preoccupations. Do you believe me when I say that I, the grandson of the Master, have been victim of painful experiences, sometimes of bitter disappointments, and always of constant anxieties – all justified – for my immediate work and future? If you have spent of late painful and trying times, my share of these troubled hours is by no means much less and my burden much lighter.

My field of study is so *vast*, I have to acquire, master and digest so many facts, courses, and books – all essential, all indispensable to my future career in the Cause. The very extent of this immense field is enough to discourage, excite, and overwhelm such a young and inexperienced beginner as myself. Think of the vast field of Economics; of social conditions and problems; of the various religions of the past, their histories and their principles and their force; the acquisition of a sound and literary ability in English to be served for translation purposes; the mastery of public speaking so essential to me, all these and a dozen more – all to be sought, acquired, and digested!

Prayer, faith, perseverance and effort will alone do it. Praying for your success from all my heart!
Shawqí Rabbání[7]

Academic Work

Academic work at Oxford is supervised by tutors who help students choose their subjects and arrange for their lectures. The students are encouraged to attend lectures offered by the University, often held in the departmental buildings or inside the colleges.

In addition to the lectures, students are required to meet with their tutors for specific work. Tutors assign particular topics to the students for study and give them roughly a week to research the topic and write an appropriate essay. The students are required to consult numerous sources in the college library and in the university Bodleian Library. When the essay is completed, the students must read the essay in the presence of their tutor and other students and receive the tutor's criticism. This exercise helps prepare them for the university's final examination.

The prestige and reputation of each college depends on how well its students perform academically in the university final examinations and later in life.

Academic Year

The academic year is divided into three terms of approximately eight weeks separated by vacation periods. The first term, the Michaelmas Term, begins early in October and ends in December before Christmas. The second term, the Hilary Term, begins in January and ends in late March. The third term, Trinity Term, begins in April and ends late in June. The Trinity term is followed by a long vacation.

Gowns

When Shoghi Effendi attended Oxford, the students were required to wear appropriate gowns most of the time. The Scholars wore floor-length black flowing gowns, the Exhibitioners and Commoners wore shorter gowns, and those students pursuing postgraduate courses wore gowns extending to mid-calf. Shoghi Effendi, being a graduate student, probably wore a gown of the latter type.

Student Accommodation

Although Shoghi Effendi did not register in Balliol during the first term, he was in the college every day, and received tuition from A. D. Lindsay. He looked forward to moving into the college living quarters from his outside lodgings at 45 Broad Street. The student living quarters surround Balliol Hall. They had been constructed over seven centuries before the student days of Shoghi Effendi. These buildings include, additionally, a Junior Common Room (JCR), a chapel, a library, and a dining hall. Students live in buildings surrounding the administrative quarters of the college.[8]

Most members of the college live in college buildings known as staircases. Others live in housing outside the college. The student quarters in college are mostly large and spacious and often include separate areas for a bedroom and a living room. Access to the living quarters is not by corridors, but by staircases, each of which leads to two or more quarters on each of its floors.[9]

The college non-academic staff consists of the porter, the kitchen staff and the scouts. The scouts are responsible for looking after the comfort of students. They wake up the students in the mornings, clean their rooms, and serve them meals in the dining hall.

Meals and Daily Routine

Most students follow a traditional basic daily routine. They are awakened every morning by their scouts. They are then served breakfast in the hall.

Breakfast consisted of fruit juice, eggs, bacon, sausage or fish, toast and honey or marmalade. After breakfast, students usually retire to the JCR to read the morning papers before attending their respective lectures. Lunch is usually served in the hall between one and two o'clock in the afternoon. After lunch the students meet their tutors or work in the library on assignments given by their tutors. Around 3:30 p.m. many students return to the JCR to have tea, often with their guests, to write letters, or to read the papers. Dinner is served in the hall around 6 to 7:30 p.m.

After dinner students return to the JCR for coffee and discussion. A few spend time in the library, study in their quarters or visit each other in their rooms. The evenings are spent studying, attending meetings, going to the Student Union debates and so on. At the time of Shoghi Effendi the students were expected to be back in the college by nine in the evening or pay a gate fine.

While this leisurely schedule was practised more or less by the majority of the students, Shoghi Effendi did not have time to waste. He took advantage of every minute to pursue the learning objective he had set for himself or to translate the writings into English.

12
Michaelmas Term 1920

The Michaelmas term was already beginning when Lindsay wrote his first letter to Baker about Shoghi Effendi. The lectures were due to start a few days later. Yet Shoghi Effendi's registration status was not clear in early October. Nevertheless, he attended lectures and continued his work.

Shoghi Effendi's notebook shows a list of lectures he was planning to attend during the week of 11–16 October 1920:[1]

Monday	Logic – Mr Ross M.A.
Tuesday	Political Economy – Sir T. H. Penson M.A. Eastern Questions – F. F. Urquhart M.A.
Wednesday	Social & Industrial Questions – Rev. Carlyle
Thursday	Political Science – Rev. Carlyle
Friday	Social & Political Problems – Mr. Smith (Master of Balliol)
Saturday	English Economic History since 1668 – Sir T. H. Penson M.A.

Despite the pressure of work and the frustration he felt related to his admission into Balliol College, Shoghi Effendi found time for service to the Cause. Dr Esslemont had sent his book to Shoghi Effendi. On 13 October 1920 Dr Esslemont wrote to Dr Luṭfu'lláh Ḥakím:

> Shoghi has kindly supplied me with the correct transliteration of all the Persian and Arabic words and names which occur in my book.[2]

On Monday, 18 October Shoghi Effendi wrote to an oriental believer:

> My dear spiritual friend . . . God be praised, I am in good health and full of hope and trying to the best of my ability to equip myself for those things I shall require in my future service to the Cause. My hope is that I may speedily acquire the best that this country and this society have to offer and then return to my home and recast the truths of the Faith in a new form, and thus serve the Holy Threshold.[3]

The dedication of Shoghi Effendi to the service of the Cause and his vigilance not to miss any opportunity of service are evident from these letters.

Shoghi Effendi officially matriculated in the Non-Collegiate Delegacy on 23 October 1920, just over a week after starting his lectures in the Michaelmas term. The official records show him registered as Showqí Rabbání, Persian, recommended by Lindsay and the Master. Shoghi Effendi's name appears in the Non-Collegiate directory between two students, Mír Maqbúl Mahmúd and William Morris Tudor. His course of study is stated on his matriculation documents as 'Economics & Social Sciences'. The same document shows a list of four lectures for which he had registered in the Michaelmas term. The lectures were: Social and Political Questions given by the Master of Balliol, Social and Industrial Questions given by Rev. Carlyle, Elementary Economics given by Penson, and Political Science also given by Carlyle.[4]

During the Michaelmas term Ali Yazdi sent a cable to Shoghi Effendi to inform him of his forthcoming trip to the United States. Shoghi Effendi immediately telegraphed his friend, 'You don't mean to tell me you are going to America without coming to see me.' Ali Yazdi sent Shoghi Effendi a note about his travel to the United States via London to which Shoghi Effendi responded on a postcard dated 3 November 1920 from 45 Broad Street:

> My dear 'Alí,
> When I received your telegram, I wondered to what address I should forward my answer. Now that I have been informed I hasten to tell you how glad I would be to meet you, shake hands with you, and perform the ceremony of *muṣáfiḥih*.[5] I am bound with my lectures and courses and feel sometimes depressed. I shall be your host when you come to see me. I don't know how you have managed for your traveling expenses.
> On Thursday and Friday a brilliant debating soc. and an address by Bryce will be delivered.
> Shoghi[6]

In response to this invitation, Ali Yazdi travelled to Oxford and stayed in Shoghi Effendi's room for a couple of nights. Shoghi Effendi took Ali all over the university and showed him the sights. The two friends talked about their difficulties and discussed their preparation for future services to the Cause. Ali Yazdi discussed his financial condition with Shoghi Effendi and expressed his concern about his ability to save enough money to pursue his education. Shoghi Effendi comforted him and extended a warm hospitality to this childhood friend.[7]

As Shoghi Effendi was intensely interested in the outstanding speakers, especially those who spoke at the Oxford Union, he wanted to take Ali to hear the address by James Bryce and discuss it together afterwards. However, Ali could not stay and had to return to London.

After this visit, Shoghi Effendi sent Ali a note dated 6 November 1920 on an Oxford Union Society card:

> Dear 'Alí:
> I have received your card, and I knew well that it would be difficult for you to come here again. I did miss you profoundly last night and the night before, particularly as I firmly anticipated that we would both enjoy and comment upon the procedures of the debate and lecture. I trust, however, that you will not be detained a long time and that you will not have any difficulties to surmount. I have written to Grandmother about you reminding her of your

difficult and strained situation yet your patience and will. I hope that some help might issue by the time you prepare yourself for entrance into college. My best and tenderest wishes be with you always. May we meet again under better circumstances![8]

Despite his own overwhelming problems, Shoghi Effendi could not ignore his friend's financial need. He had empathized with his friend before, but could not forget Ali's financial problems. Four days later, on 10 November 1920, he wrote to Ali again.

> Dear 'Alí:
> I really never realized how minute, intense, and urgent were your financial needs. I hasten, therefore, to send you all that I can for the present – namely, five English pounds banknote, which I enclose in this letter. I hope you are staying at Miss Herrick's. She has some rooms to offer to friends who come to London. If you are not there, do apply. She is so kind.
> My studies and preoccupations are exerting an effect upon me almost as distressing as your own difficulties. Believe me it is so. I don't know what I shall do at the end.
> Yours lovingly
> Shoghi
>
> For Heaven's sake think not of sending me back anything. I flatly refuse and decline. Let your mind be at rest.[9]

Shoghi Effendi's difficulty related to his studies. The question of his admission to Balliol College was no less distressing than Ali Yazdi's financial situation. Furthermore, Shoghi Effendi was extremely busy during this period. He was so fully engaged in his work that he had little time to correspond with the Bahá'í friends. Dr Esslemont wrote to Luṭfu'lláh Ḥakím on Friday 10 December, 1920:

> I have not heard from Shoghi for some time. I must write him soon. I heard that he intended going to Glasgow during his x-mas vacations.[10]

Several letters were exchanged between the College and Mr Baker, the

Censor of the Non-Collegiate Delegacy, after the end of the Michaelmas term. These letters shed some light on the discussions behind the scenes between the College and the Non-Collegiate Delegacy. They highlight the painful experience Shoghi Effendi endured in dealing with the college administration.

The Master of Balliol was aware that Shoghi Effendi might not be allowed to move or migrate into Balliol College in the second term because of the migration rule. Concerned about Shoghi Effendi's condition, he himself became involved.[11]

The decision was finally made to admit Shoghi Effendi into Balliol College during the first week of the winter vacation and this was communicated to Mr Baker through Cyril Bailey, a Fellow of Balliol College responsible for administration. The Master of Balliol mentioned to Shoghi Effendi's tutor, Lindsay, that Bailey had discussed Shoghi Effendi's situation with Baker. On 20 December 1920 Lindsay wrote to Baker from his vacation residence in London explaining the background of the situation. He asked Baker to make an exception and allow Shoghi Effendi to migrate to Balliol for the Hilary term even though the rules for migration had not been followed, that is, notice for migration had not been given in the sixth week of the Michaelmas term.

On 22 December Lindsay wrote to Baker again responding to a letter he had just received from him about Shoghi Effendi. Lindsay said that he thought Shoghi Effendi was in London and would be making an effort to get hold of Baker. He said that he had told Shoghi Effendi that he would write to Baker much earlier. In an apologetic tone, Lindsay blamed himself and was 'very sorry indeed' for not having taken the time to discuss the issue with Baker earlier. He concluded the letter saying, 'I have a great belief in him which has been confirmed from what I have seen of him.'[12]

This positive statement by Lindsay helped Baker correct an earlier impression of Shoghi Effendi that was based purely on reports Baker had received from an informant suggesting that Shoghi Effendi had kept aloof from Oxford social life. In a letter to Lindsay dated 31 December 1920 Baker admitted that his impression of Shoghi Effendi had been based on erroneous information he had received from an informant who had mixed up Shoghi Effendi with another person. Baker confirmed that in fact Shoghi Effendi was active in the social life at Oxford. He 'played football and took part in the debates'. Baker admitted that he had somewhat 'wronged the man'.[13]

In the same letter, Baker mentioned that he had seen Shoghi Effendi the previous day, Thursday, 30 December, and told him the news that an application would be submitted to the Delegacy for his migration into Balliol on 15 January and that there was no reason for it to be refused. Baker was confident that Shoghi Effendi's certificate of migration would be issued on Monday, 17 January 1921.[14]

Upon receipt of Baker's letter, Lindsay felt that he should correct Shoghi Effendi's records at Balliol College. He wrote a note to Cyril Bailey on Thursday, 6 January 1921 informing him that the unkind remarks made about Shoghi Effendi had not been true. His note to Bailey also shows that in the second term, Shoghi Effendi was to write a paper on the 'Republic and Ethics' and on 'History of Philosophy from Descartes to Kant'.[15]

On 15 January 1921 permission was issued by the Non-Collegiate Delegacy for the migration of Shoghi Effendi into Balliol. Two days later Shoghi Effendi received a certificate of migration signed by two proctors. Thus, he officially migrated to Balliol and signed the college Register, as the 1st son of Mírzá Hádí Shírází, age 23.[16]

13
Hilary Term in Balliol

Shoghi Effendi started the Hilary Term 1921 as an official Balliol student living in college, occupying a room in one of its western buildings. The room provided sleeping, study and entertainment areas. Shoghi Effendi studied in his room and in the Balliol college library as well as in the Oxford University Bodleian Library. The buildings of the college served as a wall surrounding it on three sides and a wall separated Balliol from the neighbouring Trinity College. A porter's lodge was by the college gate, which was locked at night. From the college Shoghi Effendi could walk to the important buildings of the university. Below is a brief description of the main college areas that Shoghi Effendi would have visited on a daily basis.

College Main Gate and Front Quadrangle

The layout of the porter's lodge area today is different from that seen by Shoghi Effendi in 1920. Upon entering the gate, the area immediately to the right used to have a door through which the students entered to receive their mail and to sign the porter's register. That entrance has now been replaced with a wall. After entering through the gate, one sees the front quadrangle.

The front quadrangle dates back to the 14th century, and constitutes the oldest part of the college. Every part of the quadrangle has been restored several times in its long history. Surrounding the front quadrangle is a range of buildings that includes the students' living quarters.

College Library

The building on the west side of the front quadrangle used to be the Old Hall where students had their meals. However, in 1853 the hall was converted to a library. In 1920, Shoghi Effendi would have spent many hours in this library, the entrance to which was near the Master's Lodgings. In 1920 the present entrance and floor did not exist.

Garden Quadrangle

This area is the newer part of the college and comprises a garden surrounded by staircases. The formal building bordering it dates back to the 18th century. There are several buildings which Shoghi Effendi would have visited and these are described below in a clockwise circuit of the perimeter.

The Master's Lodgings

These were constructed in 1867 when the Master of Balliol was Robert Scott. In 1920, the then Master, A. L. Smith, occupied these quarters. He would have received Shoghi Effendi here.

Staircases X through XIV

These staircases, which are known respectively as the Fisher's Building, the Bristol Building and Basevi's Building occupy the south and just over two-thirds of the western edge of the garden quadrangle. They were constructed between 1759 and 1826. Shoghi Effendi probably visited several of his friends in these staircases.

Junior Common Room

This building was erected in 1912. The Junior Common Room occupied the ground floor and the basement of the building. The main room was extended and remodelled in 1964. Shoghi Effendi used the common room for after-dinner teas and discussions. The style and decorations of the room, however, have changed since the period of Shoghi Effendi's sojourn in Oxford.

Salvin's Buildings

These buildings which constitute staircases XVI to XVIII, were designed by Salvin in 1853. They replaced earlier college buildings including the Master's stables and a building known as Caesar's Lodgings. The back gate of the college, previously located next to the Junior Common Room, was relocated to its present position and a tower constructed above it at the same time. This door opened to St Giles and is opposite Beaumont street.

Shoghi Effendi's room was most probably in the Salvin's building. He had indicated to the friends that his window opened to the Martyrs' Memorial.

The Hall

The Hall was built in 1877 and has since been used for serving meals to the students and faculty. It contains rows of tables with benches on each side. The High Table, where the Master, Fellows, and tutors dine, is situated along the opposite edge of Hall from the entrance and is set perpendicular to the other tables. The windows in the Hall were originally fully glazed. In 1910 panelling was installed inside and the lower sections were blocked up. The Hall is decorated by brightly painted heraldic decorations related to benefactors. Large portraits of the Masters of Balliol College as well as of distinguished alumni create a serious atmosphere. The Hall is where Shoghi Effendi would have eaten his meals every day while in college.

The East Side and Lawn

The buildings that stand on the northeast side of Balliol College adjacent to the Hall did not exist when Shoghi Effendi was at Balliol. The east side had a wall separating it from Trinity College. Inside the wall was a garden with gordouli and mulberry trees.

The Fellow's Garden

This area, a charming garden, faces the Old Common Room and was used by the Fellows of the college. It was enclosed and had a passage on its west side.

Holywell Annexe

In 1920 Balliol College had an annexe which was used by students during their vacations. Surrounding the annexe were sports grounds, including tennis courts where students played single or double matches with their friends.[1]

Shoghi Effendi in college

The first week of the Hilary term ended on 27 January. Shoghi Effendi was in college during this week. The record of his expenses in Balliol College shows charges in the categories 'kitchen', 'stores', and 'messenger'. The kitchen charge refers to the meals served in the dining hall for the week and was £1/16/6 (one pound, 16 shillings and six pence). The stores charge refers to supplies Shoghi Effendi bought in the college stores and was 2/9 (two shillings and nine pence). The messenger charge probably refers to the fee for delivering messages within Oxford and shows an amount of four pence.[2]

The students of Balliol College had observed Shoghi Effendi in the college grounds during the first term. However, at that time he was a student attempting to be admitted into college. When he was admitted, they were curious to know who he was. The rumour was that Shoghi Effendi was related to the head of the Bahá'í Faith and would be occupying a high position in the Faith.

It is certain that the attitudes of students during this time at Oxford were class-conscious. These attitudes were reinforced by an institution that was conscious of its own destiny to produce the leaders of tomorrow in a sheltered, intellectual atmosphere rooted firmly in the past. These attitudes prevail even today. For example, on a spring Sunday afternoon, one can still observe young people punting on the Cherwell River, spending considerable time reading newspapers and taking tea in the Junior Common Room or JCR, as it is called. One notices how these young people pride themselves on their wit, on *what* they say as well as *how* they say it. One finds students listening intently with upraised eyebrows and polite *hmms* to the discourses around them, portraying a facade of effortless superiority. These attitudes were prevalent in 1920 and the recollection of Shoghi Effendi's contemporaries may be better understood in the context of such class-conscious attitudes.

Many of the students did not take the opportunity to spend time with Shoghi Effendi or to get to know him. They observed him from a distance. Shoghi Effendi's zeal, his loftiness of purpose, his seriousness about the goal he had set for himself and his diligence in all facets of his work surprised many students who believed that a Balliol man should show his 'superiority' without appearing to be making any effort. Most other students would conceal the amount of work they had put into their assignments in order to show that their work had been completed with little effort. Boyce Gibson, one of Shoghi Effendi's contemporaries, refers to this attitude of the upper-class English students of this period:

> I wonder how much he [Shoghi Effendi] liked his experience at Balliol. I doubt if he really felt at home there. It was not a matter of being Asian: Some of the Indians who were up with me were thoroughly at home there. Possibly it was that he knew he had a mission to fulfil, and in letting it be known he both cut across the current mood of benevolent incredulity and flouted the upper-class English convention of the time, that one should not <u>appear</u> to take things too seriously. I fear that he was sometimes hoaxed and I still don't know whether he was aware of it.[3]

As time passed, the students began to see Shoghi Effendi in a different light. They observed him in a variety of situations: discussing issues with enthusiasm in the dining hall, in the Junior Common Room (JCR), attending the Oxford Union debates and discussing the debate with fellow students. Through these interactions Shoghi Effendi's popularity grew. He became well respected and admired by the majority of students.

The records of his college expenses show his increasing social activity in the college. During the third, fourth and fifth week of the Hilary term, the college weekly expense record shows charges made by Shoghi Effendi for 'JCR teas', referring to afternoon teas and sandwiches which Shoghi Effendi probably bought for himself and his guests. In the third, fifth, sixth and seventh weeks of the term, his weekly expense sheet shows charges for 'gate bill', which refers to the charge for entering the college gate after it was closed at 9 p.m.[4]

While the subjects Shoghi Effendi was studying at Oxford were of interest to him, his primary purpose was to prepare himself for his future services to the Cause by perfecting his English so that he might be able to translate adequately the sacred writings of the Faith. To a friend in London he wrote:

> I am engaged in this land, day and night in perfecting myself in the area of translation . . . I do not have a moment's rest. Thank God that to some extent at least the results are good.[5]

In a letter written on Friday, 28 January 1921 from Balliol College to a Persian friend, Shoghi Effendi expressed his happiness at having just completed the translation of the Persian Hidden Words and the Tablet of Visitation. He had also translated other Tablets and letters of the Master and was happy that to some degree he had rendered a service to the Holy Threshold. He expressed the hope that in the near future the Súriy-i-Haykal and the Tablets to the Kings would be translated in the most perfect, the most novel and the most eloquent style, thus demonstrating a clear evidence that would justify his remoteness from the holy court. He sent greetings to the friends of the region, particularly to Mírzá Dáwúd and Dr Aflátún.[6]

Shoghi Effendi sent some of the translated Tablets, together with essays he had written, to a few of the English friends for their comments and corrections of the English. The individuals who had the bounty of receiving these early translations and essays were Dr Esslemont, Lady Blomfield and Ethel Rosenberg.

In an undated letter written on Balliol College stationery to Lady Blomfield, who was often addressed as Sitárih Khánum, a title given to her by the Master, Shoghi Effendi wrote about his translation work:

> I shall send you my version of the Arabic Hidden Words & the Epistle to Queen Victoria as soon as they are ready and I hope to have the pleasure of receiving any remarks or corrections you may desire to make with regard to them . . .
>
> As I desire to submit my paper on the Cause to Dr Carpenter[7] I would be much obliged if you could return it when convenient.[8]

On 5 February 1921 Dr Esslemont wrote to Luṭfu'lláh Ḥakím:

> I had a letter from Shoghi this week. He seems to be very busy at Oxford, and more satisfied than he was last session.[9]

Shoghi Effendi wrote to Dr Esslemont on 17 February 1921 acknowledging the receipt of the essay which Dr Esslemont had corrected and sharing the news that he had been asked to read a paper on the Bahá'í movement at the Oxford University Asiatic Society, which represented twelve nationalities:

> I have gladly accepted & have a long, comprehensive and elaborate paper which I hope to read this Monday. It is a custom of the Society to invite at every meeting an official of the University or an outsider who will be fully acquainted with the subject under discussion & who will address the society after or before the discussion is made on the paper.
>
> I understand that the Society has requested Dr. Estlin Carpenter to act as their distinguished visitor on that occasion but he seems to have been unable to respond to their invitation. They have now written to Prof. Browne & presumably they have intimated to him the nature of the subject & the name of the speaker. I presume he will be present but notwithstanding the attitude he will probably take in the discussion I have decided not to modify the tone of my speech & have preserved my quotations of his account when he visited Baha'u'llah in Acre. I don't know what will ensue in the meeting & what will be the atmosphere of the discussion in his presence. It is quite an unexpected turn & we hope for the best.[10]

The 'long, comprehensive and elaborate' presentation referred to by Shoghi Effendi included a summary of the history of the Cause from its inception, recounting the extraordinary events associated with it, presenting the heroine it produced in Ṭáhirih and other devoted followers it raised up. In this paper Shoghi Effendi refers to the extraordinary spread of the Faith throughout Persia, beyond that country to other regions of Asia, and beyond the continent to Africa, Europe, America and Alaska. He emphasizes that this spread has taken place despite an absence of financial resources, of means of communication, and of propaganda. This movement, he asserts, cannot be treated as negligible.

Shoghi Effendi then gives a more detailed account of the birth of the Faith in Shiraz in the context of the social and political conditions of the nineteenth century. He explains the challenge of the Báb to the corrupt clergy, and the threat this posed to the notorious leaders of

Islam but not to Islam itself. He explains how the combined efforts of clergy and government to suppress the Cause resulted only in attracting greater attention and publicity.

He recounts the rise of Bahá'u'lláh as the leader of the community, His imprisonment in the dungeon of Tehran, and the moving words of patience and courage uttered to His companions in that prison. He summarizes the events that transpired subsequent to His release from the prison and banishment to Iraq, His declaration as 'Him Whom God Shall Make Manifest' in Baghdad, and subsequent banishments culminating in the Most Great Prison of 'Akká. Shoghi Effendi then refers to the epistles written by Bahá'u'lláh to the kings and rulers of the time and the amazing prophecies in them that were fulfilled. He quotes the statement of Edward G. Browne about his remarkable audience with Bahá'u'lláh.

Shoghi Effendi's historical account is followed by the exposition of social teachings of the Cause and the bond of fellowship these teachings have produced wherever they have penetrated – a bond that has linked the East and West in a way that no other movement has so far been able to achieve. Shoghi Effendi recounts touching examples of the noble self-sacrifice of believers everywhere in building the institutions of the Faith such as the House of Worship. He asserts that although these principles have had their origins in earlier Faiths, yet they are not realized or enforced in those religions. He concludes by posing a question to his audience – if the movement has so far succeeded in exemplifying these social teachings wherever it has shed its light, may we not hope that it may one day usher in that golden Millennium awaited by all the world's great religions?

The full text of this remarkable address was published from September 1923 to April 1924 in *The Dawn*, the monthly Bahá'í journal of Burma, and is included in the appendix of this book.

According to the college records, Shoghi Effendi probably left the college for the spring vacation a day or two before the conclusion of the eighth week of the Hilary term, which ended on 17 March 1921.[11]

14

Spring Vacation 1921

The spring vacation began in mid-March and ended late in April. Shoghi Effendi spent the earlier part of this vacation in Scotland visiting his sister Rúhangíz. The latter part of the vacation was spent in Sussex. This is stated in a letter written by Dr Esslemont to Luṭfu'lláh Ḥakím, dated 23 March 1921.[1]

Although Shoghi Effendi was extremely busy during this vacation and barely spent time in Oxford, yet spring was the season he would begin to play tennis, a game he loved and in which he excelled. He played tennis with many students during this season as well as in the summer.

One of his tennis partners, J. C. Hill, gives a picture of Shoghi Effendi's speed in hitting the ball and his enjoyment of the game:

> I used to play tennis with him in the Master's Field, and marvellously active he was . . . He was ambidextrous and switched his racket from one hand to the other for a volley or the net with lightening speed – but not in a grimly earnest manner. On the contrary he was laughing . . . most of the time.[2]

Geoffrey Meade, another Balliol student who played tennis with Shoghi Effendi, has left this description:

> He was very keen to hit vigorously at the ball, which either went out or into the net, or was a brilliant shot. When serving he would go as far back as possible and serve as he strode briskly forward. If his ball went out or into the net he would stride on, as often as not coming well inside the service line before sending the second ball. When 'fault' was called he thought it a great joke, and it is a tribute to his popularity that it was a joke in which his partner shared.[3]

SPRING VACATION 1921

Adrian Franklin remembers not only playing tennis with Shoghi Effendi but also the quality of the courts:

> I distinctly remember playing tennis with him on the very bad Balliol clay courts: he had a very hard service for so short a man. Am I right in thinking he played left handed?[4]

We also have the recollection of G. Raleigh, who claims to have defeated Shoghi Effendi at a tennis match.

> Curiously enough, I happen to recall quite well that last time I played with him, I had the good luck to beat him quite soundly – 6–2, 6–1, or something like that. We enjoyed our games together, because we enjoyed tennis in very much the same way. He was such a pleasant person to play with.[5]

We also have the recollection of J. C. Dwyer, a student who had come to Balliol one year before Shoghi Effendi. He paints a picture of the fearless spirit of Shoghi Effendi:

> An example of his intrepid spirit, I remember hearing of him that he had addressed Hopkins, an American Rhodes Scholar, with the words: 'Hopkins! I hear that you are a Tennis Blue. Let us have a game sometimes.'[6]

These recollections add to the picture we have of the serious young Shoghi Effendi, and shows his sense of humour, his love for sports, and his friendship with his contemporaries. Some of the tennis matches could have taken place during this spring vacation, despite the fact that Shoghi Effendi was away from Oxford most of the time.

On Tuesday, 29 March 1921 Shoghi Effendi wrote from Scotland to Ḍíyá'u'lláh Aṣgharzádih stating that he had arrived a few days earlier to see his sister and attend to her affairs. Aṣgharzádih, who received numerous letters from Shoghi Effendi, was a Persian believer born in Mílán in 1880. He had made pilgrimage to the Holy Land twice, in 1903 and 1920. During his second pilgrimage, he spent several months in the presence of the Master. After his pilgrimage he went to London where he carried on business as a carpet merchant.[7]

In his letter Shoghi Effendi expresses his hope of going to London a few days later to meet the friends and to attend spiritual meetings in the home of Mírzá Yúhaná Dáwúd, which was located in a secluded and quiet area. He mentions that in Glasgow there was an Indian youth who had been recently blessed with a Tablet from the Master and that he hoped to meet this young man before proceeding to London.[8]

The Master, knowing Shoghi Effendi's earlier physical condition as well as his diligence and drive, had sent clear instructions that Shoghi Effendi should spend some days resting. Shoghi Effendi obeyed the Master's wishes and spent a few days during this vacation in Fermore Villa in Sussex, which had a good climate, to engage in prayers, meditation, and services to the Cause.[9]

Although he was on holiday and away from his studies, Shoghi Effendi was busily engaged in making translations, giving him rest only from his academic work. On Monday, 16 April 1921 Shoghi Effendi wrote a letter from Sussex to a Persian friend enclosing a Tablet he had just received from the Master stating that he had been engaged in the translation work in Sussex for the previous two days. However, having forgotten to bring along with him from Oxford several important Tablets, he wished this friend to immediately mail him copies of the Tablets of Ṭarázát and Bishárát, or the blue book Shaykh Faraj had published. He stressed that he needed these Tablets and was awaiting them.[10]

On Wednesday, 20 April 1921 Shoghi Effendi was back in Oxford. He again wrote to his Persian friend indicating that the notebook containing some Tablets had arrived. He wrote that he was taking extracts from the Tablets and returning them. He was, he said, immersed in translation work. In the two days since his return to Oxford he had, on instructions from 'Abdu'l-Bahá, translated some general Tablets, prayers and the Tablet of Tajallíyát.[11]

15

Trinity Term 1921

Balliol College records for the first week of Trinity term ending 28 April 1921 show Shoghi Effendi's full participation in college activities. He took his meals in college dining hall, purchased items in the college stores, used the college messenger services and paid one shilling for bicycle repair. He spent nine full weeks in college during the Trinity term, excepting probably a day or two prior to the conclusion of the ninth week ending 23 June 1921.[1]

The Trinity term had hardly begun when Shoghi Effendi began planning ahead for the summer. To ensure he would not waste a moment of the long vacation that would soon follow, he sought a competent tutor to work with him during the summer months. His first choice was R. A. Nicholson, the Arabic scholar. On Friday, 29 April 1921 Shoghi Effendi wrote to Miss Rosenberg:

> I hope your efforts will bear fruit and a satisfactory arrangement will be entered with Nicholson as I more and more feel that he is the only fitting and competent person for the job. If that fails I don't see how I can properly and profitably spend my long vacation. Would Mrs Cropper be able to arrange my work with Nicholson? I am so anxious to do some tangible substantial work during the long vacation and I think anything short of that will lamentably fall short of my aspirations. I am working on philosophy with Mr Lindsay & on English with two Balliol tutors, one of them admirably competent in English. What I need this vacation is direct help & correction of my translations . . . an English stylist would not be desirable if he has no knowledge of Persian or Arabic. The Tajalliyat, Ishraqat, Glad Tidings have been completed and I am now filling my leisure hours in working at the Epistle to the Shah & the Suratul-Haykal.[2]

PRELUDE TO THE GUARDIANSHIP

On Friday, 29 April 1921 Shoghi Effendi wrote a letter to a Persian friend in response to an invitation to attend the Riḍván gathering of the friends. He indicated that the strict rules of the college prevented him from leaving the city and therefore he regretted that he was not able to attend such a joyous Riḍván occasion. Otherwise, he asked, who would prefer seclusion in such a place and during such joyous times to fellowship with the friends of God? However, he continued, it was certain that, God willing, living in remote regions and in isolation would be followed by worthy services to the Cause of God; and this loneliness would be followed by the closeness and good pleasure of God.[3]

One of the objectives Shoghi Effendi had stated in his application to Oxford University was to associate with 'cultured and refined people'. Shoghi Effendi was able to accomplish this goal after his migration into Balliol. He had associated with a large number of students who had an extremely high respect for him despite the fact that he was not British and did not conform to the upper-class British conventions. As mentioned above, many assumed that he would in future be the head of the Bahá'í Faith. Among his group of friends were B. J. Bevan-Petman, Paul Leroy-Beaulieu, Boyce Gibson, William Y. Elliot, Leonard Manyon and J. R. Cullen. With these friends he played tennis and conversed on philosophical and religious issues, always with high excitement. G. C. Greer stated:

> I recall that we knew him to be somehow destined to head the Baha'i Faith – a fact which made him an interesting and unusual figure in the College.[4]

Mr Soskice, a contemporary of Shoghi Effendi, also provided his impressions:

> I certainly remember that he was very friendly and easy to get on with and enjoyed laughter and conversation. He was not in the least aloof and liked making friends . . . I have an impression of him rather restless, moving about a good deal and not often to be seen sitting down for any prolonged period.[5]

Shoghi Effendi left a profound impression on some of the students at Balliol. Like many others, A.W. Davis remembered him after 50 years:

Map of Balliol from the south, 1911, by Edmund New.
Shoghi Effendi's room was probably in Salvin's buildings (left)

The Martyr's Memorial, St Giles, early 20th century

The gate facing the Martyr's Memorial. Shoghi Effendi probably used this gate, which was close to his room (Photo: Mary Gray)

Above: Elevation onto the Garden quadrangle, showing staircases XVI to XVIII. Shoghi Effendi's room was probably on one of these. The top of the Martyr's Memorial can be seen over the roof (Photo: David Lewis)

The main gate to Balliol, on Broad Street (Photo: David Lewis)

Balliol College Chapel, and interior showing the 17th-century eagle (see inset). (Photos: Mary Gray and David Lewis)

The Main Hall. Portraits of past masters line the walls
(Photos: Mary Gray and David Lewis)

Portrait of Dr A D Lindsay CBE, Shoghi Effendi's tutor, later Master of Balliol and Lord Lindsay (Photo: David Lewis)

The Master's Lodgings from the Garden Quadrangle (Photo: David Lewis)

Balliol College Gardens
(Photos: Mary Gray)

As it was, however, ours was little more than a casual acquaintance, yet even that was enough for me to remember Rabbani quite distinctly after nearly fifty years when I have forgotten even the names of almost all my contemporaries at Balliol. There was always something 'different' about him.[6]

This account by B. H. Bevan-Petman describes the respect Shoghi Effendi commanded:

> Rabbani, yes, of course I remember him.
> Rabbani was irrepressibly cheerful, always on the point of laughter, and bouncing around . . . Wherever he was, spirits were high. We all knew him destined for spiritual leadership: and believe me, in no sense of irreverence or discourtesy, he was affectionately known as 'God'. (Naughty but inevitable!)[7]

A similar account is provided by another Balliol man of that time, Geoffrey Meade:

> We were of course aware at Balliol of his high position in the Bahá'í Faith and he was affectionately referred to as 'The God Kid'. I say affectionately because there was no hint of mockery in this – he was far too well liked for that . . .
> In conclusion I would say that not only I but all at Balliol liked him very much & esteemed him & were very sorry when he left after so short a stay.[8]

J. C. Hill remembered the time he spent with Shoghi Effendi:

> He used to walk, punt, meet after Hall in various people's rooms. S. P. Streuve and D. W. Lascelles were often there. In Shoghi's room there could be Russian Caravan tea . . . to be drunk, he insisted, with Cardamon seeds. He gave me a pair of Giveh[9] I had for years, which had been sent by his family with many other things. He loved to quote Hafiz and Saadi. I got the love of Persian Poetry from him.[10]

S. P. Streuve spent much time with Shoghi Effendi and had the honour of receiving an inscription, a prayer in Arabic, from him:

During the short period of time when we were both at Balliol (I went down in 1921) we talked with each other quite often . . . for some reason he conceived a liking for me or took an interest in me . . . I seem to remember that I also attended Dr Carlyle's lecture in Political Science . . . Perhaps some light on his attitude to me will be thrown by the enclosed xerox copy of the inscription he made for me, just before leaving Oxford, on a piece of parchment-like paper. When I asked him to translate for me what he wrote there he refused to do so. I think he said that perhaps one day I would learn the language and be able to read it for myself . . .[11]

The illustrations show two passages from the writings of Bahá'u'lláh penned in Shoghi Effendi's superb handwriting. The translation of passage appearing horizontally is as follows:

He is God
  My hair is My Attributes – in which My Beauty is Concealed! Perchance the Eyes of the strangers from among My servants may fall on it, thus have We hidden from the infidels the Beauty which is Shining and Exalted.[12]

The translation of the vertical lines is as follows:

He is the Mighty, the Beloved
  My Lock is My Chain – whosoever clings to It shall never err from everlasting to everlasting, for therein is hidden the Guidance which leads to Light of Beauty.[13]

To gain insight into the meaning of these passages, one should refer to other Tablets of Bahá'u'lláh where the metaphor of the hair is used, such as prayer for the Fast.[14]

Shoghi Effendi was asked to present a paper to the Lotus Club. This club provided a forum for the discussion of intellectual issues. Two of his contemporaries, J. P. de Menasce and William Elliot, refer to the paper he presented to this club. Elliot writes:

Shoghi Rabbani, or simply Rabbani as he was more often called, was so retiring that he did not lend himself to very much discussion, even though his points of view in religion were certainly very deep and appeared from time to time in such discussion clubs as I remember taking him to. The Lotus Club principally was the outstanding club, I think, for intellectual discussion and dialogue . . . The Lotus Club appreciated the qualities of Rabbani.[15]

In her book *The Priceless Pearl*, Rúḥíyyih Khánum quotes a letter from Shoghi Effendi to a believer confirming that he had presented a paper to one of the societies at Oxford. This could have been the Lotus Club or another club.

> I shall also send you a paper on the Movement which I read some time ago at one of the leading societies in Oxford.[16]

Shoghi Effendi also presented papers to the Bahá'í community in London, as this letter from an Indian believer indicates:

> On Wednesday evening [4 May 1921] I went to attend the usual Bahá'í meeting at Lindsay Hall. Mr Shoghi Rabbani read a paper dealing with the economic problems and their solution. His paper was beautifully worded and was very good . . .[17]

On 12 May 1921 Shoghi Effendi wrote to a Persian believer, probably Ḍíya'u'lláh Aṣgharzádih, asking him to send back papers which he had earlier sent to be read in the company of the friends. He mentioned that he needed these papers for his future conversations with some of the notables of Oxford University.[18]

16

Long Vacation 1921

The long vacation started in the third week of June and continued until the first week in October. Edna True, who had met Shoghi Effendi in Haifa in 1919, wrote this account of her meeting with him in London at the beginning of the vacation.

> In June . . . when I knew I was going to London, I wrote the Guardian offering to go to Oxford to see him. He replied that he would be passing through London at that very time . . . and suggesting that we have tea together at my hotel.
>
> While we were having tea, in this rather large salon of the hotel, word was sent to me that Captain so-and-so was at the reception desk with my plane ticket over to France. The Guardian spoke up and requested that the Captain be brought to us, and when he arrived, seemed most interested in my flight, asking just where my seat was. On looking over the plan of the plane, he noticed an open cock-pit in front of the pilot's cabin, and he asked the Captain if I could not have a place there. The captain replied that passengers did not usually sit there, but he promised to do what he could about it, and when I arrived at the airfield, he appeared with the news that I had to put on a special helmet, goggles, etc.! All of this had been the Guardian's idea and wish, but it proved to be an exciting experience.[1]

During the long vacation Balliol students wishing to study during the summer moved from the college to an annexe situated near Manchester College known as the Holywell Annexe. Shoghi Effendi stayed in this annexe for a part of this long vacation. One of his contemporaries, L. Forbes-Ritte, referred to the time he spent with Shoghi Effendi in this annexe.

He was quiet, agile minded, singularly well informed about this country, and that I attribute to his always wanting to know why ... He did spend a few weeks with Abdu'l-Hamid and me in a Holywell annexe we had. It was used in the long vac. by those wishing to stay up for study. We three, so far as I can recall, breakfasted together each day, and as the only 'native' I leg-pulled a great deal, when they asked questions.²

G. E. Lavin, who had come up to Balliol in 1918, described a conversation he had with Shoghi Effendi during this vacation.

> I have clear recollections of several hours' discussion with him in the Quad one summer's evening when we debated a number of broad ethical problems and found we had much in common although our backgrounds were very different.³

Sometime before the first week of July Shoghi Effendi left Oxford. His exact itinerary is not known. We do know, however, that on 6 July 1921 Dr Esslemont received a letter from him in which he stated that he would be visiting Dr Esslemont for a few days in a fortnight's time. Dr Esslemont mentioned this in a letter to Dr Ḥakím, postmarked 7 July 1921. He also states that Shoghi Effendi was in Crowborough, Sussex, during the university vacation.⁴

On 9 July, 1921 Shoghi Effendi wrote to Ethel Rosenberg thanking her for her kindness in forwarding his correspondence and sharing his immediate plans for the vacation. He states that he was planning to leave the next day for Bournemouth and would stay there for about two weeks. On 26 July he came to London to meet his sister and went with her to Mrs Thornburgh-Cropper's. Regarding his work and translations he wrote:

> My work with my tutor has been successfully terminated & among other Tablets, the Epistle to Nap. III has been carefully & properly translated. I hope to share it with you when I meet you next in London.⁵

On 10 August 1921 Shoghi Effendi was in Torquay. He wrote in Persian to Ḍíyá'u'lláh Aṣg͟harzádih from 115 Abbey Road. In this letter he states that the Master had given instructions that he was to abstain from work, studies and meetings and was to rest outside London. This point had been repeatedly emphasized by the Centre of the Cause. Therefore, after consultation with Mrs [Thornburgh-] Cropper and Major Tudor-Pole, Shoghi Effendi was spending some time in Torquay. He hoped to make a trip with Ḍíyá'u'lláh to Manchester at the end of the vacation. He had heard of the devotion of the Manchester friends to the Centre of the Covenant.[6]

The next day, 11 August 1921, Shoghi Effendi wrote to Miss Rosenberg again:

> I am delighted with the exquisite Tablet you have received & I am afraid my modest version has failed to convey the charm & the force of the original. One doubtful word in the text, I have inserted suspension mark, & which I may discover if you tell me what its rendering has been in the original translation – I have taken the liberty to transcribe a copy both of the original and of my version & shall be much obliged if you would let me know, as soon as convenient, all your suggestions as to my version that I may revise my own copy accordingly. Your remarks touching my version of the daily prayer, are most welcome & I am surprised to know that there is such a fitting equivalent in the Bible as the render of heavens.[7]

On Monday, 29 August 1921 Shoghi Effendi wrote a letter from Torquay to Ḍíyá'u'lláh Aṣgharzádih acknowledging the receipt of his letter and saying how much he had enjoyed reading it, for it demonstrated his dedication to the Cause. In the Torquay region, he wrote, one could not sense the fragrance of spirituality as people were immersed in materialism and superstition. He hoped Ḍíyá'u'lláh would travel with him to Manchester at the end of the summer to visit the believers.[8]

To an undated letter to Miss Rosenberg on Balliol stationery, probably written during the latter part of the long vacation in September, Shoghi Effendi attached the translation of a Tablet from the Master. This Tablet had been revealed on 20 August 1921 in honour of Mrs Crossley, praising her for the contribution she had made to the Temple fund and of her self-sacrifice in the path of God:

My dear Miss Rosenberg:
    I would be indeed much obliged to you if you could glance at my version of Mrs Crossley's Tablet & make any corrections you deem necessary & return it to me immediately . . . I am asked to send copies of it to some of the friends . . .[9]

Mrs Crossley was a devoted Bahá'í in Manchester who had responded to the call for contributions for building the House of Worship in Wilmette by selling her beautiful hair and sending the proceeds to the Temple Unity fund. Her selfless action had brought joy to the heart of the Master.[10]

In an undated letter written to a Persian friend on Balliol stationery, Shoghi Effendi stated that he had just finished a translation of a sacred Tablet of the Master for Mrs Crossley, which he had sent to her through Mr Hall. He also mentioned that he was engaged in further translations and publications of the Tablets.[11]

On Friday, 23 September, Shoghi Effendi wrote to Ḍíyá'u'lláh Asgharzádih praising God that his period of rest had been completed and that the days of study were approaching. In a few days he would arrive in London in order to send his sister to school in Scotland. He wished to meet Ḍíyá'u'lláh so that they might travel together to Manchester before returning to Oxford for the forthcoming term.[12]

On the following Wednesday Shoghi Effendi sent a note to Ḍíyá'u'lláh about going to Manchester on Saturday, 1 October. He said that his sister, who had been staying with Mrs Thornburgh-Cropper, had returned and was on her way to Scotland. Shoghi Effendi would come to Ḍíyá'u'lláh's home the next evening for a visit and to arrange the Manchester trip.[13]

Two days later Shoghi Effendi wrote a letter from 20 Bloomsbury Square, London, to Lady Blomfield expressing his pleasure at having seen her the previous evening and having had a long talk with her. He mentioned that he was planning to go to Manchester the following day and hoped to see her within a week. He also told her of his translation work:

> Your interest in my work of translation has encouraged me a great deal & my hope is that I shall in the near future realize my aspiration of rendering adequately & forcibly the words of Baha'u'llah & the Master into English.

I am enclosing a copy of one of the earliest of Baha'u'llah's prayers revealed in the early days of his stay in Baghdad. The prayer in Arabic is simply exquisite & I am not sure whether my rendering it into English has any merit whatever & whether it conveys anything of the charm of the original. You may keep it, if you think it worth your while, as I have duplicates of it.

I shall very gladly submit to your kind consideration & criticism my translations of the Epistles to Nap. III & Queen Victoria, of the Book of the Covenant & of other miscellaneous writings & prayers of Bahá'u'lláh & the Master, after I reach Oxford & hope to forward later my version of the Arabic Hidden Words . . .[14]

Visit to Manchester

Dr Esslemont visited the Bahá'ís of Manchester in late August 1921 and gave them the good news that Shoghi Effendi was planning a visit to Manchester in the near future.[15]

The community of believers in Manchester was active and devoted. The community had its roots in the earliest days of the Faith in Britain. Edward Theodore Hall, one of the pillars of the Faith in Manchester, learned of the Faith as early as 1910. He read an article about the brotherhood of man in the *Christian Commonwealth* and wrote to Major Wellesley Tudor-Pole, the author of the article, to obtain further information. Major Tudor-Pole forwarded the letter to Ethel Rosenberg, who sent Bahá'í literature to Mr Hall and put him in contact with Sarah Ann Ridgeway, the only Bahá'í in Manchester, who had learned of the Faith in 1899 in Baltimore, United States. Soon Mr Hall's wife, Rebecca, and her brother, John Craven, and his wife, Hester, all embraced the Cause of God.[16]

The Faith grew during the next decade in Manchester to just over 20 believers, including a young Persian merchant, Jacob Joseph, who was from a distinguished Jewish background. Mr Joseph offered to hold Bahá'í meetings in his office in Mosley Street starting in August 1920. This office, electrically lit and heated, became the gathering place for the believers.[17]

Shoghi Effendi arrived in Manchester on Saturday, 1 October, anxious to meet this community of devoted friends. He stayed until the following Thursday as guest of the Josephs.[18]

On Saturday evening the friends in Manchester gathered in Mr Joseph's office to await the arrival of Shoghi Effendi. They were so anxious to meet him that they were in a state of animation and expectancy when he walked in with Mr Joseph. Edward Hall has described this meeting:

> [Shoghi Effendi] made everyone at ease. His eyes were bright, his voice reassuring, his manners perfect, his features beautiful. He was as one, who, having control of himself, would therefore be able to control others. He commanded respect without seeming to know it. His youthfulness attracted us and the brightness of his thoughts called out our admiration. We all became very happy, and led him to the principal chair, and, as he wished to tell us about the Master's pleasure at Mrs Crossley's action, we placed her in the chair next to his.[19]

That evening, Lucy Hall, Edward Hall's daughter, requested that Shoghi Effendi write a few words in her autograph book. Granting this request, Shoghi Effendi wrote the following inscription:

> O Divine Providence!
> Pitiful are we; grant us Thy succour! Homeless and wanderers; give us Thy shelter! Scattered; do Thou unite us! Astray; join us to the fold! Bereft; do Thou bestow upon us a share and portion! Athirst; lead us to the wellspring of Life! Frail; strengthen us! that we may arise to exalt Thy Cause and present ourselves a living sacrifice in the pathway of guidance!
> What can I offer sweeter than the words of the beloved Master? I trust you will commit them to memory and remember me.
> To Lucy Hall from Shoghi Effendi, her brother in Baha'u'llah.[20]

The meeting at Mr Joseph's office made a profound impression on Shoghi Effendi. He was so moved by the devotion of the friends that he could not sleep all night. In the early morning of 2 October 1921 he began composing a letter to the Master, which he sent later to the Holy Land. The friends had agreed to write a joint supplication to the Master to be signed by all of them and to be sent by Shoghi Effendi. Below is a translation from Persian of Shoghi Effendi's letter to the

Master in which he praises the enlightened group of devoted believers in Manchester and refers to the joint supplication they were sending.

A letter from the humble and true servant of the Blessed Beauty, Shoghi Effendi, to His Holiness 'Abdu'l-Bahá:

My Master, my ultimate goal, my Beloved, how can I express my gratitude that Thou hast manifested such sincere, firm and blessed souls in this great city, Manchester – a city whose diverse inhabitants are negligent and steeped in materialism. These friends have kindled such light and fire in this city that its like has not been seen since the dawn of the Cause of God in these British Isles. True to a promise I had made to the friends in Manchester some time ago, I joined a gathering of the friends last night with utmost zeal and in Persian outfit – that is, with Persian hat.

There are some friends that have no peer except among the friends in Iran. Numbering some 30 souls, all from the working class, poor and needy, these friends had gathered together in a basement room. Among them were men and women, with children in their arms, who had traversed some distance during the night to come to this gathering. They gave me such a warm embrace that I was unconsciously moved. The friends, especially the woman who contributed her black locks towards the House of Worship, are poor. This woman is in such poverty and need that she has no home to offer anyone, nor any means of extending hospitality. Her father has passed away from this world and her Irish mother, a devout Catholic, is disenchanted and distanced from her daughter. Despite her condition, this woman, holding the recently revealed Tablet of the Beloved in her hand, was associating and conversing with the friends in such a state of enkindlement and radiance, and was so appreciative of the Beloved's words, that I cannot describe it. It is barely three months since she has been graced with the light of faith, and every hour of her days is dedicated to deepening in the Cause, studying the *Star of the West* and the *Glad Tidings*. She is enamoured with the Persian language and has no thought but to serve the Cause. As she handed me the Tablet from the Beloved and requested that I chant it, I was so moved by the sweetness of the expressions and words in that Tablet that my tears flowed uncontrollably. Others were also similarly moved. We had a gathering lasting to midnight that resembled those of the Iranian friends.

The souls in this city are being gradually prepared, and this humble basement meeting is expanding and becoming significant through the spiritual warmth generated by these souls. Among those who have joined the friends is a priest named Mr Heald who speaks with utmost sweetness and eloquence in praise and admiration of His Holiness Bahá'u'lláh, and whose speech has amazing influence. Today we shall have two meetings, one in his home. Although this group of believers is dispersed and they are far from each other, they come together on foot with their children in their arms. leaving their families behind. The condition of their children is similar to the condition of the children of believers in Germany – whose account has been described by the Beloved and other believers who have travelled to Stuttgart.

There are three Iranian believers here, brothers from the Mottahedeh family: Jacob, Joseph and Abraham. One of them is successful in the real estate business. They provide a high level of assistance to these poor and needy believers. Having obtained subscriptions to the *Star of the West* and *Glad Tidings* for a group of these friends, they are distributing the publications in this city. Some time ago he had sent 19 guineas as a contribution to the London community through Miss Rosenberg. This same Persian youth, Mr Joseph, has begged me to submit to Your holy presence his offer that should You wish to send teachers to these regions, he would pay all their expenses, as his business affairs are, praise be to God, prospering.

The spiritual father of this community of friends is Mr Hall. He has even set aside concern for earning his livelihood and is moving from place to place, from church to church, striving with enthusiasm to teach the souls. He has a daughter who, in her love for the Faith and her warmth of devotion, reminds one of the maidservants of God in Iran with longstanding training in the Cause. Truthfully, I never imagined that there were such souls in this city. The centre of the Cause is really Manchester, not London. Mr Remey, together with an Indian youth who was studying close to this city, and Dr Esslemont have set this group of believers on fire during the previous few months, and whatever I say will not do justice to the praise these friends deserve. It is amazing how enthusiastically they strive to learn about the history and the teachings of the Cause. They are thirsty for news of the progress of the Cause and have such attachment to the person of 'Abdu'l-Bahá. They have composed a joint supplication bearing each person's signature, which is being attached to this supplication to the Most Holy Presence. My plea is that a Tablet be revealed in their honour mentioning each person's name and that this Tablet be sent to this servant so that I may translate it with the most eloquent phrases and send it to these sincere souls. This would heighten their devotion and dedication. They are truly worthy and deserving.

I am planning to spend three to four days here, and will visit each home to the extent possible, regardless of how humble the home is. In truth these people are deserving of favours – as there are few souls in the West, whether Europe or America, who are as worthy as these friends to receive Thy favours and bounty. This Mr Hall will render great services to the Cause and his service cannot be compared with any of the London friends, even with the early believers. Meeting with these friends brings such spiritual warmth that I cannot describe. They became enkindled and joyful to learn of the Tablet of the Master to the believers in Najaf-Ábád two months ago, in which mention was made of this woman and the House of Worship. What steadfastness and certitude! They are confident as a mountain that this Cause will spread worldwide. The actions and efforts of these friends are beyond words.

My other request is that favours be bestowed upon Joseph even if it is in couple of words, as he is providing material assistance to the needy friends, and his contribution is not only material, but he is warm and loving. He and his two brothers are truly devoted. They have asked and pleaded with me to beg for confirmations on their behalf in order that they might gain the power of speech and writing for service to the Cause. My hope is that their prayer will be answered.

This supplication has become lengthy and has taken the Beloved's time. However, I was so moved by meeting these true servants of the Blessed Beauty that I could not sleep comfortably last night, until the morning arrived and I penned this supplication to describe their condition. I had heard about the devotion of these friends a few months ago but never had imagined that it would be so. What souls have been manifested such as Mr and Mrs Hall! And what rapid progress they are making in the service of the Cause! Last year according to what I have heard from the friends, these believers were not in this condition. They are becoming stronger and more steadfast day by day. My hope is that the glance of the favour of God will continually be directed upon them.

I visited Lady Blomfield in London. She is hoping to visit the Holy Land on pilgrimage this winter. I also met Tudor-Pole's sister who asked me to mention her name and say that she will never forget the memories of ... Yuhannah Dawood and Ḍíyá'u'lláh both express their servitude and selflessness to the holy threshold.

Soon I shall return to Oxford to continue again the course of my work, and according to Ladies Rosenberg and Cropper the Tablets of the Blessed Beauty have been translated far better and more eloquently than before. As always I beseech and long for the holy confirmations for my success.

The servant of the dust of Thy threshold,
Shoghi

2 October 1921[21]

Shoghi Effendi met the friends again in the afternoon of 2 October, at the same location, and was present at their gathering that evening in the home of Mr and Mrs Heald. The singing of hymns by the friends pleased Shoghi Effendi and reminded him of the days in the Holy Land when Lua Getsinger would sing a hymn for the Master. Shoghi Effendi told the friends that Lua's singing so pleased the Master that He would ask her 'to go out on the terrace of the house at Haifa, in the cool fragrant night ... and sing the hymn which always pleased Him – "Nearer my God to Thee". Her voice would rise and fall clear as a nightingale's, to the joy of the Master.'[22]

Shoghi Effendi shared with the friends some Persian poems that could be used as hymns. Lucy Hall recalled:

Shoghi Effendi told me the words of a hymn in Persian ... and he asked me for a hymn tune to fit. I played 'The Old Hundredth' from C. of E. Hymns *Ancient and Modern*. I can only remember the first two lines and do not know Persian but here they are, if you can translate them: 'Sínáy-i-haq pur núr shud; vádíy-i-muqadas túr shud...'[23]

These words are from the writings of 'Abdu'l-Bahá and give the glad tidings of the new revelation of God that has once again illuminated the Sinai of the Lord.

The next day, Monday, 3 October, Shoghi Effendi and Ḍíya'u'lláh Aṣgharzádih visited the Hall family. Shoghi Effendi presented to them a photograph of the Master on which he inscribed a few words. He then expressed his love for the children and gave them each a Persian name.[24]

Later in the afternoon, Mr Hall took Shoghi Effendi and Ḍíya'u'lláh to the house of the Reverend H. H. Johnson, in Cheetham Hills. Johnson had heard of the Cause when 'Abdu'l-Bahá had been in London in 1911. His reading of Bahá'í books and his search had led him to the Unitarian ministry. He told Shoghi Effendi that he had written an article on the Bahá'í Faith and had submitted it to the Master. He was happy that this article had been published in the *Times Educational Supplement*.[25]

Following this visit Shoghi Effendi joined the friends for the evening at Mr Joseph's office. He chanted a prayer and later shared some purple grapes he had bought earlier at a fruit stand on his way to Mosley Street. During the meeting, Shoghi Effendi showed the friends a small bottle of attar of rose which the Greatest Holy Leaf had given him and instructed him to share it with the friends when moved by the spiritual atmosphere of a meeting.[26] Here is Lucy Hall's recollection of that evening nearly 50 years later.

> I can still remember quite clearly standing in the room with him whilst he explained to me how it was the 'quintessence' and how this was made. The perfume lingered well over twenty years on the handkerchiefs and in the box in which they were treasured.[27]

Edward Hall also remembered the event:

> He asked us each to hold out a hand, palm upwards, and as he passed around the room he placed a little of this quintessence of rose-fragrance upon it; then we each, following the example of Joseph... rubbed our hands together and stroked our palms over

our hair and forehead, until ourselves and the whole atmosphere were deliciously fragrant. Then he told us beautiful things of the great Fellowship and tender things of the Holy Places, until we were no longer in Manchester, but rather in the spirit of the Holy Land.[28]

That evening, the friends signed the following joint supplication to the Master:

Our dear Lord and loving Master,
   At this moment when we are full of joy that we have attained to the meeting with thy richly illumined, beautiful, and radiant grandson, Shoghi Effendi, and have become re-inspired and re-invigorated by the pure flame of his love and his message to us, the strength of which is reinforced by the pure spirit of his honour [Ḍíyá'u'lláh], (whose every thought and act is in Thy service), we append our humble signatures to this earnest appeal for Thy supplications on our behalf – who are so small and insignificant in the midst of this great city, which is in such need of the Love of God. We are beginners in the school of the Word of God; we are attracted to the Blessed Perfection through the teachings of 'Abdu'l-Bahá, and we have turned our faces to His Glory.
   We know that all Thou doest is for our own good and for the good of the world, and in the sunshine of this knowledge we want to be one with Thee, living with Thee in the Divine Kingdom – radiant in Thy radiance in the Glory of God.
   We know that this is impossible save by Thy prayers on our behalf. We desire earnestly and ardently to be faithful and true to Thee, as Thou art to the Blessed Perfection, pure mirrors of Thee as Thou art the pure Mirror of the Graces of God. Thy prayers will assist us to this mighty end, beloved Master; and we pray for the everlasting success of Thy Divine Mission, rejoicing that Thou art in good health, and full of love towards us.
   We remain with love and deep reverence for Thee and for Thy people, and for Thy Holy Cause.
   Your faithful servants [29]

Edward Hall begged Shoghi Effendi to send this supplication without changing a word. Although Shoghi Effendi did not wish his own name to be mentioned in the supplication, he graciously granted Edward's request to make him happy and agreed to send it to the Master the way it was worded.[30]

On Tuesday, 4 October 1921, Shoghi Effendi visited the premises of the Linotype Works where John Craven worked, and in the evening went to John Craven's home where some of the believers and their friends had gathered. The next day, 26 Bahá'ís gathered again at Mr Joseph's office and each received a silk handkerchief and carnelian stones and was anointed with attar of rose by Ḍíya'u'lláh Aṣgharzádih. At eight o'clock in the evening everyone walked to a photographer's studio on Oldham Street to pose for a group photograph. Mr Hall wanted Shoghi Effendi to sit in the middle and hold the photograph of 'Abdu'l-Bahá, but Shoghi Effendi insisted that as Mr Hall was chairman of the group, he should sit there. Mr Hall accepted.[31]

On Thursday morning, 6 October 1921, Shoghi Effendi left Manchester with Ḍíya'u'lláh Aṣgharzádih.

17

Michaelmas Term 1921

At last the long vacation was over, and Shoghi Effendi was happy to be back at university. The Michaelmas term began on 6 October 1921. The college records indicate that Shoghi Effendi participated in various college activities during the first week of term, and that he used the college services for eight weeks. The last week for which there are any charges against his account is the week ending 1 December 1921. The college records for the Michaelmas term 1921 shows Shoghi Effendi's name in the list of students:[1]

+ Prendergast, V., J. R. D.
+ Rabbani, S., A. D. L.
+ Russell, J. A., McL.

The initials following each name correspond to the initials of each student's tutor; 'A. D. L.' was Shoghi Effendi's tutor A. D. Lindsay.

One of Shoghi Effendi's contemporaries, Paul Leroy-Beaulieu, recalls this period:

> I remember him quite well although I became acquainted with him a few months only before he left. He . . . spoke both French and English fluently . . . liked to talk about the Baha'i movement. He visited me several times in my rooms which were in College, on the first floor on the left hand side of the hall, but I am sorry that I don't remember where his own rooms were located. We both attended the lectures given by T. H. Penson on economics.[2]

Shoghi Effendi was eager to take maximum advantage of the time he had at Oxford in pursuit of his main objective of perfecting his English.

He carried with him a notebook in which he listed hundreds of words and typical English phrases for reference.³

He demanded much of himself and of his tutor: Lindsay tells of a specific encounter when Shoghi Effendi asked him for time during his dinner hour.

> I had posted my schedule . . . Shoghi Effendi came to me asking, 'What do you do between seven and half past eight?' 'Why man,' I cried, 'I dine!' 'Oh', said Shoghi Effendi with obvious disappointment, 'but must you have all that time?' I had not found so much eagerness for knowledge at Oxford. So I gave him another quarter-hour and went with less dinner. So it was – I suffered for him.⁴

One of Shoghi Effendi's contemporaries, Christopher Cox, a Balliol student of 1918–19, confirmed Shoghi Effendi's demand for Lindsay's time, an indication of his eagerness to take advantage of every minute he was at Oxford:

> The only story of him that I heard – viz his eagerness to obtain an hour a week tutorial with A. D. Lindsay, i.e. difficulty in accepting that the latter's timetable was almost full, when Lindsay showed him his timetable packed with postwar engagements, the remark that there was an hour's gap at lunchtime!⁵

Another contemporary, G. W. Wrangham, a Balliol student who matriculated in 1919, relates the following:

> I remember Shoghi Effendi quite well, and in particular remember that he was then destined for his exalted position in the Bahá'í Faith. I remember also the story that when he wanted to consult his philosophy tutor [A. D. Lindsay] on some matter of high religious or philosophical significance he was astounded to be told that he must wait until Lindsay has finished his lunch, such purely material matters as lunch ought not to have interfered with the investigation of philosophical truth.⁶

On Sunday, 9 October 1921 Shoghi Effendi took time from his work to write to the friends in Manchester. Here are excerpts from the letter he wrote from Balliol to Edward Hall:

> My dearest Baha'i brother:
> The sweet perfume of the friends in Manchester has clung to us wherever we have gone and now that I find myself again in the cold and academic atmosphere of Oxford, my thoughts go back to the sweet hours I have spent in your midst.
> The joint supplication, one of the most potent messages ever sent to the Beloved from these shores, is now on its way to the Holy Land and as the eyes of the Master are turned towards your great city, I am confident that ere long He will respond to your joint and earnest prayers.
> I shall never fail, immersed as I am in my work, to transmit to you all the joyful tidings I may receive from anywhere regarding the Cause, and my first and last request is that the friends, one and all, may persevere to the very end in holding their regular meetings . . .[7]

In an undated letter written in Persian on Oxford Union letterhead, Shoghi Effendi stated that he had received a Tablet in honour of the believers in Manchester which contained urgent matters.[8] He translated it immediately and sent them to Mr Hall. He also stated that he was enclosing several moving prayers of the Ancient Beauty and the Master, which he had carefully translated. He mentioned that electric lights were being installed in the vicinity of the Shrine of Bahá'u'lláh by an engineer together with a few of the friends and Mírzá Luṭfu'lláh.[9]

The Tablet of the Master to the Manchester Bahá'ís was in response to their joint supplication. It was dated 18 October 1921:

> To the beloved of the Lord in the city of Manchester:
> Your letter hath been received, and the contents thereof have imparted the utmost joy and gladness. Praised be the Lord, ye have eyes that see and ears that hear. Ye beheld the Light of Truth and are accounted, even as Christ hath said, among the Chosen rather than among the Called . . . Wherefore, praise ye the Lord, that in the lamp of your hearts the Flame of Divine guidance is kindled and ye have entered the Kingdom of God. It is incumbent upon you, however, to act with utmost discretion and not rend the veil asunder, for the enemy, though he be near or afar, lieth in wait and

stirreth the negligent to arise against His Holiness Baha'u'llah; Be ye prudent; be ye discreet.[10]

In addition to this Tablet to the believers in Manchester, the Master revealed a few individual Tablets. On 20 October 1921 the following Tablet was revealed in honour of Jacob Joseph and his brother Ibrahím. This is a paragraph from Shoghi Effendi's translation:

> O ye that stand fast and firm in the Covenant!
> The faithful servant of the Ever-Blest Beauty, Shoghi Effendi, hath written a letter, and therein hath praised you most highly, namely, that these blessed souls are true Baha'is, are verily self-sacrificing, burn brightly, even as twin candles, with the Light of Guidance, serve with heart and soul the Cause of God, succour the needy amongst the faithful, and seek fellowship with the poor.[11]

Another Tablet was revealed on the same day in honour of Samuel Heald. Here is Shoghi Effendi's translation of this Tablet:

> O son of the Kingdom of God!
> Praised be the Lord, thou hast rent asunder the veil of the Pharisees and winged thy flight unto the Kingdom of God. Thou hast accepted the Teachings of His Holiness Bahá'u'lláh and been drawn unto the Holy Spirit. In truth, thy faith is now sincere and thou hast come to know Jesus Christ better...[12]

On Tuesday, 1 November 1921 Shoghi Effendi wrote to Dr Esslemont about his translation of the Hidden Words. He enclosed his version of the Ishráqát and the Epistle to Queen Victoria and pointed out the immensity of the task of translation:

> My Dear Dr. Esslemont:–
> I have been of late extremely busy with my work & hope to give soon the final touch to my rendering of the Hidden Words ... What a difficult task translation is! The more you work on it the more difficult it appears. There is simply no end to it. You can go perfecting the art ad infinitum. My only ambition however at present is to achieve a certain relative success by improving on the

previous translations & if I attain this aim I am fully satisfied.[13]

On Saturday, 12 November Shoghi Effendi wrote to a Persian friend who had sent him pictures of the Manchester friends. In his letter he mentions that he had finished translating Tablets of the Master in honour of the Manchester Baháʼís.[14]

On 22 November 1921 Shoghi Effendi wrote to John Craven from the college Junior Common Room expressing his happiness that the speedy response of the Master to the joint supplication of the friends in Manchester had so refreshed the friends, and mentioning progress on his translation work:

> ... I have been of late immersed in my work, revising many translations and have sent to Mr Hall my version of Queen Victoria's Tablet which is replete with most vital and significant world counsels, so urgently needed by this sad and disillusioned world! If you have not perused it, be sure to obtain it from Mr Hall as it is in my opinion one of the most outstanding and emphatic pronouncements of Baháʼuʼlláh on world affairs.
>
> I am enclosing for all of you extracts, some new and some old, in the course of my readings at the Bodleian on the movement. I have also with me startling revelations on the Cause by the well-known orientalist Le Comte de Gobineau. I shall also later send you a paper on the movement which I read some time ago at one of the leading societies of Oxford.[15]

During his studies at Oxford, Shoghi Effendi became familiar with a book of extreme importance, which captured his interest and left an enduring mark on the style of English that emerged in his later writings. He saw the similarity of the historical events described in the book with the decline of the social and political institutions of his time. Furthermore, he found in this book the germ of a style of English that could serve as the vehicle for the exposition of the spiritual and intellectual verities of the Faith of Baháʼuʼlláh. This book, *The Decline and Fall of the Roman Empire*, Gibbon's famous work, was Shoghi Effendi's constant companion.[16]

One of Shoghi Effendi's contemporaries at Balliol, who later received the title Lord Stow Hill of Newport, describes Shoghi Effendi's fascination with this book:

I seem to remember him walking up and down the inner quad in the grass on many occasions reading Gibbon's *Decline and Fall* as he walked, sometimes I believe aloud. It was quite a thing to watch, and I always thought he would trip over something. However, dignity and a look of profound inspiration always seemed to be preserved.[17]

Another Balliol student, J. M. Russell, who attended Oxford the same year as Shoghi Effendi, also refers to Shoghi Effendi walking in the quadrangle:

> Perhaps my clearest memories are of him walking round in the Garden Quad on summer evenings & clearly reading a small volume.[18]

In addition to Gibbon's work, Shoghi Effendi loved the style of English in the King James version of the Bible, which he read while he was at Balliol. One of his fellow students, J. C. Hill, who knew him well, has related the following:

> He read the whole of the Bible, from cover to cover in about a week. He told us he was a lover of the midnight oil.[19]

Another Balliol student, Adrian Franklin, confirms Shoghi Effendi's interest in the Bible. Franklin remembered an anecdote that circulated in the college about Shoghi Effendi:

> There was an anecdote in the college at about this time that when he came up he had never heard of the Jewish/Christian bible but, when told of it, read it Genesis to the end of New Testament in one week. I believed this at the time – I was only just 18 – but on reflection now I see the story must have been rubbish.[20]

That story was indeed inaccurate. As well as having been exposed to the Bible at the Jesuit School, Shoghi Effendi had taken four formal courses on the Bible during his freshman and sophomore years at the American University of Beirut.

Rúḥíyyih Khánum confirms that Shoghi Effendi was interested both in the Bible and in Gibbon's work:

He was a great reader of the King James version of the Bible, and of the historians Carlyle and Gibbon, whose styles he greatly admired, particularly that of Gibbon whose *Decline and Fall of the Roman Empire* Shoghi Effendi was so fond of that I never remember his not having a volume of it near him in his room and usually with him when he travelled. There was a small Everyman's copy of part of it next to his bed when he died. It was his own pet bible of the English language and often he would read to me excerpts from it, interrupting himself with exclamations such as 'Oh what style; what a command of English; what rolling sentences; listen to this.' . . . I particularly remember one peaceful hour (so rare, alas) when we sat on a bench facing the lake on a summer afternoon in St James' Park in London and he read me Gibbon out loud. He revelled in him and throughout Shoghi Effendi's writings the influence of his style may clearly be seen, just as the biblical English is reflected in his translations of Bahá'u'lláh's Prayers, *The Hidden Words* and Tablets.[21]

18

The Last Days in England

On 29 November 1921 at 9:30 a.m. a cable reached the office of Major Tudor-Pole in London:

> His Holiness 'Abdu'l-Bahá ascended Abhá Kingdom. Inform friends. Greatest Holy Leaf[1]

Major Tudor-Pole immediately notified the friends by wire. Rúḥíyyih Khánúm, in her book *The Priceless Pearl*, suggests that Tudor-Pole must have telephoned Shoghi Effendi and asked him to come to his office. Shoghi Effendi reached London about noon, went to 61 St. James's Street and was shown into Tudor-Pole's private office.

> Tudor Pole [sic] was not in the room at the moment but as Shoghi Effendi stood there his eye was caught by the name of 'Abdu'l-Bahá on the open cablegram lying on the desk and he read it. When Tudor Pole entered the room a moment later he found Shoghi Effendi in a state of collapse, dazed and bewildered by this catastrophic news. He was taken to the home of Miss Grand, one of the London believers, and put to bed there for a few days.[2]

In his letter to the *Star of The West* a few days later Major Tudor-Pole wrote:

> Shoughi Rabbani and his sister will be returning to Haifa towards the end of the present month, and they will be accompanied by Lady Blomfield, and by Ziaoullah Asgarzade.[3]

On 29 November Dr Esslemont wrote to Shoghi Effendi with words of

THE LAST DAYS IN ENGLAND

comfort and invited him to spend a few days in Bournemouth:

> Just send me a wire . . . and I shall have a room ready for you . . . if I can be of any help to you in any way I shall be so glad. I can well imagine how heart-broken you must feel and how you must long to be at home and what a terrible blank you must feel in your life . . . Christ was closer to His loved ones after His ascension than before, and so I pray it may be with the beloved and ourselves. We must do our part to shoulder the responsibility of the Cause and His spirit and power will be with us and in us.[4]

On 1 December 1921 Dr Esslemont went to London. In his diary letter to Luṭfu'lláh Ḥakím of 8 December he recalls visiting Shoghi Effendi after the passing of 'Abdu'l-Bahá:

> [I] found poor Shoghi in bed, absolutely prostrate with grief. At first he seemed absolutely overwhelmed by the loss, unable to eat, to sleep, to think. During the day, however, he recovered, and after tea he got up and came through to the drawing room, where we had a little meeting – Miss Grand, Lady Blomfield, Mirza Dawud, Ziaoullah and myself. Shoghi read and translated to us the last tablet he had received from the Master, and chanted for us . . . the following day we all gathered at Miss Grand's again. We decided that Lady Blomfield would go with Shoghi and Ruhangiz Khanom to Haifa, as soon as the journey could be arranged. Ziaoullah also offered to go, and to bear all expenses of the journey, so far as necessary. That afternoon Shoghi came to Bournemouth with me, as we thought the rest and change at Bournemouth, while the necessary preparations were being made for the journey, would be best for him.[5]

According to Dr Esslemont, Shoghi Effendi spent the evening of 2 December through to the morning of 7 December in Bournemouth. From there he wrote this significant letter to a Bahá'í student in London, reflecting the spiritual connection he had established with the Master:

> The terrible news has for some days so overwhelmed my body, my mind and my soul that I was laid for a couple of days in bed almost

senseless, absent-minded and greatly agitated. Gradually His power revived me and breathed in me a confidence that I hope will henceforth guide me and inspire me in my humble work of service. The day has come, but how sudden and unexpected. The fact however that His Cause has created so many and such beautiful souls all over the world is a sure guarantee that it will live and prosper and ere long will compass the world! I am immediately starting for Haifa to receive the instruction He Has left and have now made a supreme determination to dedicate my life to His service and by His aid to carry out His instructions all the days of my life . . .

The stir which is now aroused in the Bahá'í world is an impetus to this Cause and will awaken every faithful soul to shoulder the responsibilities which the Master has now placed on every one of us.

The Holy Land will remain the focal centre of the Bahá'í world; a new era will now come upon it. The Master in His great vision has consolidated His work and His spirit assures me that its results will soon be made manifest.

I am starting with Lady Blomfield for Haifa, and if we are delayed in London for our passage I shall then come and see you and tell you how marvellously the Master has designed His work after Him and what remarkable utterances He has pronounced with regard to the future of the Cause . . .[6]

On 5 December Edward Hall wrote to Shoghi Effendi expressing his appreciation for Shoghi Effendi's letter, which had given the friends spiritual strength during such a time of sorrow:

Your noble letter uplifted us all and renewed our strength and determination; for if you could gather yourself together and rise above such grievous sorrow and shock, and comfort us, we, too, must do no less . . .[7]

In his diary letter to Dr Ḥakím of 8 December, Dr Esslemont wrote that Shoghi Effendi had remained in Bournemouth until the previous day, when he had received a cable from the Greatest Holy Leaf urging him to return. Thereupon, Shoghi Effendi left for London to see if arrangements could be made for an earlier passage. Dr Esslemont states that Shoghi Effendi was, at times,

... very sad and overcome with grief, but on the whole he kept up very bravely, and gradually, the conviction that, although the bodily presence was removed, the Spirit of the Beloved was as near, as powerful and as accessible to us as ever, seemed to revive his strength and hope. We had a small meeting of friends on Sat. evening, and the usual weekly meeting on Sunday evening, and at both he spoke with real power.[8]

Florence Pinchon, an early believer, describes the inspiring words Shoghi Effendi shared with the friends during the meeting in Bournemouth:

Even in such distressful circumstances he sought, like the Master, to cheer and encourage us. We must not consider the smallness of our numbers. To illustrate, he related the story of how a very small, bent and wrinkled old woman asked Abdu'l-Baha's permission to introduce her three sons. Whereupon three tall stalwart young men came forward and stood around her. 'Behold', exclaimed the Master smilingly, to the believers present, 'from how tiny an acorn these mighty oaks have sprung!'[9]

According to Isobel Slade, Shoghi Effendi was in London on 8 December 1921. Miss Grand had invited Mrs Slade to her flat that evening. It was a solemn occasion. The friends bade farewell to Shoghi Effendi who was leaving for Haifa with Lady Blomfield to be present for the reading of 'Abdu'l-Bahá's Will. Here are Mrs Slade's recollections of that evening:

I was particularly impressed by this very young man, whom I saw for the first time. He seemed dazed and bewildered with sadness. It was late evening and the room was very heated but he wore an overcoat. He was asked if he would not like to remove it. He replied that when he set out for England his grandfather had told him always to wear it in winter.[10]

E. C. Forster, a British believer who had met Shoghi Effendi during this period, described a meeting of Shoghi Effendi with the friends in Chelsea. The impression retained by Mrs Forster was 'that of a very grave young figure who moved quietly and with great dignity among the assembled friends'.[11]

Owing to difficulties with his passport, Shoghi Effendi could not leave as soon as he wished. He sent a cable to Haifa informing the Greatest Holy Leaf that he could not arrive until late December. 'He sailed on 16 December, accompanied by Lady Blomfield and Rouhangeze, and arrived in Haifa by train at 5.20 P.M. on 29 December from Egypt where his boat from England had docked.'[12]

A few days after his arrival in the Holy Land, Shoghi Effendi heard the provisions of the Master's Will read to him:

> O my loving friends! After the passing away of this wronged one, it is incumbent upon the Aghṣán (Branches), the Afnán (Twigs) of the Sacred Lote-Tree, the Hands (pillars) of the Cause of God and the loved ones of the Abhá Beauty to turn unto Shoghi Effendi – the youthful branch branched from the two hallowed and sacred Lote-Trees and the fruit grown from the union of the two offshoots of the Tree of Holiness, – as he is the sign of God, the chosen branch, the Guardian of the Cause of God, he unto whom all the Aghṣán, the Afnán, the Hands of the Cause of God and His loved ones must turn . . .
>
> The sacred and youthful branch, the Guardian of the Cause of God, as well as the Universal House of Justice to be universally elected and established, are both under the care and protection of the Abhá Beauty, under the shelter and unerring guidance of the Exalted One (may my life be offered up for them both). Whatsoever they decide is of God. Whoso obeyeth him not, neither obeyeth them, hath not obeyed God; whoso rebelleth against him and against them hath rebelled against God; whoso opposeth him hath opposed God; whoso contendeth with them hath contended with God; whoso disputeth with him hath disputed with God; whoso denieth him hath denied God; whoso disbelieveth in him hath disbelieved in God; whoso deviateth, separateth himself and turneth aside from him hath in truth deviated, separated himself and turned aside from God.[13]

An inscription written by Shoghi Effendi for Professor G. Struve

BALLIOL COLLEGE,
OXFORD.

Sunday

My dear Sitárih Khánum:—

We had a delightful gathering at Lady B.'s the night after I met you & I read to the friends the Tablet of the Master with regard to the 'Save the Children Fund.' I am herewith enclosing the Tablet as well as the article on the Mashriqu'l-Adhkár, which you were so kind as to lend them both to me.

I shall send you my version of the Arabic Hidden Words & the Epistle to Queen Victoria as soon as they are ready

and I hope also to have the pleasure of receiving any remarks or corrections you may desire to make with regard to them.

Zia'u'lláh has expressed the wish of having facsimile copies of the original Tablet printed & distributed together with your article enclosing the translation of it in English & Russian. I am therefore transcribing the Tablet & condensing it in one page written in a very minute & artistic Persian fashion & will send it to Zia'u'lláh for reproduction. With kind regards & best wishes

Yours very sincerely
Shoghi

Letter from Shoghi Effendi to Lady Blomfield from Balliol College

Balliol men, 1919–1920, photograph taken on the steps of the Main Hall. Shoghi Effendi is in the group on the left (see opposite page)

Shoghi Effendi among students at Balliol College (detail)

Shoghi Effendi with Bahá'ís in Manchester, October 1921

Left to right, from the back: Albert Joseph, John Craven, Jim Birch, Sam Joseph, H. Jarvis, Rebecca Hall, Lucy Hall, Mrs Heald, Mrs Chessell, Jeff Joseph, Olive Jarvis, Mrs Hoferer, Mrs Birch, Nora Crossley, Jas Chessell holding Helen, Shoghi Effendi, Edward T. Hall, Ḍíá'u'lláh Aṣgharzádih, Mr Heald, Norman Craven, Mrs Craven, Harold Taylor, Edward P. Hall, Ronald Craven, Mabel Chessell

In Manchester with the three Joseph brothers

Balliol, Oxford,
Nov. 1. 1921

My dearest Dr. Esslemont:—

I have been of late extremely busy with my work & hope to give soon the final touch to my rendering of the Hidden Words.

I enclose my version of the Lah-ráját & Queen Victoria's Epistle which you may keep for yourselves & trust you will be pleased with their general style & presentation.

What a difficult task Translation is! The more you work on it the more difficult it appears. There is simply no end to it, you can go on perfecting the art ad infinitum. My only ambition however at present is to achieve a certain measure of success by improving on the previous translations & if I attain this aim I am fully satisfied.

Yours most affectionately
Shoghi

I hear from home that an electric plant has been installed at each of the Holy Shrines & electric light has been supplied to the interior as well as the vicinity of the Sacred Tombs.

Letter from Shoghi Effendi to Dr John Esslemont, 1 November 1921

BALLIOL COLLEGE.
OXFORD.
Nov. 22.

My dear brother:—

I was so touched by your letter & am so glad to know that the Master really has so refreshed your soul & restored to our fold your child. I have seen of late numerous in my visits, persons many travellers & have been to Mr. Hall my vision of Queen Victoria's faith—which is replete with most vital & significant counsels, so recently made by this holy & distinguished lady.

If you have not yet formed the desire to consult it from Mr. Hall as it is in my opinion one of the most outstanding & emphatic pronouncements of 'Abdu'l-Bahá on world affairs.

I am enclosing for all of you extracts, some new & some old, in the course of my readings at the Pensions on the movement. I have also with me something invaluable on the Cause by the well-known orientalist & critic & professor. I shall also later send you a review of the movement which I read some time ago as one of the leading societies in Oxford.

Meantime I wish you from all my most spiritual devotional in your lives, in your meetings, in your collective ac-
tivities, to the promising & potent centre of the Cause in Manchester. I shall not fail to ask from the Master in my most supplication his fervent & pious regard regarding your reference in your letter. It has pleased him so much to hear of you all & I am sure your beautiful faith alone will make you worthy of the Great Trust he reposes in you.

With my loving attempts to Mr. Craven & all the friends yours in His Service,
Shoghi.

Letter from Shoghi Effendi to John Craven, 22 November 1921, one week before the passing of 'Abdu'l-Bahá

Shoghi Effendi, Guardian of the Bahá'í Faith, 1922

PART IV

At the World Centre

19

The Beloved Guardian

When the Will and Testament of 'Abdu'l-Bahá was read, it became clear to all the believers that the centre of the Cause of God was Shoghi Effendi. This was the wish of the Master and the Will of God. The young Shoghi Effendi, now confronted with great responsibilities, submitted to the will of his beloved Master and accepted to take charge of the destiny of the Cause of God. This meant leaving behind the painstaking tasks of learning academic facts and of perfecting his command of English in the great intellectual centre of the west. Shoghi Effendi assumed the challenges of an office that required of him a far greater degree of discipline and commitment, a field of service for which his entire past was but a divinely ordained preparation.

This chapter surveys a few highlights of the work of the Guardian during the span of 36 years, so short and yet so eventful. We who are close enough to the period of the Guardianship to have lived during Shoghi Effendi's days, to have received his stirring communications, his soul-inspiring directives, to have had the great blessing of attaining his presence – we cannot comprehend what God has wrought through His noble scion, His beloved Chosen Branch of the tree of holiness. We live in a time that is too close to his days to fully appreciate Shoghi Effendi or to gain an adequate perspective of the significance of a mission thrust upon him since time immemorial, a mission which was prophesied by the great prophet Isaiah:

> And there shall come forth a rod out of the stem of Jesse, and a Branch shall grow out of his roots: And the spirit of the Lord shall rest upon him, the spirit of wisdom and understanding, the spirit of counsel and might, the spirit of knowledge and of the fear of the Lord; And shall make him of quick understanding in the fear of the

PRELUDE TO THE GUARDIANSHIP

Lord ... and he shall smite the earth with the rod of his mouth, and with the breath of his lips shall he slay the wicked ... The wolf also shall dwell with the lamb, and the leopard shall lie down with the kid; and the calf and the young lion and the fatling together; and a little child shall lead them.[1]

That little child, Shoghi Effendi, the grandson of 'Abdu'l-Bahá, the apple of His eye, was now given the mantle of the Guardianship of the Cause of God.

Retrospect

This beloved grandson of 'Abdu'l-Bahá, in whose eyes and bearing was imprinted the sign of God, had undergone the most thorough preparation for the high office he was destined to assume after the passing of the Master, a preparation that had lasted all through his childhood and youth.

Although he had actively participated in student social activities at Oxford and earlier, and was remembered by his contemporaries for his eagerness, cheerful disposition, laughter and high spirits, Shoghi Effendi had experienced, throughout his student years, a series of circumstances that were difficult and often painful. During his childhood, he had attended a French Jesuit school in Haifa he did not like; neither had he liked the French school he had attended in Beirut. When the Master invited him to join His entourage on the North American teaching trip, he was prevented from making that exciting trip in the company of his beloved grandfather.

During his college years, the perilous days when Palestine was involved in the world war and the life of 'Abdu'l-Bahá was in great danger, he had continued his studies away from the Master. When the war was over, he had thrown himself into the difficult, laborious and all-consuming task of translation, transcription and correspondence. In his zeal to serve the Master he had exhausted his physical energies, requiring him to leave the land of his beloved for rest in a sanatorium in Paris. Alone in Paris, he had undergone treatment and, submissive to a strong inner urge and to the wish of the Master to pursue his further education at Oxford, he had proceeded to England to perfect his English in order to render a worthy service to the Cause of God.

At Oxford he had endured painful experiences associated with his registration and had struggled with the inner anxiety of having to learn so much in so short a time to justify his remoteness from the Holy Land. And while engaged in acquiring the knowledge he felt he needed, he was robbed of the presence of his beloved Master.

The pain this radiant youth suffered we can never comprehend. The agony of his separation from the Master during his childhood and youth, and especially immediately before the passing of the Master, none can fathom. And now that the Will and Testament of the Master was made known, Shoghi Effendi faced infinitely greater challenges.

The Task before the Guardian

Among the entire family of the Master, including his own brothers and sisters, the only person who genuinely welcomed Shoghi Effendi's appointment as the Guardian of the Cause of God and stood behind him was the Greatest Holy Leaf, the sister of 'Abdu'l-Bahá. Many felt that, owing to their seniority, they were in a position to give advice and counsel to the young Guardian. Such individuals, with petty minds and shallow faith, had forgotten the power of God's revelation and that self-serving ideas have no place in the Cause of God. They failed to realize that the Cause of God would not be corrupted and manipulated by self-interest.

The burden Shoghi Effendi bore in having so much to study in so short a time was insignificant compared with the overwhelming responsibilities he now faced as the Guardian. Before him lay an array of difficult tasks, all to be accomplished in a short span of time.

The vast majority of the writings of Bahá'u'lláh and 'Abdu'l-Bahá, their Tablets, epistles and books, were not yet adequately translated. Bahá'u'lláh's vision that 'all that dwell on earth' would soon 'be enlisted' under the 'banners of light'[2] that welcomed Him as He set foot in 'Akká towards the Most Great Prison, was far from reality. Those holy souls whom Bahá'u'lláh had promised during His last days would be raised up to bring victory to His Cause were few in number or had not yet been born. The mighty institutions that would facilitate the coming into the Cause of the masses of humanity and which would usher in the Kingdom of God on earth were barely established. The understanding of the believers worldwide of the station of the Báb, Bahá'u'lláh, the Master and the Guardian was inconsistent. The vision of how the

Cause of God would emerge out of the chaos of a decadent age to exert its healing influence on humanity was blurred. There was only a small band of believers in the East and West who, though devoted to the Cause, were unprepared to minister to the dire needs of an ailing humanity. And not least, the army of light marshalled by the Guardian faced bitter opposition from both old and new Covenant-breakers and fierce attacks by the external enemies of the Cause.

After a few months, Shoghi Effendi's physical condition declined. He needed rest. He retired to the mountains of Switzerland for two periods to recuperate and the Greatest Holy Leaf performed prescribed duties on his behalf during his absence. After his much-needed rest, the Guardian returned to the Holy Land ready to discharge his responsibilities, to fulfil the promise of God recorded in Isaiah, and to execute the divine Will for humanity.

What transpired during the period of his Guardianship is the exhilarating story of the operation of the divine Will.

Translation and Transliteration

While he was in England, the Guardian had already translated several of the major Tablets of Bahá'u'lláh. The Persian Hidden Words and the Tablet of Visitation had been completed in the winter of early 1921. The Súriy-i-Haykal, the Tablet to the Kings, the Arabic Hidden Words, the Epistle to Queen Victoria, the Tablets of Ṭarázát and Bishárát, the Epistle to Napoleon III and the Epistle to the Shah of Iran, had been translated in the spring and summer of 1921.

The beloved Guardian finalized these translations and completed several others, including the Will and Testament of 'Abdu'l-Bahá, during the period that followed his assumption of the mantle of Guardianship. His translations of the writings of Bahá'u'lláh such as the *Kitáb-i-Íqán*, the *Epistle to the Son of the Wolf* and other Tablets continued one after the other.

To familiarize the Western believers with the station of the Báb and to make them aware of the early history of the Cause, the Guardian took on the task of translating parts of Nabíl's immortal narrative. But his was not merely a translation; it was a phenomenal work integrating in its footnotes the vast collection of essays, articles and letters written by travellers and orientalists of earlier generations, which the beloved

Guardian had assembled or discovered during his studies in the Bodleian Library at Oxford.

The transliteration of the Persian and Arabic names had hitherto been inconsistent in English Bahá'í literature, such as *Star of the West*. Shoghi Effendi adopted a standardized method of transliteration which he used in *The Dawn-Breakers* to help the believers of all lands with the Persian and Arabic names of individuals and places that fill the pages of this book.

Building the Foundations of the World Order of Bahá'u'lláh

Concurrent with his translation work, and in conformity with the Will and Testament of 'Abdu'l-Bahá, the charter for the World Order of Bahá'u'lláh, the Guardian directed the attention of the Bahá'í world during the years 1921 to 1937 to the World Order of Bahá'u'lláh. In letters written during the period 1921–1937, he explained the principles and structure of the Administrative Order. He developed the constitutional structure of local and national spiritual assemblies – the fundamental institutions that would usher in the World Order – clarified their relationships with the community of the believers and elucidated the manner of their election and operation. He emphasized that the Administrative Order is the channel through which the spirit of God would flow, that the Bahá'ís must be ever watchful lest 'the means supersede the end' – lest too much attention to the details of the administration deter them from its spirit.

In particular, during the period 1929 to 1936 the beloved Guardian wrote seminal letters describing the characteristics of the World Order of Bahá'u'lláh. His conviction of the uniqueness of that World Order, as explained in these letters, was awe-inspiring. Having been thoroughly immersed at Oxford in understanding the forces that advance the evolution of the social order, having studied logic, political economy and political science, social and industrial questions, and economic history in that great centre of learning, having become familiar with the many schemes devised by the great statesmen of the world, he saw the inadequacy of human systems and schemes based on special interests and was certain that despite the best efforts of the world's statesmen, nothing short of the Revelation of Bahá'u'lláh could address the needs of an ailing humanity.

PRELUDE TO THE GUARDIANSHIP

In November 1931 he gave the Bahá'í world the gift of this clear understanding in a significant letter entitled 'The Goal of a New World Order', in which he introduced the vision of the emergence of a federated and united humanity against the backdrop of a war-weary world immersed in chaos and confusion.

> Dearly-beloved friends! Humanity, whether viewed in the light of man's individual conduct or in the existing relationships between organized communities and nations, has, alas, strayed too far and suffered too great a decline to be redeemed through the unaided efforts of the best among its recognized rulers and statesmen – however disinterested their motives, however concerted their action, however unsparing in their zeal and devotion to its cause. No scheme which the calculations of the highest statesmanship may yet devise; no doctrine which the most distinguished exponents of economic theory may hope to advance; no principle which the most ardent of moralists may strive to inculcate, can provide, in the last resort, adequate foundations upon which the future of a distracted world can be built.
>
> No appeal for mutual tolerance which the worldly-wise might raise, however compelling and insistent, can calm its passions or help restore its vigour. Nor would any general scheme of mere organized international cooperation, in whatever sphere of human activity, however ingenious in conception, or extensive in scope, succeed in removing the root cause of the evil that has so rudely upset the equilibrium of present-day society. Not even, I venture to assert, would the very act of devising the machinery required for the political and economic unification of the world – a principle that has been increasingly advocated in recent times – provide in itself the antidote against the poison that is steadily undermining the vigour of organized peoples and nations.
>
> What else, might we not confidently affirm, but the unreserved acceptance of the Divine Programme enunciated, with such simplicity and force as far back as sixty years ago, by Bahá'u'lláh, embodying in its essentials God's divinely appointed scheme for the unification of mankind in this age, coupled with an indomitable conviction in the unfailing efficacy of each and all of its provisions, is eventually capable of withstanding the forces of internal

disintegration which, if unchecked, must needs continue to eat into the vitals of a despairing society. It is towards this goal – the goal of a new World Order, Divine in origin, all-embracing in scope, equitable in principle, challenging in its features – that a harassed humanity must strive.[3]

To help the believers understand that the civilization toward which Bahá'u'lláh's teachings impel mankind will not emerge from mere adjustments to the existing order, the beloved Guardian gave the Bahá'í world the vision that what the world will witness will be 'an organic change in the structure of present-day society, a change such as the world has not yet experienced':

> Let there be no mistake. The principle of the Oneness of Mankind – the pivot round which all the teachings of Bahá'u'lláh revolve – is no mere outburst of ignorant emotionalism or an expression of vague and pious hope. Its appeal is not to be merely identified with a reawakening of the spirit of brotherhood and good-will among men, nor does it aim solely at the fostering of harmonious cooperation among individual peoples and nations. Its implications are deeper, its claims greater than any which the Prophets of old were allowed to advance. Its message is applicable not only to the individual, but concerns itself primarily with the nature of those essential relationships that must bind all the states and nations as members of one human family. It does not constitute merely the enunciation of an ideal, but stands inseparably associated with an institution adequate to embody its truth, demonstrate its validity, and perpetuate its influence. It implies an organic change in the structure of present-day society, a change such as the world has not yet experienced. It constitutes a challenge, at once bold and universal, to outworn shibboleths of national creeds – creeds that have had their day and which must, in the ordinary course of events as shaped and controlled by Providence, give way to a new gospel, fundamentally different from, and infinitely superior to, what the world has already conceived. It calls for no less than the reconstruction and the demilitarization of the whole civilized world – a world organically unified in all the essential aspects of its life, its political machinery, its spiritual aspiration, its trade and finance, its script

and language, and yet infinite in the diversity of the national characteristics of its federated units.[4]

On 8 February 1934 the Guardian gave the Bahá'í world a superb gift, one that was needed to clarify once and for all the inconsistent views among the believers about the stations of the central figures of the Faith and their relationship to the Administrative Order. In this marvellous document, entitled 'The Dispensation of Bahá'u'lláh', he shared the references from the writings of the Báb and Bahá'u'lláh about the station of Bahá'u'lláh. He expounded on the 'greatness, the inconceivable greatness' of the Revelation of Bahá'u'lláh, and referred to the promises that have been fulfilled by Him as 'Jehovah', the 'Lord of Hosts', the 'Father'. Yet, to prevent any confusion in the minds of the believers about the relationship of the Manifestation of God with the divine essence, he clarified that the 'divinity attributed to so great a Being and the complete incarnation of the names and attributes of God in so exalted a Person should, under no circumstance be misconceived or misinterpreted'. He explained that the

> human temple that has been made the vehicle of so overpowering a Revelation must . . . ever remain entirely distinguished from that 'innermost Spirit of Spirits' and 'Eternal Essence of Essences' – that invisible yet rational God Who . . . can in no wise incarnate His infinite . . . Reality in the concrete and limited frame of a mortal being.[5]

Further, in this letter the Guardian clarified the twofold station ordained by the Almighty for the Báb, explaining that

> the greatness of the Bab consists primarily, not in His being the divinely appointed Forerunner of so transcendent a Revelation, but rather in His having been invested with the powers inherent in the inaugurator of a separate religious Dispensation, and in His wielding, to a degree unrivalled by the Messengers gone before Him, the scepter of independent Prophethood.[6]

Having clarified the stations of the twin Manifestations, the Guardian explained the unique station of 'Abdu'l-Baha, Who, moving in a sphere of His own and holding a rank radically different from that of the Author and the Forerunner of the Baháʼí Revelation . . . forms together with them what may be termed the Three Central Figures of a Faith that stands unapproached in the world's spiritual history. He towers, in conjunction with them, above the destinies of this infant Faith of God from a level to which no individual or body ministering to its needs after Him, for no less a period than a full thousand years, can ever hope to rise.[7]

As to his own station, the Guardian made it clear that although he is

> overshadowed by the unfailing, the unerring protection of Baháʼuʼlláh and of the Báb, and however much he may share with ʻAbduʼl-Bahá the right and obligation to interpret the Baháʼí teachings, he remains essentially human and cannot . . . arrogate to himself . . . the rights, the privileges and prerogatives which Baháʼuʼlláh has chosen to confer upon His Son.[8]

Two years after sending this letter, the Guardian felt it necessary to give the Baháʼí World a glimpse of the world commonwealth of Baháʼuʼlláh, a document that surveyed fifteen years since the passing of the Master. Entitled 'The Unfoldment of World Civilization', it examines 'the forces of disintegration which batter at the fabric of a travailing society'.[9] It was in this letter that the Guardian introduced a theme he would expound eight years later: the twofold process that would bring to a climax the forces transforming our planet:

> A twofold process, however, can be distinguished, each tending, in its own way and with an accelerated momentum, to bring to a climax the forces that are transforming the face of our planet. The first is essentially an integrating process, while the second is fundamentally disruptive. The former, as it steadily evolves, unfolds a System which may well serve as a pattern for that world polity towards which a strangely-disordered world is continually advancing; while the latter, as its disintegrating influence deepens, tends to tear down, with increasing violence, the antiquated barriers that seek to block humanity's progress towards its destined goal. The constructive process stands associated with the nascent Faith

of Bahá'u'lláh, and is the harbinger of the New World Order that Faith must erelong establish. The destructive forces that characterize the other should be identified with a civilization that has refused to answer to the expectation of a new age, and is consequently falling into chaos and decline.[10]

After describing the evidences of the signs of moral downfall, the collapse of Islam, the deterioration of Christian institutions, and the breakdown of political and economic structures, the beloved Guardian envisions the world commonwealth of Bahá'u'lláh emerging from the realization of the unity of the human race. Here are the opening themes from that remarkable vision:

> The unity of the human race, as envisaged by Bahá'u'lláh, implies the establishment of a world commonwealth in which all nations, races, creeds and classes are closely and permanently united, and in which the autonomy of its state members and the personal freedom and initiative of the individuals that compose them are definitely and completely safeguarded. This commonwealth must, as far as we can visualize it, consist of a world legislature, whose members will, as the trustees of the whole of mankind, ultimately control the entire resources of all the component nations, and will enact such laws as shall be required to regulate the life, satisfy the needs and adjust the relationships of all races and peoples . . . The economic resources of the world will be organized, its sources of raw materials will be tapped and fully utilized, its markets will be coordinated and developed, and the distribution of its products will be equitably regulated.[11]

As a result of these and other communications during the period 1921–1937, the Bahá'í community learned about the World Order of Bahá'u'lláh, its forerunner, its author, its architect, the processes that humanity would go through on the path of its realization, and a picture of its future state. The Guardian had thereby established the basic elements – the administrative machinery of the Cause and the necessary embryo of the future World Order of Bahá'u'lláh. The embryo would need to grow, develop, evolve and mature within the womb of the mighty administrative institutions Bahá'u'lláh Himself has created.

The emphasis on administration and group decision-making was hard for many star teachers of the Faith to understand. A few could not accept the authority of the local spiritual assemblies, and lost their faith. The majority, however, forfeited their will to the will of the institutions, and stayed firm in the Covenant. They realized that the authority of the local and national assemblies was undeniable, even when such institutions were in their infancy.

Executing the Divine Teaching Plan

Referring to the Tablets of the Divine Plan, revealed by the Master to the North American Bahá'í community (including Canada), as the charter for the worldwide expansion of the Cause, the beloved Guardian initiated the first Seven Year Plan for that community in 1937. He reminded the believers of the distinction and primacy conferred upon them by the Master, and inspired them to safeguard that primacy by arising to fulfil the goals of that Plan.

One year later, the Guardian gave the North American Bahá'í community an illuminating and momentous document, a book-length letter entitled *The Advent of Divine Justice* in which he reiterated the Will of God for that community, portrayed the role it was destined to fulfil in the spiritual transformation of the planet, praised the devoted souls who had rendered sacrificial services to the Cause, conferred upon its members the distinction of being the spiritual descendants of the Dawn-Breakers of an heroic age, explained the challenges the friends of God would have to overcome and outlined the spiritual prerequisites required for success in fulfilling their responsibility of spiritual leadership among all nations. He gave them as his special gift a soul-stirring selection from the ocean of Bahá'u'lláh's matchless utterance to inspire their hearts and comfort their souls. This immortal document, which has been and will continue to be a frame of reference for North America for decades and centuries to come, will continue to serve as both the diagnosis and the remedy for its social ills.

Just over two years later, at the height of World War II, the Guardian gave to the Bahá'í communities 'throughout the West' yet another significant document, a second book-length letter entitled *The Promised Day is Come* in which he provided an overview of the operation of the Divine Will in the social affairs of humanity. In this letter, which was a further development of the letter he had sent the believers in the West eight years earlier, he explained that the maladies afflicting humanity must be viewed as the interposition of providence. He stated that a tempest of unprecedented violence was sweeping the face of the earth, that no one except the followers of Bahá'u'lláh could comprehend whence it came and where it was leading. He attributed the turmoil engulfing the human race and the sufferings resulting from it as consequences of humanity's dismissal of the revelation sent by God to heal the sickness with which it was afflicted. The closing passage of the letter offers a remarkable analogy summarizing the central theme of the book and bears witness to the eloquence evident in all of the Guardian's writings:

> Not ours, puny mortals that we are, to attempt, at so critical a stage in the long and checkered history of mankind, to arrive at a precise and satisfactory understanding of the steps which must successively lead a bleeding humanity, wretchedly oblivious of its God, and careless of Bahá'u'lláh, from its calvary to its ultimate resurrection. Not ours, the living witnesses of the all-subduing potency of His Faith, to question, for a moment, and however dark the misery that enshrouds the world, the ability of Bahá'u'lláh to forge, with the hammer of His Will, and through the fire of tribulation, upon the anvil of this travailing age, and in the particular shape His mind has envisioned, these scattered and mutually destructive fragments into which a perverse world has fallen, into one single unit, solid and indivisible, able to execute His design for the children of men.
>
> Ours rather the duty, however confused the scene, however dismal the present outlook, however circumscribed the resources we dispose of, to labour serenely, confidently, and unremittingly to lend our share of assistance, in whichever way circumstances may enable us, to the operation of the forces which, as marshalled and directed by Bahá'u'lláh, are leading humanity out of the valley of misery and shame to the loftiest summits of power and glory.[12]

In this magnificent book, which will serve as a beacon of light amidst the gloom associated with trials and ordeals that will continue to engulf humanity during the dark years ahead, the Guardian explained that the sufferings meted out to the children of men serve a dual purpose

– as the punishment of God because of His justice, and the purging of humanity because of His love. Consistent with this theme, the Guardian further developed the Bahá'í view of the unfolding of dual and concurrent processes in human history – the destructive process associated with the rolling up of the old order, and the constructive process identified with the birth and growth of the World Order of Bahá'u'lláh.

> We are indeed living in an age which, if we would correctly appraise it, should be regarded as one which is witnessing a dual phenomenon. The first signalizes the death pangs of an order, effete and godless, that has stubbornly refused, despite the signs and portents of a century-old Revelation, to attune its processes to the precepts and ideals which that Heaven-sent Faith proffered it. The second proclaims the birth pangs of an Order, divine and redemptive, that will inevitably supplant the former, and within Whose administrative structure an embryonic civilization, incomparable and world-embracing, is imperceptibly maturing. The one is being rolled up, and is crashing in oppression, bloodshed, and ruin. The other opens up vistas of a justice, a unity, a peace, a culture, such as no age has ever seen. The former has spent its force, demonstrated its falsity and barrenness, lost irretrievably its opportunity, and is hurrying to its doom. The latter, virile and unconquerable, is plucking asunder its chains, and is vindicating its title to be the one refuge within which a sore-tried humanity, purged from its dross, can attain its destiny.[13]

These twin gifts of the Guardian, *The Advent of Divine Justice* and *The Promised Day is Come*, served to deepen the Bahá'ís in the West and enabled them to gain a more profound sense of their mission amidst the confusion and darkness in humanity's most devastating war.

The North American Bahá'í community completed the Seven Year Plan in victory, and at its end in 1944 celebrated the centenary of the declaration of the Primal Point, the Báb. On this occasion, the Guardian gave the Bahá'í community yet another gift of love, a book of unsurpassed eloquence and of significant content covering the first one hundred years of the Faith of Bahá'u'lláh. This historical account, so full of heroism, so replete with evidence of the noblest demonstration of self-sacrifice the world has ever seen, so fraught with acts of barbarism and brutality toward the infant Faith of God and the inevitable culmination of such acts in the victory of that Cause – this historical account must convince every unbiased reader of the mysterious power latent in this revelation that continues to shape the destinies of the human race. The Guardian's closing paragraph to this outstanding work, *God Passes By*, will inspire generations of believers:

> Whatever may befall this infant Faith of God in future decades or in succeeding centuries, whatever the sorrows, dangers and tribulations which the next stage in its world-wide development may engender, from whatever quarter the assaults to be launched by its present or future adversaries may be unleashed against it, however great the reverses and setbacks it may suffer, we, who have been privileged to apprehend, to the degree our finite minds can fathom, the significance of these marvellous phenomena associated with its rise and establishment, can harbour no doubt that what it has already achieved in the first hundred years of its life provides sufficient guarantee that it will continue to forge ahead, capturing loftier heights, tearing down every obstacle, opening up new horizons and winning still mightier victories until its glorious mission, stretching into the dim ranges of time that lie ahead, is totally fulfilled.[14]

The Expansion of the Cause

The expansion of the Cause continued after the first Seven Year Plan through a series of national plans in Great Britain, Germany, Iran and other countries, including the first international teaching plan, which enlisted the cooperation of five national communities in the Africa Project of 1950–52. These plans, including the second Seven Year Plan for the American believers, spanned the period 1944 to 1953 and centred on the teaching of the Cause to the diverse peoples in new territories and on the establishment of Bahá'í administrative institutions.

During the momentous years when the plans were in progress, the Guardian communicated with each national community, reminding it of its high destiny, inspiring the believers to higher levels of service, and appealing in soul-inspiring language to every adherent of the Cause of God not to allow the precious opportunities of the hour to be irretrievably lost. Here are a few examples of the Guardian's appeals:

Once again – and this time more fervently than ever before – I direct my plea to every single member of this strenuously labouring, clear-visioned, stout-hearted, spiritually endowed community, every man and woman, on whose individual efforts, resolution, self-sacrifice and perseverance the immediate destinies of the Faith of God, now traversing so crucial a stage in its rise and establishment primarily depends, not to allow, through apathy, timidity and complacency, this one remaining opportunity to be irretrievably lost.[15]

Appeal to members of the community so privileged, so loved, so valorous, endowed with such potentialities to unitedly press forward however afflictive the trials their countrymen may yet experience . . . however onerous the tasks still to be accomplished, until every single obligation under the present Plan is honourably fulfilled . . .[16]

The prizes within reach of this community are truly inestimable. Much will depend on the reaction of the rank and file of the believers to the plea now addressed to them with all the fervour of my soul.

To act, and act promptly and decisively, is the need of the present hour and their inescapable duty. That the American Bahá'í community may, in this one remaining field, where so much is at stake, and where the needs of the Faith are so acute, cover itself with a glory that will outshine the splendor of its past exploits in the far-flung territories of the globe, is a prayer which I never cease to utter in my continual supplications to Bahá'u'lláh.[17]

As a result of these and other appeals of the Guardian and the response of the friends, the teaching plans initiated by him ended in victory and the message of God was spread to the diverse elements of humanity. Local and national spiritual assemblies were established and consolidated. By 1953, the number of national spiritual assemblies had reached twelve. In that year, the Bahá'í communities throughout the world celebrated the centenary of the occasion in the Síyáh-Chál of Tehran when Bahá'u'lláh received the first intimation of the revelation that was to flood His person and flow from His Supreme Pen for a period of nearly 40 years.

Two other events coincided with this centenary celebration. The first was the dedication of the Mother Temple of the West, the Bahá'í House of Worship in Wilmette, and the second was the announcement by the beloved Guardian of the commencement of a ten-year long world spiritual crusade to conquer the hearts of men.

The Ten Year Crusade involved the entire Bahá'í world. It called for the cooperation of all twelve National Spiritual Assemblies as well as the believers in all lands, 'be they in active service or not, of either sex, young as well as old, rich or poor, whether veteran or newly enrolled'.[18] This Crusade would culminate in the first Bahá'í World Congress in 1963, and would celebrate the centenary of the declaration of Bahá'u'lláh in the Garden of Riḍván.

The response of the believers of the East and the West to this plan of their beloved Guardian was overwhelming. Within the short span of one year the majority of the virgin territories that constituted the pioneering goals for this plan were filled. By October 1957 the number of countries, territories and islands in which the Cause of God had penetrated had reached 254.[19]

Building the City of God

This was not all. Whilst executing the Divine Plan of the Master, the Guardian paid careful attention to the provisions of another charter for the new World Order, the Tablet of Carmel in which Bahá'u'lláh refers to the City of God, prophesied in the scriptures of the past, a City that would be raised on Mount Carmel to serve as the seat of His dominion, from which the signs and evidences of His revelation, His laws and ordinances would flow to all nations and embrace all humanity.

The Guardian meticulously raised the superstructure of the Shrine of the Báb in whose vicinity he laid to rest the sacred remains of the Greatest Holy Leaf, the sister of 'Abdu'l-Bahá. Adjacent to this holy spot, the Guardian raised monuments for Navváb, the wife of Bahá'u'lláh; the Purest Branch, Mírzá Mihdí, the brother of 'Abdu'l-Bahá; and Munírih Khánum, the wife of 'Abdu'l-Bahá. Years later he conceived the idea of a far-flung arc embracing these resting-places.

On this arc, he explained, would be raised the mighty institutions that would administer the Cause of God at its spiritual centre, thus uniting both the spiritual and administrative elements of the Faith of

God on the same holy mountain. Shoghi Effendi completed the construction of the first of these structures, the Archives building, at a spot closest to the Shrine of the Báb.

The Guardian applied the same level of attention to beauty, excellence and execution of detail to all the holy places in 'Akká. He purchased, restored and beautified the holy sites where the Blessed Beauty had passed His days. This included the Mansion of Bahjí and its surroundings, the Riḍván Garden, Mazra'ih and the House of 'Abbúd.

Defending the Faith against External Attacks

As the Faith marched forward under the guidance of the Guardian, the Bahá'í community suffered repeated attacks by its enemies, particularly in Iraq, Egypt and Iran.

In Iraq the House which had been occupied by Bahá'u'lláh for nearly the entire period of His exile in that country, which had been acquired by Him and had been ordained as a place of pilgrimage, was unlawfully seized by the Shí'í community.

In Egypt, the fanaticism of the local inhabitants of a village in the district of Beba precipitated shameful acts by its notary, authorized by the Ministry of Justice, who demanded that the Muslim wives of three Bahá'ís be divorced from them. The grounds for such an absurd judgement was that these individuals had abandoned Islam after their legal marriages as Muslims had been registered.

In Iran, the cradle of the Faith, the persecution of the believers reached a climax towards the end of the Guardian's ministry when a premeditated campaign was launched over the air, from the pulpit and through the press, aimed at the extermination of the Bahá'í community. The disgraceful acts that emerged from this campaign were directed not only towards innocent believers but also against Bahá'í properties. The House of the Báb, ordained by Bahá'u'lláh as the most important place of pilgrimage in the cradle of the Faith, was twice desecrated, the dome of the central Bahá'í administrative headquarters was demolished, and other Bahá'í administrative headquarters throughout the provinces were seized and occupied.

The believers who were victims of persecution endured these difficulties with radiant acquiescence. Their Guardian, however, while deeply saddened by the events, took steps to avert the crises and the suffering by appealing to the world's highest tribunals. In each of these situations the Guardian directed the Baháʼí community to seek justice through the court systems. Hence, the Baháʼí case in Iraq was considered in successive tribunals including the Court of Appeal in Iraq and finally the League of Nations. The Baháʼí case in Egypt was considered by the Appellate religious court of Beba, and won for the Faith the acknowledgement of its status as an independent religion. The Baháʼí case in Iran was brought to the attention of that country's highest authorities as well as to the Secretary-General of the United Nations and the President of the Social and Economic Council.

These repeated crises abated, the Cause of God emerged triumphant and stronger through the ordeals, and the Baháʼí community established a method of confronting attacks on its members or its institutions. The community demonstrated its resolve to continue its fight against persecution and injustice through the agencies of the international community.

Protecting the Covenant

Nor was this all. The Guardian, persistently and painstakingly, purified the Faith from those who broke the Covenant, who for 65 years tried unsuccessfully every possible scheme to cause a rift within the community of the Most Great Name. By the time of Shoghi Effendi's passing, this band of faithless relatives of Baháʼu'lláh and ʻAbdu'l-Bahá had attempted repeatedly to undermine the authority of the Guardian. By appealing to authorities, by claiming rights of inheritance, by spreading false rumours and accusations against the Head of the Faith, by seizing the key to the Shrine of Baháʼu'lláh, and by continuing to occupy the Mansion of Bahjí, these misguided opponents of the Faith of God inflicted severe blows on the body of the Cause and saddened the radiant heart of the Guardian. Yet, despite these attacks and temporary setbacks, the Cause of God continued its onward march, purified and stronger than before, along its destined course. It was the Will of God that His Covenant remain intact in order to serve, in the fullness of time, as the axis for the oneness of humankind.

By the time of the Guardian's passing, all the holy sites in the Holy Land legally belonged to the Baháʼí community and were permanently secured from the influence of the Covenant-breakers. The Shrine of

Bahá'u'lláh and the Mansion of Bahjí had been returned, restored and beautified. The buildings occupied by Covenant-breakers adjacent to the Mansion had been acquired and demolished. The gardens surrounding the most sacred spot on earth, the Ḥaram-i-Aqdas, the Qiblih of the people of Bahá, had been designed and filled with beautiful plants and flowers under the Guardian's close supervision.

Preparing the Transition to the Future

Finally, the Guardian, faithful to the provisions of the Will and Testament of 'Abdu'l-Bahá, the charter of the World Order of Bahá'u'lláh, was inspired to break with his past practice of elevating only posthumously certain devoted believers to the exalted rank of Hand of the Cause of God. He selected from among the living faithful friends a number of dedicated believers and elevated them to this exalted rank. These souls responded with utmost devotion and loyalty to the call of their beloved, ready to sacrifice their all at his command. The Guardian inspired, nurtured, trained and developed this small band of heroic and self-sacrificing servants, who numbered 27 at the time of his passing, and entrusted them with the stewardship of the Cause of God, confident that they would be capable of keeping the ship of the Cause on its predestined course and of steering it to its ultimate destination. These are the words of Shoghi Effendi announcing the appointment of the last contingent of the Hands of the Cause just before his passing:

> So marvellous a progress, embracing so vast a field, achieved in so short a time, by so small a band of heroic souls, well deserves, at this juncture in the evolution of a decade-long Crusade, to be signalized by, and indeed necessitates, the announcement of yet another step in the progressive unfoldment of one of the cardinal and pivotal institutions ordained by Bahá'u'lláh, and confirmed in the Will and Testament of 'Abdu'l-Bahá, involving the designation of yet another contingent of the Hands of the Cause of God, raising thereby to thrice nine the total number of the Chief Stewards of Bahá'u'lláh's embryonic World Commonwealth, who have been invested by the unerring Pen of the Centre of His Covenant with the dual function of guarding over the security, and of insuring the propagation, of His Father's Faith.[20]

The intrepid souls who had now been given the chief stewardship of the World Commonwealth of Bahá'u'lláh, became aware as never before of their responsibility to protect the Cause. They could not fathom the wisdom behind such a responsibility while the Guardian was still on this earthly plane. It became clear to them only after the passing of their beloved. It was this body of steadfast and dedicated Hands of the Cause who, though heart-broken and bewildered by the passing of their beloved leader, stood firm at the hour of trial, and refused, except in a single case,[21] to act in any manner that would inflict the slightest harm on the unity of the Faith of God. Theirs was the supreme challenge of preserving the integrity of the Cause whose custodianship had been entrusted to them, a challenge which they met superbly. It was they who set the unprecedented example of handing over the reins of authority of a Bahá'í world community undivided and undeterred, to that infallible institution, the Universal House of Justice, in 1963. It was these god-intoxicated heroes and heroines, the legacy of the Guardian, who then strove until their last breath to sacrifice their energies, their talents, their time, their all at the threshold of the newly elected institution whose birth they had helped facilitate.

Transition

Just before the mid-point of the Ten Year Plan, on the cold autumn day of 4 November 1957, the Blessed Beauty called Shoghi Effendi to His other dominions. The ark of salvation, the ship of the Cause of God, would continue its course under the leadership of its chief stewards toward its ultimate destiny. The Guardian, having finished his work on this earthly plane, ascended to the realms beyond, leaving an army of bereaved, yet dedicated and determined souls to complete the execution of the processes which he had set in motion, processes whose unfoldment would engage hundreds of future generations.

The Beloved Guardian's Legacy

The writings of the Faith had been translated by Shoghi Effendi into the most perfect English, conveying accurately and forcefully the revelation of God to the western world. Future translations would follow his standard.

The salient features of the Faith's history, laws and promised World Order had been delineated and fully explained in a language and in a style comprehensible to the believers of both the East and the West. A standardized transliteration system of the names associated with the heroes and heroines of the Apostolic Age and the sacred spots associated with that age had been adopted and references to such names in later Bahá'í literature would follow the same system.

The principles of the Administrative Order of the Faith, rooted in the writings of Bahá'u'lláh and in the Will and Testament of 'Abdu'l-Bahá had been fully explained to the believers. The machinery of the administration had been reared by him and used to accomplish seemingly impossible tasks. Now that he was gone, this Administrative Order would continue to grow to maturity following the standard he had set, without the slightest deviation from principle.

The pattern for executing the Divine Plan of the Master for the conquest of the hearts of men had been established, and incremental plans for the execution of that plan had been executed. Future plans would evolve from this example.

The standard for the buildings on Mount Carmel, mighty institutions that would serve as the beacon of light in a dark and confused world, had been established. The gardens surrounding those buildings had been laid out, the style of architecture that would express the spirit of those buildings had been defined through the first structure, the Archives building. The remaining part of the edifices of the arc would be constructed in the same style.

The claims of the Covenant-breakers to Bahá'í properties had been greatly reduced and most rights transferred to the institutions of the Faith. The influence of the Covenant-breakers was overshadowed by the onward march of the Cause of God, and the community was purified from their poison. The responses to those who would attempt to violate the Covenant in the future would follow the same standard.

Looking back at the life and work of Shoghi Effendi, we see how marvellous was his handiwork, how beautiful his design, and how perfect the sequence of events that transpired after his assumption of the mantle of Guardianship. The longing of his heart, so often expressed to the friends while he was a student at Oxford – that he properly equip himself for service to the Cause – had been fulfilled.

Mansion of Love

Shoghi Effendi, that young Oxford student who became the Guardian of the Cause of God, left a legacy which will astound generations of humanity. No words of ours can adequately convey the admiration, love, gratitude, and devotion which are his due. The words that befit him best are his own, written on the passing of the Greatest Holy Leaf:

> Whatever betide us, however distressing the vicissitudes which the nascent Faith of God may yet experience, we pledge ourselves, before the mercy-seat of thy glorious Father, to hand on, unimpaired and undivided, to generations yet unborn, the glory of that tradition of which thou hast been its most brilliant exemplar.
>
> In the innermost recesses of our hearts . . . we have reared for thee a shining mansion that the hand of time can never undermine, a shrine which shall frame eternally the matchless beauty of thy countenance, an altar whereon the fire of thy consuming love shall burn forever.[22]

APPENDIX

Shoghi Effendi's Address to the Oxford University Asiatic Society, February 1921[1]

It is with no sense of trepidation that I approach this vast subject – but rather with an overwhelming 'embarras de richesses' that I feel confronted, in attempting to condense even the salient features of my theme in so small a compass.

For a movement which appeared at one of the most economically restless, politically agitated, yet scientifically remarkable periods in European History; born in the midst of what historians have maintained to be one to the most corrupt regions within the pale of civilization; launched by the son of a woolmonger in Shiraz, who as a herald after chastisement, humiliation, and confinement was in the prime of his youth made the target of two volleys of fire, and to whose eloquence, piety, fervour, simple and courteous manners, such as Le Comte de Gobineau and even some of his sworn adversaries testified; whose founder, though a wealthy Persian Nobleman, discarded all his riches, was thrown for months in the Imperial, subterranean dungeons with the mark of adamantine chains indelibly graven upon his neck; was four times exiled, fifty years in captivity and though deserted, yea denounced by his closest kinsmen, promoted his cause while in chains and fetters, apostrophising and rebuking the very monarchs in whose prison he lay; foretold with his power of clairvoyance the fall of Napoleon III on the one hand and the 'lamentations of Berlin' and the tragic end of the 'king' on the other – such a movement appears to be well worth consideration and serious study. Furthermore, a movement that displays a history stained with the blood of a noble army of martyrs, the record of whose agonies finds hardly any parallel in the annals of the persecution of the world, which in a country whose men however degraded were still decidedly superior to its women, produced a heroine whose career the Marquess Curzon of Kedleston has characterized as 'one of the most affecting episodes in Modern History'; 'whose appearance in any country and any age', the well known orientalist Edward Granville Browne regards as 'a rare phenomenon in a country like Persia, a prodigy almost a miracle'; and whom the graphic pen of Le Comte de Gobineau portrays as 'the most extraordinary manifestation of this most extraordinary movement'; a movement which unlike others through its present vigorous spirit has dispelled every apprehension that time might damp its zeal, which advocates the solution of the economic problems of the age and has exerted a profound influence on Persian literature, not to mention Persian intellect and character, a movement which is in process of linking the East with the West removing all barriers of race, creed and colour and that exemplified by the conduct of its devotees during the racial riots that convulsed the American States after the war as well as by the privations undergone by the poorer followers of the faith in Persia in their contributions towards a 'Temple of worship' to be erected across the Atlantic by their co-workers whom they have never seen or known; a movement that has despite the relentless opposition of a firmly entrenched hierarchy of fanatic clergy that has hurled at it its charges of Nihilism, Anarchism, and Pantheism, and, in the absence of proper means of publicity, of systematic raising of funds and propaganda organisation has invaded almost the whole of Persia and has within less than a century notwithstanding the growing materialism of the west, and the coalition of two of the most autocratic potentates of the East to suppress it, burst the confines of Persia, crossed the limits of Asia, affected Europe, penetrated Africa down to its southernmost limit, enrolled within its ranks thousands in the American continent, reaching northwards to the Esquimaux of Alaska, and southward to the foot of the Andes, spread over the mid-Pacific Islands, and thence reaching the Antipodes, has encircled Japan, Burma, and Afghanistan, and is today stretching out to Indo-China – that such a cause should be treated as negligible, I for one, refuse to believe.

It was the year 1844 towards the middle of the 19th century, 'a century of revolution – revolution in Government, revolution in the material conditions and circumstances of life, and revolution in knowledge and in mental outlook' that still another revolution in religious

SHOGHI EFFENDI'S ADDRESS TO THE OXFORD UNIVERSITY ASIATIC SOCIETY

ideas and conceptions was introduced in the city of Shiraz by young scion of the house of the Prophet of Islam, 'Ali Muhammad by name, who appeared heralding the advent of 'Him who shall usher in a new and golden age' and, with religion as his lever effect peacefully and steadily the regeneration of mankind. The century which witnessed the birth of such a movement was indeed a most remarkable one.

But brilliant as the whole century was, yet the decade in which the movement was born was one of the darkest yet the most potent and significant of all. The years 1840 to 1850 were years of great political upheaval that convulsed the whole of Central Europe signalising the rising spirit of liberalism and of nationality that had been so long kept in check by the reactionary dictators of Europe, the sovereigns of the Holy Alliance. And not only was the decade politically an agitated one but it was also socially [as] a result of the failure of the Chartist movement a period of restlessness and disillusionment. At such a time this young Persian Seer appeared in the very heart of the Orient, the home of world religions and in the native land of Zoroaster, whose religion the Orientalist James Darmesteter, describes as 'the last reflex of the ideas which prevailed in Toran during five centuries which preceded and the seven which followed the Birth of Christ, a period which gave to the world the Gospels, the Talmud and the Quran exerting much influence on each of the Movements which produced or proceeded from those three books, lending much to the Rabbis, and much to Muhammad'.

Nor was the East, and particularly Persia in a state of peace and harmony, though its unrest was of a different character. Wrapped in the gloom of denominational, sectarian, racial, and social fanaticism, the whole land afforded a scene of a most deplorable nature. It is no exaggeration to state that if by some unfortunate mishap a Jew's garment brushed that of a Muhammadan the latter would immediately discard, nay destroy it, deeming it polluted. Similarly the Muslim, far from drinking from a cup that had touched the lips of a Nazarene, would, regarding it defiled, smash it to pieces.

In the midst of such circumstances, abroad and at home, this young Siyyid 'Ali Muhammad who was born on 20th of October 1819 declared his mission. His father, a wool-merchant in Shiraz, died during his infancy and the child was brought up under the care of his maternal uncle. Destined as he was originally for commercial pursuits, his early youth was spent in partnership with his uncle at Shiraz after which he independently conducted business in the town of Bushire, on the Persian Gulf. But trade and commerce were not in keeping with his thoughts and nature which were given from the very beginning to religious meditation, and pious devotion. He spent therefore, the main part of his life prior to the declaration of his mission, in religious pursuits, in prayer, and in contemplation. His extreme piety and virtue, his liberal ideas, the charm of his manner, the beauty of his person, the sweetness of his disposition, and the eloquence of his words kindled a spirit of devotion in the hearts of his entourage; and when on May 23rd 1844 he laid claim to be the *Bab* meaning 'gate', the 'forerunner' of him who should purify the perverted religions and sects of his time from fanaticism, and establish the promised era of peace, and of freedom, it was felt by those whose conduct was the very negation of such ideals that the death-knell of their supremacy was being sounded. The young prophet, appearing among people predominantly Islamic in faith, started with the Quran in his hand, to denounce the life, the conduct, the precepts, and even the dogmas of the corrupt clergy which he asserted and proved to be in flagrant contradiction to the Book. He preached a cause that was subversive to the interests of the notorious leaders of Islam but not to the pristine teachings of Islam itself. Soon after his declaration, when he under-took the pilgrimage to Mecca, the few yet zealous followers he had left behind started to arouse the masses from their lethargy. Thirsty souls who for years had chafed under the baleful influence of an orthodox clergy began to read his writing, and that in the uttermost secrecy, for the alarmed body of the Ulamas, Mullas, Siyyids, and Mujtahids were beginning to incite the Government to come to their aid in their campaign of suppression. On his return from pilgrimage, his cause which had already advanced rapidly, was given a fresh impetus and this made the problem of quenching its fire imperative and extremely difficult. He was arrested, summoned before councils, interrogated, cross-examined, threatened, humiliated, bastinadoed, and after a period of confinement in the citadels of Maku, and Chihriq he was suspended in public square of Tabriz and made the target of two volleys of bullets. To the clergy and the Government, it seemed the extinction of this threatening fire; but the martyring of a Siyyid, of the lineage of the prophet while inspiring the few votaries of the faith with a new ardour and courage, attracted the attention of the whole country and gave the faith a much greater publicity. Meanwhile a grave incident took place which afforded a fresh opportunity to the clergy, to press their demand to supplement the martyrdom of the leader with the extermination of his followers, precipitating that period of persecution which the history of the Movement so remarkably exhibits.

Two years after the martyrdom of the Bab, two unbalanced impassioned Babis in desperate grief at the loss of their master, fired at the *Shah* with a fowling-piece. They were instantly seized and put to death, that being the signal for and an episode of the long period of persecution that followed. The clerical element pressed now their contention that the movement aimed at the overthrow of all forms of Government, that it had political motives and that the only remedy would be a wholesale massacre of its adherents. Government and clergy, hand in hand, after this attack on the person of the Sovereign, started on a campaign of unspeakable atrocities. Every conceivable means of torture which the cruel tyrant of the East and his torture-mongers could devise was mercilessly used to force the adherents of the faith to apostatize. But all was in vain.

Among countless cruelties a woman, to whom I have already alluded, of highly esteemed clerical parentage, endowed with great beauty, intellect, tenacity and eloquence without meeting the Bab responded to his call. In spite of the dissuasion of her kindred she deserted rank, family, renown and to the great scandal of her devout yet bigoted kinsmen discarded the veil, and preached far and wide the gospel of love, of justice and of purity to men and women alike and was at last strangled by a colored slave, thrown into a pit and stoned.

No wonder that Lord Curzon referring to these abominable acts comments as follows: –

> Tales of magnificent heroism illumine the blood stained pages of Babi history. Ignorant and unlettered as many of its votaries are and have been, they are prepared to die for their religion, and fires of Smithfield did not kindle nobler courage than has met and defied the more refined torture-mongers of Tihrán. Of no small account then must be the tenets and creed that can awaken in its followers so rare and beautiful a spirit of self-sacrifice.

Among the many victims of such tortures, thrown into the Imperial dungeons of he *Shah* was a young Persian nobleman, Husayn 'Ali by name and later entitled Bahá-u-lláh (the splendour of God) the first-born son of one of he foremost ministers of the Crown, born on November 12, 1817, and belonging to an ancient family of Nur in the province of Mazindaran which in later times returned the most prominent councillors and ministers of he *Shah*. Immediately the call from S͟hiráz had reached the capital, Tihran, he responded and disregarding honour and public esteem, and giving up high rank and riches, (the latter being soon after pillaged and plundered), he enlisted himself as a resolute advocate of the cause braving all peril, extending his help, morally and materially to the early propagators of the faith and gaining thereby notoriety in the sight of the clergy and the Government. His open and undaunted behaviour in diffusing the liberal ideas of the martyred chief made him, to be suspected of complicity in the attempt on the life of the *Shah* and, thus arrested, was thrice imprisoned, his last confinement lasting four months in the subterranean dungeons of the *Shah*. There was no doubt that he had, through his talents, personality, eloquence, courage, and indomitable will, earned the admiration of his co-workers and was gradually coming up to be regarded as the unquestioned leader of a cause that was left leaderless. The farewell scenes, marked with confidence and imbued with gaiety and transport that ensured around him, whenever the executioner would penetrate the darkness of the gaol and summon one or two of the languishing Babi prisoners to the gallows; the moving word of patience, of courage and hope which he uttered to the departing companions; the leading role he took in the songs of exultation and the hymns of praise and in the other manifestations of joy that cheered the damp and foul atmosphere of the prison; his persuasive tone in preaching the faith to the other inmates of the dungeon, the spirit of dignity and contentment which he evinced whenever a relaxation was effected or a gift bestowed by the *Shah* – all these made him, if spared, a promising figure in the future course of the Movement.

Soon, however, his complicity being disproved, he was released and as his personal prestige had immensely increased he was shortly after, as a result of an agreement with the Ottoman and Persian Governments, exiled with his family and some of his companions on October 14, 1852 to Baghdad, in Mesopotamia. The handful of exiles, thus severed apart from the remnants of the faith in Persia, stayed there about eleven years, two of which Bahá-u'-lláh spent in solitude and meditation in the mountains of Sulaymanniah in the province of Kurdistan. Friends, even his family knew not his whereabouts. When he returned, he declared, at first to his entourage and later to the world his mission as 'him whom the Bab had expressly foretold'.

The declaration of Baha'u'lláh again filled the Government as well as the clergy with alarm and through the persistent efforts of the Persian ambassador at Constantinople, authorization from Sultan 'Abdu'l'Aziz was obtained for the transference of the growing community to the Turkish Capital – a spot distant from Persia and remote from the resort of pilgrims. This transference was effected on May 1st 1863. His second exile, followed after four months by a third to Adrianople, and its consequent remoteness from the land of its birth, where the few adherents that remained were threatened with extinction by the persecutions that still raged intermittently all over the land, did not arrest the onward march of the Cause. On the contrary, during his sojourn in Adrianople and during the early years of his incarceration in the prison of Acre, Baha'u'lláh, in his writings through a series of detailed epistles addressed himself to Queen Victoria, Napoleon III, the Pope Pius IX, the Czar of Russia, the Emperor of Germany, the Sultan of Turkey, the Shah of Persia, and the Presidents of the American Republics, revealing to them his mission, expounding his principles, admonishing them to rule with justice, praying for their guidance and enlightenment, reminding them of the Past, warning them of the Future and summoning them to disarm and to usher in the era of Universal Peace. By some these messages were received with admiration and respect [, by] others with indifference, and still others by derision and contempt. Queen Victoria, is reported to have remarked that if this Cause is of God it would stand, and if not no harm would result. She was assured a long and prosperous reign, while her influence in the abolition of slave traffic, her start towards democratic representative institutions, and her form of Government as constitutional monarchy were highly extolled.

These epistles as well as the vast amount of writings revealed at that time by the Pen of Baha'u'lláh filled again the Governments concerned with alarm, but increased the ardour of the adherents of the faith who were now in increasing numbers scattered throughout Persia, Mesopotamia and India. The Ottoman and Persian Governments, again in concert decided on the exile of the community for a fourth time to the

PRELUDE TO THE GUARDIANSHIP

distant penal colony of Acre in Syria, wherein political suspects, convicts, criminals of the worst types, brigands and highway robbers were strictly confined and hardly survived. Its climate was so unhealthy that it was referred to as a spot which if a bird flew over, it would instantly drop dead. When Bahá'u'lláh and his seventy companions were transferred to that remote colony reaching it on August 30, 1868, the Persian ambassador in Constantinople assured his Government in Tihran that the doom of the sect was sealed. Yet it was during the twenty-five remaining years of his life which he spent in the prison of Acre in a most insalubrious climate, the early part of which years was spent in utter privation, and strict confinement that his movement spread far and wide, that Europe, the Far East and later, America caught its spark, that his Book of Laws the 'Kitabu'-Aqdas' was revealed and his epistle to the Shah of Persia forwarded, that his predictions were fulfilled and that the number of his followers swelled from a mere handful of apprehensive exiles to almost a million and that in Persia alone.

About that time in the year 1890, Edward Granville Browne of the University of Cambridge, on the occasion of his visit to Acre and his meeting the Prisoner in his Mansion and Garden at Bahji wrote the following: –

> Of the culminating event of this my journey some few words at least must be said . . . Though I dimly suspected whither I was going, and whom I was to behold (for no distinct intimation had been given to me), a second or two elapsed ere, with a throb of wonder and awe, I became definitely conscious that the room was not untenanted. In the corner where the divan met the wall sat a wonderous and venerable figure, crowned with a felt head-dress of the kind called *taj* worn by *'dervishes'* (but of unusual height and make), round the base of which was wound a small white turban. The face of him on whom I gazed I can never forget, though I cannot describe it. Those piercing eyes seemed to read one's very soul; power and authority sat on that ample brow; while the deep lines on forehead and face implied an age which the jet-black hair and beard flowing down in indistinguishable luxuriance almost to the waist seemed to belie. No need to ask in whose presence I stood, as I bowed myself before One who is the object of a devotion and love which kings envy and emperors sigh for in vain.

A mild dignified voice bade me be seated, and then continued 'Praise be to God that thou has attained . . .Thou hast come to see a prisoner and an exile . . . We desire but the good of the world and the happiness of the nations; yet they deem us a stirrer up of strife and sedition worthy of bondage and banishment . . . That all nations should become one in faith and all men as brothers; that the bonds of affection and unity between the sons of men should be strengthened, that diversity of religion should cease, and differences of race be annulled – what harm is there in this . . . Yet so it shall be; these fruitless strifes, these ruinous wars shall pass away and the "Most Great Peace" shall come. Do not you in Europe need this also? Is not this that which Christ foretold? Yet do we see your kings and rulers lavishing their treasures more freely on means for the destruction of the human race than on that which would conduce to the happiness of mankind . . . These strifes and this bloodshed and discord must cease, and all men be as one kindred and one family . . . Let not a man glory in that he loves his country; let him rather glory in this, that he loves his kind . . .'

Such, so far as I can recall them, were the words which, besides many others, I heard from Baha. Let those who read them consider well with themselves whether such doctrines merit death and bonds and whether the world is more likely to gain or lose by their diffusion.

With the declaration of the Counter-revolution of 1909 and the deposition of Abdul Hamid, the long period of forty years' incarceration came to an end, and in the year 1911 'Abdu'l-Baha his appointed son set out for a four years' extensive travel to Europe and America proclaiming the cause of his father to Jews, Christians and Muhammadans alike, propounding its fundamental, social and religious principles to Atheists, Agnostics, Theodophists, Mormons, Quakers, Socialists, and followers of various other schools of thought, asserting in synagogues on purely historical grounds the validity of Christ's mission and his fulfilment and propagation of the Mosaic dispensation; proclaiming in mosques the fundamental unity underlying the religions of the past and establishing in Temples and Churches the truth of the Prophet's mission deriving scientific incontestable evidences from the Quran itself. Before starting on his Western journey he raised a stately Mausoleum for the

Bab on Mount Carmel, the 'Vineyard of God' in Palestine, whither the mutilated body of the harbinger of the Movement was borne from Tabriz, the scene of his martyrdom. He also enhanced the beauty and the stateliness of the Sacred Sepulchre of his father, which lies on the verdant plains of Acre, in the heart of a land unsurpassed in its religious traditions, hallowed to the Jew, the Christians and the Muslims alike.

Between these two hallowed shrines and in such a region dwells, free and in peace, at present, the aged leader of the faith, gathering around his table every night the American, the European, the African and the Asiatic and sending out unceasingly through his epistles and the many pilgrims who flock to his doors dynamic messages of love and of hope to a bleeding and weary world.

With regard to the teachings of the Movement its cardinal principle is the existence of One Supreme Being manifesting Himself like the revealing rays of the Sun in the burnished mirrors of Messengers and Prophets who at various times, have appeared, expounded the same truth, preached the same gospel, but garbed in every time in an attire that would conform with the understanding of their age. Hence the explanation of the various religious ordinances, and the diverse conceptions [of] the state of after life; should the peoples of the world, of whatever race, creed or colour seek truth diligently and with an unbiased mind, they will inevitably converge around the same centre for truth is one and indivisible. Thus the principle of the Oneness of mankind is established. Baha'u'llah addressing mankind says 'Of one tree are all ye the fruits, and of one Bough the leaves.' Diversity of colour and form should not lead to conflict but should as is the case with a bed of flowers of various scents, forms, and hues enhance the excellence and power of mankind. The exaltation of humanitarianism over patriotism expressed in the saying 'Let not man glory in that he loves his country, let him rather glory in this that he loves his kind'; the conception of the world as one home and mankind as one family; the establishment of the Parliament of man in the form of a comprehensive representative international assembly that shall equitably and peacefully adjust international dispute; drastic measures of disarmament consistent with national safety; the Ideal of Universal Peace to be realised not through human efforts exclusively but confirmed and guided by the Divine Spirit [:] these have been repeatedly expressed and emphasized by the Pen of Baha'u'llah in his epistles to the individuals, assemblies and sovereigns of the world. The equality in rights of men and women is proclaimed.

Mankind has two wings, one is woman, the other man. So long as the two wings are unequally developed the bird cannot fly. Hence the need for compulsory Universal education, with particular stress on the training of women as the mothers of the future on whom primarily will depend the direction and education of the coming generation. Religion is regarded as 'the supreme and mighty bulwark'. 'If the edifice of religion shakes and totters commotion and chance will ensue . . . for in the world of mankind there are two safeguards that protect man from wrong doing. One is the law which punishes the criminal, but the law prevents only the manifest crime and not the concealed sin; whereas the ideal safeguard, namely the Religion of God prevents both the manifest and the concealed crime.' Religion (and the term is used throughout to denote the true monotheistic form of religion) too would conform to reason and science, for both are but manifestations of Truth which is one and indivisible. Adoption of one universal tongue and script with the national tongue and script has been enjoined facilitating thereby international understanding and saving time and energy.

Another express provision in the teachings of the Movement is the institution of the House of Justice called the 'Baytu'l-'Adl'. Although the details touching its structure and operation have not yet been fully laid down yet the broad principles guiding its future activities has been established. Its duties are religious, educational, economic and political. Its different spheres of activity will be departmental, national and international. It is broadly speaking the nucleus of the Bahai State. Church and State thus far from being divorced from one another are harmonized, their interests are reconciled, are brought to co-operate for the same end, yet for each is reserved its special and definite sphere of activity. Indeed if one glances at the outstanding precepts of the Movement comprehensive and practical as they are, as the suppression of all dogmas, superstitions, religious organisations, rituals and verbal traditions, the abolition of priesthood, the discouragement of celibacy, the emphasis laid on deeds rather than words, the conception of labour as an act of worship, the belief that the criterion of every true living religion must be its conformity with reason and science and its aiming at the betterment of mankind, the body of its social and economic teachings which while denouncing force and violence and retaining the institution of private property seeks on one hand to infuse by its spirit a sense of justice and goodwill in both employer and workman alike and on the other provides the means whereby the status of the wage-earning class will be raised, – the details governing the institution of the Mashriqu'l-Adhkar – all these teachings go to show that religion far from being excluded from man's social life should on the contrary quite stabilize and protect it. The belief in the existence and the immortality of the soul; of its future reward and punishment; the condemnation of the life of the hermit and of all forms of austerities; the confession of sin to none but God; the repudiation of mendacity and idleness; the prohibition of all intoxicants; the necessity of cleanliness and the stress laid on piety, love, justice, service, pardon, steadfastness, co-operation, humility, these are among the features of its basic principles.

A concrete embodiment of the conception that faith and worship though essential are not sufficient in themselves but should be supplemented by social service is to be found in the institution of the Mashriqu'l-Adhkar, 'the Dawning-place of Praise,' a Temple of worship, to be provided if possible in every city and town, and open to all men and women irrespective of creed, colour, race, and language. Its adorning is to be simple and unostentatious, its prayer direct, simple in their wording and simply recited, the best hours for devotion being at dawn, then the state of nature and of human mind admirably lend themselves to prayer and meditation. But prayer does not constitute the only purpose of this Temple, for, various accessories such as hostels, asylums, hospitals, orphanages, elementary as well as advanced educational institutions, are to exemplify and embody the other essential element in worship namely social services.

The first of such temples has been built in what was before the Revolution an integral part of the Russian Czarist Empire, in the city of Ishqabad, Turkistan for the erection of which the East and West have amply contributed. The example has been followed by the Bahais in the United States, where soon the corner-stone of such a temple will be laid in the shores of Lake Michigan in the vicinity of Chicago. Contributions from their Persian, Hindu, Japanese, Burmese, English, French, German, Turkish, Armenian, Kurdish, Syrian, and Jewish Co-workers are pouring in and it is no exaggeration to state that when the work will reach its final consummation, it will be one of the most concrete and sublime embodiments of inter-religious, inter-racial, and inter-national brotherhood.

We see to-day the East after the convulsion of the Great War is alienated from the West in its customs, its traditions, its religion, its political standards, its conceptions of freedom and of civilization, its economic interests and its standard of living. Hardly any thing short of a fresh superhuman power, can bridge the chasm that is sundering today the two halves of humanity. And it is not much to say that wherever the spirit inculcated by this movement has penetrated, a bond of fellowship has originated that links as no human interest has so far proved to link, the East with the west.

In the capital of Persia, Tihran, where its torture-mongers have inflicted such atrocities and where the black shadow of religious sectarianism, and social fanaticism was so predominant, we see to-day in one home, around one table, Jews, Christians, Muslims, Zoroastrians, Persians, Arabs and Kurds associating in a spirit of real brother-hood, giving wherever an occasion has arisen their property, their comforts, yea their lives one for the other. Such a transformation in Persia was certainly a century ago inconceivable.

For the erection of the 'Temple of Worship' in the United States of America, the poor and needy adherents of the Faith in Persia have contributed to their utmost and with a spirit that deserves mention: –

Eye witnesses have reported that in the outlying province of Khorasan in a village consisting of thirty families – all fired with the spirit of the Movement and afflicted with poverty – a single rug is owned by a group of families and whenever an itinerant Bahai teacher would arrive the rug would be passed around from one house to another that it might provide partial comfort to the wayworn traveller. Living on barest bread, the father of each family would gather every day one or two handfuls of wheat and store them for the use of the expected teacher. Despite such misery they would manage to gather a penny or half a penny every day to be sent as contribution to the Temple in the United States. If they own two pence one of it is surely to go to the Temple. If they obtained a monthly pay of twenty Shillings, they purchase with it some wool to weave it into cloth and sell it for thirty Shillings reserving half of it as future capital while the other half is divided between the price of their daily bread and their contribution to the Mashriqu'l-Adhkar.

In conclusion it may be observed that many of these teachings have been advocated by past philosophers, poets, and prophets from the dawn of History till now, that they are in no wise new and original. But in return may I ask whether any of these ideals have been realised and these teachings enforced. Has Christianity as it stands to-day or Islam, Judaism, and other religious schools of thought achieved their aims? And if the movement has wherever it has shed its light, so far succeeded in that direction may we not hope that it may one day usher in that golden Millennium, the awaited Time embodied for the Jew in his promised Messiah, for the Christian in the second coming of Christ, for the Muslim in the return of the Mahdi (Christ), for the Gabr in the purification of the world and the annihilation of the Ahriman by the hand of the new Saviour Saoshyant, for the Hindu in the anticipation of hearing again the voice of the divine Krishna and to the Buddhist for the advent of the great fifth Buddha who will regenerate the world.

Bibliography

'Abdu'l-Bahá. *Selections from the Writings of 'Abdu'l-Bahá.* Haifa: Bahá'í World Centre, 1978.

Bahá'í World, The. Vols 1–12, 1925–54. RP Wilmette, Ill: Bahá'í Publishing Trust, 1980; vol. 13, Haifa: Bahá'í World Centre, 1970; vol. 14, Haifa: Bahá'í World Centre, 1974; vol. 15, Haifa: Bahá'í World Centre, 1976.

Bahá'u'lláh. *Tablets of Bahá'u'lláh Revealed after the Kitáb-i-Aqdas.* Haifa: Bahá'í World Centre, 1978.

— *Prayers and Meditations by Bahá'u'lláh.* Wilmette, Ill: Bahá'í Publishing Trust, 1938.

Balyuzi, H. M. *'Abdu'l-Bahá.* Oxford: George Ronald, 1971.

Blomfield, Lady. *The Chosen Highway.* London: Bahá'í Publishing Trust, 1940; RP Oxford: George Ronald, 2007.

Carless Davis, H. W. *A History of Balliol College.* Oxford: A. R. Mowbray & Co., 1963.

Commonwealth Universities Yearbook, vol. 3, 1994.

Dictionary of National Biography, 1901–1960. Oxford: Oxford University Press, 1971.

Gail, Marzieh. *Arches of the Years.* Oxford, George Ronald, 1991.

Hall, E. T. *Bahá'í Dawn: Early Days of the Bahá'í Faith in Manchester.* Manchester: Bahá'í Assembly, 1925.

Jones, John. *Balliol College Oxford: A Brief History and Guide.* Abingdon: Leach's, 1993.

Momen, Moojan. *Dr John Ebenezer Esslemont.* London: Bahá'í Publishing Trust, 1975.

Nabíl-i-A'ẓam. *The Dawn-Breakers: Nabíl's Narrative of the Early Days of the Bahá'í Revelation.* Wilmette, Ill: Bahá'í Publishing Trust, 1970.

Penrose, Stephen B. L. *That They May Have Life*. Princeton: Princeton University Press, 1941.

Rabbaní, Rúḥíyyih. *The Priceless Pearl*. London: Bahá'í Publishing Trust, 1969.

Randall-Winckler, Bahíyyih, and M. R. Garis. *William Henry Randall: Disciple of 'Abdu'l-Bahá*. Oxford: Oneworld, 1996.

Rutstein, Nathan. *Corinne True: Faithful Handmaid of 'Abdu'l-Bahá*. Oxford, George Ronald, 1987.

Shoghi Effendi. *Bahá'í Administration*. Wilmette: Ill: Bahá'í Publishing Trust, 1968.

— 'The Bahai Movement: A paper read by Shoghi Effendi at Oxford', in *The Dawn, A monthly Bahai Journal of Burma*, Vol. 1, Nos. 1–8 (September 1923–April 1924).). Rangoon: Syed Mustafa Roumie.

— *Citadel of Faith: Messages to America 1947–1957*. Wilmette, Ill: Bahá'í Publishing Trust, 1965.

— *God Passes By*. Wilmette, Ill: Bahá'í Publishing Trust, rev. edn 1974.

— *Messages to the Bahá'í World*. Wilmette, Ill: Bahá'í Publishing Trust, 1971.

— *The Promised Day Is Come*. Wilmette, Ill: Bahá'í Publishing Trust, rev. edn. 1980.

— *The World Order of Bahá'u'lláh: Selected Letters*. Wilmette, Ill: Bahá'í Publishing Trust, RP 1991.

Star of the West. RP Oxford: George Ronald, 1984.

Syrian Protestant College. *Student Union Gazette*, SPC (First Number, Nov. 1915). Available at: http://bahai-library.com.

Weinberg, Robert. *Lady Blomfield: Her Life and Times*. Oxford: George Ronald, 2012.

— *Ethel Jenner Rosenberg: The Life and Times of England's Outstanding Bahá'í Pioneer Worker*. Oxford: George Ronald, 1995.

Whitehead, O. Z. *Some Bahá'ís to Remember*. Oxford: George Ronald, 1983.

Who's Who, 1920.

Yazdi, Ali M. *Blessings Beyond Measure: Recollections of 'Abdu'l-Bahá and Shoghi Effendi*. Wilmette, Ill: Bahá'í Publishing Trust, 1988.

BIBLIOGRAPHY

Unpublished sources

American University of Beirut. College records.

— Jafet Library. Blatchford collection; Moore collection, available at: http://ddc.aub.edu.lb/projects/jafet/moore/.

Archives of the National Spiritual Assembly of the Bahá'ís of the United Kingdom. Copy of Shoghi Effendi's diary letters (typescript by Lucy Hall).

— Letters from individuals, various collections.

— Florence Pinchon. *Memoirs of Dr Esslemont.*

Author's collection. Letters from various individuals (see 'Notes and References' for details).

Balliol College, Oxford. College records.

St Catherine's College, Oxford. College records.

United States Bahá'í National Archives. Shoghi Effendi Collection, Pre-1922 letters.

Notes and References

Preface
1. Excerpts from Shoghi Effendi's diary are included here without editorial changes for punctuation, grammar or style, as it was considered important to show Shoghi Effendi's growing mastery of the English language, which it was his intention to perfect during his period of study at Oxford.
2. Letter from the Universal House of Justice to the author, 21 July 1967.
3. Letters from St Catherine's College and Balliol College to the author, 1 September 1993 and 25 August 1993.

Chapter 1: Childhood and Youth
1. Rabbaní, *The Priceless Pearl*, p. 4.
2. The date mentioned in *The Priceless Pearl* is the most reliable date as it appears to be consistent with several instances when Shoghi Effendi had to declare his age, although not all. The early registration forms at the Syrian Protestant College did not require a birth date, only the age of the student; it was only in 1917 that the registration forms began to require a birth date. This may be because a person's birthday was not given the great emphasis as it is in the West and many people born in the latter part of the 19th century and early part of the 20th century did not have any idea when they were born. My father was among them. He used to tell his family that the time of his birth was recorded in a volume that contained the sacred writings of the Faith, but that the book was lost. He chose 1 January 1904 as a close estimate because it was easy to remember.
3. Nabíl-i-A'ẓam, *Dawn-Breakers*, genealogy chart.
4. Quoted in Rabbaní, *The Priceless Pearl*, p. 5.
5. ibid. p. 4.
6. ibid. p. 17.
7. ibid. p. 9.
8. ibid.
9. According to Rabbaní, *The Priceless Pearl*, pp. 15–17, this school was located in Haifa.

PRELUDE TO THE GUARDIANSHIP

10. Interview with Dr Mo'ayyid, 1970.
11. Rabbaní, *The Priceless Pearl*, p. 17.
12. Yazdi, *Blessings Beyond Measure*, p. 50.
13. Rabbaní, *The Priceless Pearl*, p. 19.
14. Yazdi, *Blessings Beyond Measure*, pp. 51–3.
15. Rabbaní, *The Priceless Pearl*, pp. 19–20.
16. Interview with Dr Mo'ayyid, 1970.
17. Rabbaní, *The Priceless Pearl*, pp. 20, 24.
18. Quoted ibid. p. 21.
19. ibid.

Chapter 2: Syrian Protestant College (SPC)
1. Rabbaní, *The Priceless Pearl*, p. 17.
2. Interview with Dr Mo'ayyid, 1970.
3. College records, American University of Beirut, sent to the author by the university registrar.
4. This section on the history and background of the Syrian Protestant College is taken from Penrose, *That They May Have Life*.
5. ibid. p. 2.
6. ibid. pp. 8–10.
7. ibid. p. 29.
8. Rabbaní, *The Priceless Pearl*, p. 21.
9. ibid. p. 22.
10. Transcripts of Shoghi Effendi, sent to the author by the American University of Beirut.
11. College Records, American University of Beirut, sent to the author by the university registrar.
12. *Student Union Gazette*, SPC (1914–1915), pp. 28–30. Available at: http://bahai-library.com.
13. College Records, American University of Beirut, sent to the author by the university registrar.
14. Quoted in *The Bahá'í World*, vol. 13, p. 67.
15. USBNA, Shoghi Effendi Collection, Pre-1922 letters.
16. Quoted in *The Bahá'í World*, vol. 13, p. 67.
17. Penrose, *That They May Have Life*, p. 150.
18. USBNA, Shoghi Effendi Collection, Pre-1922 letters.
19. Penrose, *That They May Have Life*, p. 151.
20. ibid. p. 153.
21. USBNA, Shoghi Effendi Collection, Pre-1922 letters.
22. Transcripts of Shoghi Effendi, sent to the author by the American University of Beirut.

REFERENCES

23. College Records, American University of Beirut, sent to the author by the university registrar.
24. *Star of the West*, vol. 9, no. 9, p. 99.
25. Interview with Dr Mo'ayyid, 1970.
26. Yazdi, *Blessings Beyond Measure*, pp. 55–7.
27. Transcripts of Shoghi Effendi, sent to the author by the American University of Beirut.
28. *Student Union Gazette*, SPC (First Number, Nov. 1915), pp. 21–24. Available at: http://bahai-library.com.
29. Transcripts of Shoghi Effendi, sent to the author by the American University of Beirut.
30. College Records, American University of Beirut, sent to the author by the university registrar.
31. Penrose, *That They May Have Life*, p. 159.
32. College Records, American University of Beirut, sent to the author by the university registrar.
33. Rabbaní, *The Priceless Pearl*, pp. 25–6.
34. For the Moore collection see http://ddc.aub.edu.lb/projects/jafet/moore/.

Chapter 3: In the Service of the Master, Autumn and Winter 1918

1. Rabbani, *Priceless Pearl*, pp. 25–6.
2. See, for example, *Bahá'í Year Book*, vol. 1, pp. 12–15.
3. *Bahá'í World*, vol. 15, p. 431.
4. Momen, *Esslemont*, p. 10.
5. Archives of the National Spiritual Assembly of the Bahá'ís of the United Kingdom. See also *Star of the West*, vol. 9, no. 17, pp. 194–5.
6. *Star of the West*, vol. 10, no. 1, pp. 8–10.
7. ibid. vol. 9, no. 17, p. 196.
8. ibid. vol. 10, no. 1, p. 3.
9. ibid. vol. 9, no. 17, p. 197.
10. United States Bahá'í National Archives (USBNA), Shoghi Effendi Collection, Pre-1922 letters.
11. For example, Blomfield, *Chosen Highway*.
12. Diary of Shoghi Effendi, copy in the Archives of the National Spiritual Assembly of the Bahá'ís of the United Kingdom.
13. A slightly different version is recorded in Yazdi, *Blessings Beyond Measure*, p. 62.
14. *Star of the West*, vol. 10, no. 2, pp. 17–19 and vol. 10, no. 1, pp. 7–12.
15. ibid. vol. 10, no. 1, p. 11.
16. *Star of the West*, vol. 10, no. 1, pp. 3, 9, 13.

Chapter 4: In the Service of the Master, Early 1919

1. Diary of Shoghi Effendi, copy in the Archives of the National Spiritual Assembly of the Bahá'ís of the United Kingdom.
2. ibid.
3. Archives of the National Spiritual Assembly of the Bahá'ís of the United Kingdom.
4. *Star of the West*, vol. 9, no. 19, p. 223; vol. 10, no. 1, pp. 8, 13–14; vol. 10, no. 2, pp. 28–9, 338–40; vol. 10, no. 19, p. 340.
5. ibid. vol. 10, no. 3, p. 39.
6. ibid. vol. 10, no. 1, pp. 12–13; no. 2, pp. 29–32; no. 3, pp. 42–3; no. 7, p. 143.
7. Diary of Shoghi Effendi, copy in the Archives of the National Spiritual Assembly of the Bahá'ís of the United Kingdom.
8. *Star of the West*, vol. 10, no. 2, p. 31.
9. Diary of Shoghi Effendi, copy in the Archives of the National Spiritual Assembly of the Bahá'ís of the United Kingdom.
10. *Star of the West*, vol. 10, no. 3, pp. 40–41; no. 4, pp. 76–8; no. 7, pp. 136–7, 144.
11. Diary of Shoghi Effendi, copy in the Archives of the National Spiritual Assembly of the Bahá'ís of the United Kingdom.
12. *Star of the West*. vol. 9, no. 19, p. 220.
13. Diary of Shoghi Effendi, copy in the Archives of the National Spiritual Assembly of the Bahá'ís of the United Kingdom.
14. *Star of the West*. vol. 10, no. 1, pp. 10–11; no. 3, pp. 41–2; no. 4, pp. 79–80; no. 6, p. 110; no. 17, p. 316.
15. ibid. vol. 10, no. 2, p. 23.
16. *Star of the West*, vol. 10, no. 11, pp. 217–220; vol. 11, no. 3, pp. 48-54.
17. Later married to Ahmad Sohrab, the recipient of these diary letters, whom she divorced when he broke the Covenant.

Chapter 5: In the Service of the Master, Spring 1919

1. *Star of the West*, vol. 10, no. 5, p. 96; vol. 10, no. 9, p. 185.
2. ibid. vol. 10, no. 5, p. 96.
3. ibid. vol. 10, no. 3, p. 36.
4. ibid. pp. 43–4.
5. ibid. p. 44.
6. ibid. vol. 10, no. 4, p. 73.
7. ibid. vol. 10, no. 7, p. 143; vol. 10, no. 9, pp. 184–5.
8. ibid. vol. 10, no. 9, p. 184.
9. ibid. vol. 10, no. 6, p. 109.
10. ibid. vol. 10, no. 11, p. 221; vol. 10, no. 19, pp. 340–41.
11. ibid. vol. 10, no. 11, p. 221.

12. ibid. vol. 10, no. 8, p. 153.
13. ibid. vol. 10, no. 6, pp. 104–6.
14. ibid. vol. 5, no. 5, pp. 94–5.
15. USBNA, Shoghi Effendi Collection, Pre-1922 letters.
16. *Star of the West*, vol. 5, no. 5, pp. 94–5.
17. USBNA, Shoghi Effendi Collection, Pre-1922 letters.
18. *Star of the West*, vol. 10, no. 7, pp. 135–6.
19. ibid. vol. 10, no. 8, pp. 156–64.
20. USBNA, Shoghi Effendi Collection, Pre-1922 letters.
21. Archives of the National Spiritual Assembly of the Bahá'ís of the United Kingdom.
22. *Star of the West*, vol. 10, no. 8, p. 155.
23. ibid. p. 168.

Chapter 6: In the Service of the Master, Summer 1919

1. USBNA, Shoghi Effendi Collection, Pre-1922 letters.
2. *Star of the West*, vol. 11, no. 1, pp. 15–19.
3. ibid. vol. 10, no. 8, p. 165 (partial transcription; opening and closing transcribed from a copy of the original postcard).
4. Archives of the National Spiritual Assembly of the Bahá'ís of the United Kingdom.
5. USBNA, Shoghi Effendi Collection, Pre-1922 letters.
6. *Star of the West*, vol. 10, no. 12, p. 233; vol. 10, no. 14, p. 267.
7. Archives of the National Spiritual Assembly of the Bahá'ís of the United Kingdom.
8. *Star of the West*, vol. 10, no. 8, p. 155.
9. USBNA, Shoghi Effendi Collection, Pre-1922 letters.
10. *Star of the West*, vol. 10, no. 12, pp. 233–4, 236; vol. 10, no. 14, pp. 267–8, 272; vol. 10, no. 17, pp. 318–19.
11. ibid. vol. 10, no. 12, pp. 234–6; vol. 10, no. 13, pp. 250–51; vol. 10, no. 14, p. 268; vol. 11, no. 10, pp. 159–64, 166–8; vol. 11, no. 16, p. 276.
12. ibid. vol. 10, no. 13, p. 246; vol. 10, no. 14, pp. 268–70; vol. 10, no. 17, pp. 319–20; vol. 10, no. 18, pp. 329–30; vol. 11, no. 3, p. 54; vol. 11, no. 4, p. 76; vol. 11, no. 6, p. 104.
13. ibid. vol. 10, no. 13, p. 245 ; vol. 10, no. 19, pp. 339–40.
14. ibid. vol. 10, no. 13, p. 246 ; vol. 11, no. 5, p. 92; vol. 11, no. 10, p. 165, vol. 11, no. 14, pp. 240–43.
15. ibid. vol. 10, no. 17, p. 319 ; vol. 11, no. 16, pp. 277–8.
16. ibid. vol. 10, no. 14, pp. 270–71; vol. 10, no. 19, p. 342; vol. 11, no. 10, pp. 165–6.
17. ibid. vol. 10, no. 13, pp. 247–9.
18. ibid. vol. 10, no. 13, pp. 246–7.

PRELUDE TO THE GUARDIANSHIP

19. ibid. vol. 11, no. 16, p. 276.
20. ibid. vol. 10, no. 12, p. 236.
21. ibid. vol. 10, no. 18, pp. 329–30.
22. USBNA, Shoghi Effendi Collection, Pre-1922 letters.
23. ibid.
24. Diary of Shoghi Effendi, copy in the Archives of the National Spiritual Assembly of the Bahá'ís of the United Kingdom.
25. ibid.
26. ibid.
27. ibid.
28. ibid.
29. ibid.
30. ibid.
31. ibid.
32. ibid.
33. ibid.
34. ibid. This is the translation by Shoghi Effendi in his diary; the later authorized translation of the Tablet may be found in *Selections from the Writings of 'Abdu'l-Bahá*, no. 28, p. 57.
35. ibid. This is the translation by Shoghi Effendi in his diary; the later authorized translation of the Tablet may be found in *Selections from the Writings of 'Abdu'l-Bahá*, no. 17, pp. 35–7.
36. ibid.
37. ibid.
38. ibid.
39. ibid.
40. ibid.

Chapter 7: In the Service of the Master, Autumn 1919

1. USBNA, Shoghi Effendi Collection, Pre-1922 letters.
2. ibid.
3. ibid.
4. ibid.
5. Diary of Shoghi Effendi, copy in the Archives of the National Spiritual Assembly of the Bahá'ís of the United Kingdom.
6. ibid.
7. ibid.
8. ibid.
9. USBNA, Shoghi Effendi Collection, Pre-1922 letters.
10. Diary of Shoghi Effendi, copy in the Archives of the National Spiritual Assembly of the Bahá'ís of the United Kingdom.
11. ibid.

REFERENCES

12. ibid.
13. ibid.
14. *Star of the West*, vol. 8, no. 3, p. 37.
15. Diary of Shoghi Effendi, copy in the Archives of the National Spiritual Assembly of the Baháʼís of the United Kingdom.
16. ibid.
17. *Star of the West*, vol. 10, no. 19, p. 342; vol. 11, no. 16, pp. 278–80.
18. USBNA, Shoghi Effendi Collection, Pre-1922 letters.
19. ibid.
20. ibid.
21. Diary of Shoghi Effendi, copy in the Archives of the National Spiritual Assembly of the Baháʼís of the United Kingdom.
22. ibid.
23. ibid.
24. ibid.
25. ibid.
26. USBNA, Shoghi Effendi Collection, Pre-1922 letters.

Chapter 8: Last Months with the Master

1. Diary of Shoghi Effendi, copy in the Archives of the National Spiritual Assembly of the Baháʼís of the United Kingdom. Edna True had been serving in France with the Smith College Relief Unit during the war. This pilgrimage was to be the last of the many times Corinne True was in the presence of the Master.
2. ibid.
3. ibid.
4. ibid.
5. ibid.
6. ibid.
7. ibid.
8. ibid.
9. ibid.
10. ibid.
11. ibid.
12. *Star of the West*, vol. 10, no. 17, p. 306; also in Shoghi Effendi's diary.
13. Interview by Nathan Rutstein with Edna M. True, in Rutstein, *Corinne True: Faithful Handmaid of ʻAbduʼl-Bahá*.
14. For the Randalls' account of this pilgrimage see Bahíyyih Randall-Winckler and M. R. Garis: *William Henry Randall: Disciple of ʻAbduʼl-Bahá* (Oxford: Oneworld, 1996).
15. Diary of Shoghi Effendi, copy in the Archives of the National Spiritual Assembly of the Baháʼís of the United Kingdom.

16. ibid.
17. ibid.
18. Bahá'u'lláh, *Tablets*, p. 28.
19. Diary of Shoghi Effendi, copy in the Archives of the National Spiritual Assembly of the Bahá'ís of the United Kingdom.
20. ibid.
21. ibid.
22. ibid.
23. ibid.
24. ibid.
25. ibid.
26. ibid.
27. ibid.
28. ibid.
29. ibid.
30. ibid.
31. ibid.
32. ibid.
33. USBNA, Shoghi Effendi Collection, Pre-1922 letters.
34. ibid.
35. Momen, *Esslemont*, pp. 19–20.
36. Yazdi, *Blessings Beyond Measure*, p. 70.
37. ibid. p. 71.
38. *Star of the West*, vol. 11, no. 10, p. 166. This Tablet was retranslated for *Selections from the Writings of 'Abdu'l-Bahá*, no. 1.
39. *Star of the West*, vol. 11, no. 15, pp. 259–60; vol. 11, no. 18, pp. 306–8.
40. Momen, *Esslemont*, p. 20.
41. USBNA, Shoghi Effendi Collection, Pre-1922 letters.
42. ibid.

Chapter 9: Recuperation in Paris

1. Rabbaní, *Priceless Pearl*, p. 32.
2. Letter from the collection of Mr Z. Khadem.
3. *Bahá'í World*, vol. 14, p. 352. See also Gail, *Arches of the Years*, pp. 179–86.
4. Letter from the collection of Mr Z. Khadem.
5. Yazdi, *Blessings Beyond Measure*, pp. 72–3.
6. Letter from the collection of Mr Z. Khadem.
7. ibid.
8. Letter in St Catherine's College Office.
9. Archives of the National Spiritual Assembly of the Bahá'ís of the United Kingdom.
10. Yazdi, *Blessings Beyond Measure*, pp. 74–5.

REFERENCES

11. Archives of the National Spiritual Assembly of the Bahá'ís of the United Kingdom.
12. Letter from the collection of Mr Z. Khadem.
13. ibid.
14. Rabbaní, *Priceless Pearl*, pp. 11–13.

Chapter 10: Arrival in England

1. For an account of her life see Robert Weinberg, *Lady Blomfield : Her Life and Times* (Oxford : George Ronald, 2012).
2. After Lord Lamington's death, Lady Lamington sent the ring given to her husband by the Master to the National Spiritual Assembly of the Bahá'ís of Great Britain.
3. Letter from Shoghi Effendi, Archives of the National Spiritual Assembly of the Bahá'ís of the United Kingdom.
4. Archives of the National Spiritual Assembly of the Bahá'ís of the United Kingdom.
5. *Who's Who*, 1920.
6. Balyuzi, *'Abdu'l-Bahá*, p. 156.
7. Weinberg, *Ethel Jenner Rosenberg*, p. 173.
8. Letter in the Archives of the National Spiritual Assembly of the Bahá'ís of the United Kingdom. See also Weinberg, *Ethel Jenner Rosenberg*, pp. 173–4.
9. Letter in the Archives of the National Spiritual Assembly of the Bahá'ís of the United Kingdom.
10. This section on the history and background of Balliol College is taken from Carless Davis, *History of Balliol College*.
11. Carless Davis, *History of Balliol College*, p. 2.
12. ibid. pp. 6–9.
13. Letter from Shoghi Effendi in Persian, in the Archives of the National Spiritual Assembly of the Bahá'ís of the United Kingdom.
14. Jones, *Balliol College Oxford: A Brief History and Guide*, p. 8.
15. Carless Davis, *History of Balliol College*, p. 239.
16. ibid. p. 244.
17. *Dictionary of National Biography*, 1901–1960. See also Carless Davis, *History of Balliol College*, pp. 261–7. In 1922 Lindsay left Balliol to accept the post of Professor of Moral Philosophy at Glasgow but returned in 1924 as Master of the college upon the death of A. L. Smith. In 1935 he was appointed Vice-Chancellor of the University of Oxford.
18. Carless Davis, *History of Balliol College*, pp. 260–61.
19. *Who's Who*, 1920.
20. ibid.
21. Letter in the Archives of the National Spiritual Assembly of the Bahá'ís of the United Kingdom. See also Rabbaní, *Priceless Pearl*, pp. 32–3.

22. Quoted in Rabbaní, *Priceless Pearl*, p. 33.
23. Letter in the Archives of the National Spiritual Assembly of the Bahá'ís of the United Kingdom.
24. Balzuyi, *'Abdu'l-Bahá*, p. 356.
25. Esslemont letters in the Archives of the National Spiritual Assembly of the Bahá'ís of the United Kingdom.
26. Letter in the Archives of the National Spiritual Assembly of the Bahá'ís of the United Kingdom.

Chapter 11: Matriculation and Student Life at Oxford
1. Letter from A. D. Lindsay to J. B. Baker, collected by the present author from St Catherine's College.
2. Located in the centre of the city of Oxford.
3. *Commonwealth Universities Yearbook*, 1994, vol. 3.
4. Copy of letter in the present author's collection.
5. St Catherine's College records.
6. Ali Yazdi had been sent by the Master to Germany to prepare for his further education in the United States. The sum given to him by the Master was dwindling, and Ali was concerned about saving enough to make the trip.
7. Yazdi, *Blessings Beyond Measure*, pp. 80–82.
8. Jones, *Balliol College Oxford: A Brief History and Guide*, pp. 33–34.
9. This is based on the experience of the author during the academic years 1964–1968. The description of life at Oxford in this chapter reflects the conditions of the university in 1964, which were not very different from those in 1920.

Chapter 12: Michaelmas Term 1920
1. Adapted from Rabbaní, *Priceless Pearl*, p. 36.
2. Letter from Dr Esslemont to Luṭfu'lláh Ḥakím, Archives of the National Spiritual Assembly of the Bahá'ís of the United Kingdom.
3. Quoted in Rabbaní, *Priceless Pearl*, p. 37.
4. College records, St Catherine's College.
5. A form of greeting performed by Persian men.
6. Yazdi, *Blessings Beyond Measure*, pp. 82–3.
7. ibid. p. 83.
8. ibid. p. 85.
9. ibid. pp. 85–6.
10. Letter in the Archives of the National Spiritual Assembly of the Bahá'ís of the United Kingdom.
11. Inter-college correspondence, St Catherine's College.
12. Letter from Lindsay to Baker, St Catherine's College.

REFERENCES

13. Letter from Baker to Lindsay, St Catherine's College.
14. ibid.
15. Letter from Lindsay to Bailey, Balliol College.
16. Balliol College records.

Chapter 13: Hilary Term in Balliol

1. Jones, *Balliol College Oxford: A Brief History and Guide*, pp. 33–9.
2. Bursary files, Balliol College.
3. Letter from A. Boyce Gibson to the author, 3 May 1969.
4. Bursary files, Balliol College.
5. Quoted in Rabbaní, *Priceless Pearl*, p. 37.
6. Letter from Shoghi Effendi in Persian, Archives of the National Spiritual Assembly of the Bahá'ís of the United Kingdom.
7. Dr J. Estlin Carpenter was the Principal of Manchester College when the Master visited there in 1913. He presided at the meeting where 'Abdu'l-Bahá spoke and paid an eloquent tribute to His work and the message He was delivering to the western world. Further, in his book *Comparative Religion* he refers to the Bahá'í Faith and asks, '. . . has Persia, in the midst of her miseries, given birth to a religion which will go around the world?' (Quoted in Balyuzi, *'Abdu'l-Bahá*, p. 354).
8. Letter in the Archives of the National Spiritual Assembly of the Bahá'ís of the United Kingdom.
9. Letter in the Archives of the National Spiritual Assembly of the Bahá'ís of the United Kingdom.
10. Letter in the Archives of the National Spiritual Assembly of the Bahá'ís of the United Kingdom.
11. College records, Balliol College.

Chapter 14: Spring Vacation 1921

1. Letter in the Archives of the National Spiritual Assembly of the Bahá'ís of the United Kingdom.
2. Letter from J. C. Hill to the author, 29 May 1969.
3. Letter from Geoffrey Meade to the author, 18 April 1969.
4. Letter from Adrian Franklin to the author, 17 April 1969.
5. Letter from G. Raleigh to the author, 23 June 1969.
6. Letter from J. C. Dwyer to the author, 24 May 1969.
7. *Bahá'í World*, vol. 13, pp. 881–2.
8. Letter from Shoghi Effendi in Persian, Archives of the National Spiritual Assembly of the Bahá'ís of the United Kingdom.
9. Archives of the National Spiritual Assembly of the Bahá'ís of the United Kingdom.
10. Letter from Shoghi Effendi in Persian, Archives of the National Spiritual

Assembly of the Bahá'ís of the United Kingdom.
11. Letter from Shoghi Effendi in Persian, Archives of the National Spiritual Assembly of the Bahá'ís of the United Kingdom.

Chapter 15: Trinity Term 1921
1. Bursary files, Balliol College.
2. Letter in the Archives of the National Spiritual Assembly of the Bahá'ís of the United Kingdom.
3. Letter from Shoghi Effendi in Persian, Archives of the National Spiritual Assembly of the Bahá'ís of the United Kingdom.
4. Letter from G. C. Greer to the author, 23 June 1969.
5. Letter from Lord Snow Hill of Newport, Mr Soskice, to the author, 19 May 1969.
6. Letter from A. W. Davis to the author, 21 April 1969.
7. Letter from B. H. Bevan-Petman to the author, 18 May 1969.
8. Letter from Geoffrey Meade to the author, 18 April 1969.
9. Persian shoes made of cloth.
10. Letter from J. C. Hill to the author.
11. Letter from S. P. Streuve to the author, 27 May 1969.
12. *Bahá'í News*, no. 121, p. 11.
13. ibid.
14. Bahá'u'lláh, *Prayers and Meditations*, pp. 288–93.
15. Letter from William Elliot to the author, 15 July 1969.
16. Quoted in Rabbaní, *Priceless Pearl*, p. 34.
17. ibid.
18. Letter from Shoghi Effendi in Persian, Archives of the National Spiritual Assembly of the Bahá'ís of the United Kingdom.

Chapter 16: Long Vacation 1921
1. Letter from Edna True to the author, 23 April 1969.
2. Letter from L. Forbes-Ritte to the author, 1969.
3. Letter from G. E. Lavin to the author, 1969.
4. Letter in the Archives of the National Spiritual Assembly of the Bahá'ís of the United Kingdom.
5. Letter in the Archives of the National Spiritual Assembly of the Bahá'ís of the United Kingdom.
6. Letter from Shoghi Effendi in Persian, Archives of the National Spiritual Assembly of the Bahá'ís of the United Kingdom.
7. Letter in the Archives of the National Spiritual Assembly of the Bahá'ís of the United Kingdom.
8. Letter from Shoghi Effendi in Persian, Archives of the National Spiritual Assembly of the Bahá'ís of the United Kingdom.

REFERENCES

9. Letter in the Archives of the National Spiritual Assembly of the Bahá'ís of the United Kingdom.
10. Whitehead, *Some Bahá'ís to Remember*, p. 55.
11. Letter from Shoghi Effendi in Persian, Archives of the National Spiritual Assembly of the Bahá'ís of the United Kingdom..
12. ibid.
13. ibid.
14. Letter in the Archives of the National Spiritual Assembly of the Bahá'ís of the United Kingdom.
15. Whitehead, *Some Bahá'ís to Remember*, p. 57.
16. ibid. pp. 31–4.
17. ibid. p. 53.
18. Hall, *Bahá'í Dawn*.
19. ibid. p. 22–3.
20. Lucy Hall's autograph book.
21. *Payám-i-Bahá'í*, No. 208 (March 1997), pp. 18-20. Translation by the author.
22. Hall, *Bahá'í Dawn*, p. 23.
23. Letter from Lucy Hall to the author, 1 July 1969.
24. ibid.
25. Hall, *Bahá'í Dawn*.
26. Letter from Lucy Hall to the author, 1 July 1969.
27. ibid.
28. Hall, *Bahá'í Dawn*, p. 24.
29. Whitehead, *Some Bahá'ís to Remember*, pp. 59–60.
30. Letter from Lucy Hall to the author, 1 July 1969.
31. ibid.

Chapter 17: Michaelmas Term 1921

1. Balliol College records.
2. Letter from Paul Leroy-Beaulieu to the author, 1969.
3. Rabbaní, *Priceless Pearl*, p. 37.
4. Quoted in ibid. p. 35.
5. Letter from Christopher W. M. Cox to the author, 1969.
6. Letter from G. W. Wrangham to the author, 1969.
7. Letter from Shoghi Effendi to E.T. Hall, Lucy Hall's papers.
8. Letter from Shoghi Effendi in Persian, Archives of the National Spiritual Assembly of the Bahá'ís of the United Kingdom.
9. Letter from Shoghi Effendi in Persian, Archives of the National Spiritual Assembly of the Bahá'ís of the United Kingdom.
10. Hall, *Bahá'í Dawn*, p. 27.
11. ibid.
12. Quoted in Whitehead, *Some Bahá'ís to Remember*, p. 63.

PRELUDE TO THE GUARDIANSHIP

13. Letter in the Archives of the National Spiritual Assembly of the Bahá'ís of the United Kingdom.
14. Letter from Shoghi Effendi in Persian, Archives of the National Spiritual Assembly of the Bahá'ís of the United Kingdom.
15. Letter in the Archives of the National Spiritual Assembly of the Bahá'ís of the United Kingdom.
16. Rabbaní, *Priceless Pearl*, pp. 37–8.
17. Letter from Lord Stow Hill of Newport, Mr Soskice, to the author, 11 July 1966.
18. Letter from J. M. Russell to the author, 1969.
19. Letter from J. C. Hill to the author, 29 May 1969.
20. Letter from Adrian Franklin to the author, 1969.
21. Rabbaní, *Priceless Pearl*, pp. 37–8.

Chapter 18: The Last Days in England

1. Quoted in Rabbaní, *Priceless Pearl*, p. 39.
2. ibid.
3. *Star of the West*, vol. 12, no. 16, p. 252.
4. Quoted in Rabbaní, *Priceless Pearl*, p. 40.
5. Letter in the Archives of the National Spiritual Assembly of the United Kingdom.
6. Quoted in Rabbaní, *Priceless Pearl*, pp. 40–41.
7. ibid. pp. 41–2.
8. Letter in the Archives of the National Spiritual Assembly of the United Kingdom.
9. Florence Pinchon's Memoirs of Dr Esslemont, in the Archives of the National Spiritual Assembly of the United Kingdom.
10. Letter from Isobel Slade to the author, 19 May 1969.
11. Letter from E. C. Forster to the author, 10 May 1969.
12. Rabbaní, *Priceless Pearl*, p. 42.
13. 'Abdu'l-Bahá, *Will and Testament*, p. 11.

Chapter 19: The Beloved Guardian

1. Isaiah 11:6.
2. Quoted in Shoghi Effendi, *God Passes By*, p. 184.
3. Shoghi Effendi, 'The Goal of a New World Order', in *The World Order of Bahá'u'lláh*, pp. 33–4.
4. ibid. pp. 42–3.
5. Shoghi Effendi, 'The Dispensation of Bahá'u'lláh', in *The World Order of Bahá'u'lláh*, p. 112.
6. ibid. p. 123.
7. ibid. pp. 131–2.
8. ibid. p. 151.

9. Shoghi Effendi, 'The Unfoldment of World Civilization', in *The World Order of Bahá'u'lláh*, p. 161.
10. ibid. p. 170.
11. ibid. pp. 203–4.
12. Shoghi Effendi, *The Promised Day is Come*, p. 124.
13. ibid, p. 17.
14. Shoghi Effendi, *God Passes By*, p. 412.
15. Shoghi Effendi, *Citadel of Faith*, p. 157.
16. ibid. p. 50.
17. ibid. p. 150.
18. Shoghi Effendi, *Messages to the Bahá'í World*, p. 120.
19. ibid. p. 126.
20. ibid. p. 127.
21. Charles Mason Remey.
22. Shoghi Effendi, *Bahá'í Administration*, p. 196.

Appendix: Shoghi Effendi's Address to the Oxford University Asiatic Society

1. 'The Bahai Movement: A paper read by Shoghi Effendi at Oxford', in *The Dawn, A monthly Bahai Journal of Burma*, Vol. 1, No. 1 (September 1923); No. 2 (October 1923); Nos. 3 and 4 (November & December 1923); No. 5 (January 1924); No. 6 (February 1924); No. 7 (March 1924); and No. 8 (April 1924). No attempt has been made here to impose editorial consistency as regards punctuation, transliteration or capitalization; the address is printed here as it appears in the journal *The Dawn*.

www.ingramcontent.com/pod-product-compliance
Lightning Source LLC
Chambersburg PA
CBHW071655160426
43195CB00012B/1471